For Your Freedom and Ours

FOR YOUR FREEDOM AND OURS

Polish Progressive Spirit from the 14th Century to the Present

Second, enlarged edition

Edited by

Krystyna M. Olszer

Frederick Ungar Publishing Co.
New York

The first edition of *For Your Freedom and Ours*
was published in 1943, with the subtitle
"Polish Progressive Spirit Through the Centuries."
Edited by
Manfred Kridl
Wladyslaw Malinowski
Józef Wittlin
Preface by Malcolm W. Davis
Translation and Editorial Assistance by
Ludwik Krzyżanowski

CONTENTS

v

CONTENTS

vii

CONTENTS

PREFACE

(TO THE SECOND EDITION)

Nearly forty years have passed since the first edition of this book. During these years Europe's frontiers have changed, as have its political configurations and social systems. This book's major theme, however, remains relevant. The slogan that serves as title, "For Your Freedom and Ours," initially formulated by the Polish historian Joachim Lelewel, first appeared on the banners of the November Insurrection of 1830–31. Thus, the new edition coincides with the one hundred and fiftieth anniversary of the November Insurrection. It gives an overview of the Polish progressive spirit as it developed through the centuries and updates the original book with supplementary chapters, taking the reader from 1943 to the present, when the Polish people struggle yet again for their human rights and political independence.

Thus, the book's original character as it was conceived by a group of Polish refugee writers and scholars during the war is preserved. They encountered great difficulties, since the primary sources for their work were left in their occupied homeland, and they had to locate material in the West. Yet they accomplished their task, and therefore, this edition of *For Your Freedom and Ours,* a testament to their scholarship and patriotism, is now presented with only minor changes. By dealing with Poland's post-World War II history, the final chapter presents the background of the anti-Communist opposition movement. Although the majority of these texts have never been openly published in Poland, they have circulated throughout the country in secretly produced mimeographed sheets. In these articles, declarations, and resolutions the reader will hear the true voice of human conscience—a voice that exemplifies the progressive spirit of Poland's centuries-old tradition.

January 1981   KRYSTYNA M. OLSZER

PREFACE

(TO THE FIRST EDITION)

At the key-point of northern Europe, the Polish land has long been a major objective in the play for power. It stretches, rolling and open, from the Carpathian mountain ranges northward to the Baltic Sea. Between these two barriers, it has been a highway for migration and a fighting ground for military movement. For the Slav, finding a way to the west, and the Teuton, driving to the east, it has been a meeting-place of rivalry and war. During much of their history, alien imperial rulers have divided the territory and dominated the life of the Polish people, and have used Polish resources and strength for purposes of their own that held nothing in common with the popular spirit or will.

Nevertheless, throughout the centuries, from the time in the middle ages when Poles ventured to question the divine right of kings, the demand for freedom has always been renewed by leaders of Polish thought and has more and more rallied support. It has broadened and deepened in emphasis, during recent times, as democratic ideas gained influence, and has laid stress on the struggle for social welfare. Even now from Nazi-occupied Poland, as these pages show, the cry re-echos still for liberty and justice.

If memory serves, there should be no surprise that this is so, nor should the terrible present mean lack of hope for the future. During the first World War Poland was repeatedly over-run by invasions. Thousands of square miles were ravaged. Populations were driven from their homes. Millions died from epidemics and hunger, while the occupying troops requisitioned food and livestock. As the armistice came, all of the country was in the grip of foreign forces. After one hundred and fifty years of partition, some thirty millions of people had their nationhood restored amidst chaos and famine, with contagious diseases taking thousands as toll, communications disrupted and ralways largely destroyed. Yet within a year government had been set up and was working, responsible to a legislative assembly, which held under the Constitution the reserved right to dissolve itself; local administrations were functioning; land reform had been initiated; public schools were teaching; transport and industry and farming were in operation; the plague menace was being mastered; social strife was under control, and order was restored.

In the twenty years that followed, the Poles gave proof of their quality in many forms of high achievement. Yet they were uneasy years everywhere in Europe, increasingly so, and particularly in the central and eastern regions where the strains and stresses were strong and the pressures were powerful from outside upon the newly-restored nations. During this period, no solid and satisfactory relationship was realized between Poland and the neighboring other states of the area. Many and diverse attempts were made to form economic and political systems among them. Ideas of associating the Baltic States and Finland with Poland, Rumania, and in some cases either Czechoslovakia or Hungary, were advanced, while another project aimed at relating the first group, with Rumania and Czechoslovakia, to Hungary, Bulgaria and Greece. Efforts were carried far towards the realization of a Polish-Czechoslovak accord of collaboration. With Rumania, Poland concluded a convention of military alliance. A project was discussed likewise for a mutual assistance agreement to include Poland, Rumania, Czechoslovakia, Yugoslavia and Greece. Poland and the Little Entente nations — Czechoslovakia, Rumania and Yugoslavia—correlated their action as far as possible on matters of common interest. In the economic field, at the beginning of the depression in 1930, on Polish initiative there was organized an agrarian block of countries including Poland, Czechoslovakia, Rumania, Yugoslavia, Hungary, Bulgaria, and two of the Baltic states, Latvia and Estonia, with the objective of preferential tariffs. Later, in the crisis days of 1934 and 1935 with the menace of military pressures thrusting towards war, there were determined endeavors for an Eastern European security structure to be supported by all the continental powers.

Yet throughout the twenty years to the onset of the second World War it was apparent that among the countries of the region, as they had come out of the first World War, the feeling of their individual rights and traditions was prevailing by its established natural strength over the newer sense of mutual interdependence and community of interests. Undertakings to act together, to consult and to cooperate, were restricted in scope by the desire to avoid general obligations and risks remote from home. The inevitable linking of such risks in a chain of dangers for all was consequently demonstrated by events, as it has been to other states throughout the world whose peoples have shown themselves more reluctant to face and grasp the issues.

The new time to follow today's deadly conflict will offer, with victory, a fresh opportunity. In its different circumstances, after this tribulation, the spirit that is voiced in these pages, given effect in that association of a revived Poland relations with neighboring peoples of the region, may work out the relationships and reconciliations, never before achieved, which are indispensable for safety and welfare.

MALCOLM W. DAVIS

INTRODUCTION

(TO THE FIRST EDITION)

Polish political thought has had a long history, in which periods of very real development alternated with periods of decline. At all times, however, the ideas of progress and democracy have held a prominent place in it. Throughout its development, too, it has retained both the interest of the nation and a high ideological level.

The progressive and democratic traditions in Poland can be traced as far back as the fifteenth and sixteenth centuries, to the works of Polish writers whose ideas, far in advance of the rest of the nation, were highly regarded throughout Europe. These writers cannot, of course, be spoken of as representatives of modern democracy, for such democracy did not exist anywhere at the time, but they were the early forerunners of future development, and were themselves, to a certain extent, the products of their age, for the seeds of democracy already existed in the political organization of Poland.

Sixteenth century Poland was a limited monarchy, governed chiefly through the houses of parliament. Of course, political rights were vested solely in the nobility, and the nation as a whole had no share in the government, but the nobility was rather numerous, comprising about 10 per cent of the total population, and exercised their rights in parliament with a full degree of democratic freedom. They were able to restrict sharply the power of the king, and to acquire certain basic rights which rendered Poland one of the most advanced countries of the time. The freedom of speech, religious tolerance, inviolability of person and property which reigned in Poland, provided a favorable climate for the rise of courageous reformers and fighters for new ideas.

In the seventeenth century this remarkably advanced political organization began to decline rapidly. Poland was plunged into a period of almost continual wars, both foreign and internecine, accompanied by economic disintegration and leading inevitably to a breakdown of the political system. Parliament functioned badly; at the same time the authority of the executive was progressively being undermined even further. The last years of the 18th century witnessed the complete collapse of the Polish State.

However, decades before the loss of its independence, the Polish nation began a cultural and political rebirth. The many statesmen, political writers, and poets active at that time were reviving the great traditions of progress and democracy, shaping a new philosophy which combined the historic heritage of 16th century Poland with the ideals of 18th century European enlightenment. Men like Krasicki, Staszic, Kołłątaj, Stanislaw Potocki, and Małachowski were, above all, great Europeans in the broadest sense of the word. They had broken with the narrow nationalism dominant among the Polish gentry of the preceding century, who instilled isolation from Western European culture, and reliance solely on national strength. They knew that all great human ideals are universal, and that each nation must rise to those ideals. But while they were *universalists*, they were also ardent *patriots*, who felt that their foremost duty was to help their nation to rise to a higher intellectual, moral, and social level. They were the great educators of their people, and their patriotism, which was combined with Europeanism and universalism, as well as their rejection of narrow chauvinism, was largely responsible for the moral atmosphere in which subsequent generations of great Poles thought and lived. The words of the great Polish poet, Adam Mickiewicz, "Wherever there is a struggle for freedom, there is also a struggle for Poland", stem from the spirit of these 18th century Polish thinkers.

The Polish writers of the 18th century refused to accept social inequality and the disenfranchisement of the great mass of the people; they rebelled against the exploitation and subjection of a large part of the population. They demanded major, even radical, reforms, frequently referring to the traditions of the 16th century, when many Polish writers had already begun to raise their voices for the betterment of the conditions of peasants and town dwellers. These demands were now taken up with increased force by the 18th century writers, and, combined with the general trend towards reform of the political system in Poland, brought about the promulgation of a new Constitution, which was voted on May 3, 1791.

This Constitution, the product of the best minds of the generation, was a compromise between progressive trends and the need to reckon with existing conditions. The landed gentry would not accept more radical reforms. The country was menaced by Prussia, Russia, and Austria. The economic situation was also critical. Although neither the peasant problem, nor the burgher question could be fully solved by the Constitution under these circumstances, it was nevertheless an important step in the direction of establishing a modern political system. Its educational value was particularly great, for it served as a beacon for subsequent Polish generations. It was also highly regarded by progressive thinkers throughout Europe, and men like Mirabeau and Edmund Burke considered it one of the foremost political achievements of the age.

The whole history of Poland, from the last partition, in 1795, to the rebirth of the Polish Republic in 1918, was a series of heroic efforts on the part of the best men of the nation to realize the ideas set forth by the Constitution, the ideals of freedom, equality, independene, and social justice. These ideals were the rallying call of the long Polish struggle for freedom, of the Kościuszko insurrection, of the Polish Legions in Napoleon's Army, of the insurrections against Russian rule in 1830 and 1863, of the uprisings against Prussia and Austria in 1846 and 1848, of the revolutionary movement against Czarism in 1905, and of Piłsudski's Legions in the First World War.

During the long period of national bondage which began with the partition of Poland, the restoration of the nation's independence became the paramount issue to politically conscious Poles. To them, as to all the most eminent representatives of Polish culture, national independence became inseparably linked with democracy and progress. A democratic Poland, a people's Poland, governed by the people and for the people, a Poland of free and equal men, the home of social justice and a creative member of the great family of free nations—such was the ideal for which the best force of the nation fought.

After the defeat of the Polish insurrection of 1830 refugee groups which found asylum in France and, to a lesser extent, in Great Britain and the United States, worked for this goal. These groups, known in Poland's political history as "The Great Emigration", became the heralds of a new Poland. The humanist and humanitarian ideals of the Polish struggle for independence found their best expression in the activities and writings of Adam Mickiewicz, the greatest of Polish poets. The struggle for the liberation of all peoples and for a just world order were, in his mind, inseparable from or even synonymous with the fight for Poland's freedom, As editor-in-chief of the revolutionary-democratic daily, *"The Tribune of the Peoples"*, published in Paris in 1848 and 1849, Mickiewicz gathered around himself outstanding representatives of all the oppressed nations of the time.

The manifesto of the "POLISH DEMOCRATIC SOCIETY" was also published in Paris (1836). This organization played a major role in the history of the development of modern political thought in Poland. Its manifesto expanded and further clarified the ideas of the May Constitution. The policies of the landed aristocracy were sharply condemned, and the peasantry was viewed as the class which was socially most important and constructive. The Poland of the future was envisaged as a democratic nation, the home of the working people.

The democratic approach was emphasized even more strongly by the group of social thinkers affiliated with the "POLISH PEOPLE", which included Worcell, Kamieński, Heltman, and many others. These men were the forerunners of the powerful current of social radicalism which is an important element in present-day Polish culture.

Social ideals were dominant in Polish political thought throughout the second half of the 19th century and the beginning of the twentieth. During that period a new school of thought, Positivism, made its appearance. Its representatives stressed the importance of what they called "organic work", or "work at the foundation". In its practical application this program aimed at the acquisition of wealth (analogous to the French slogan, "Enrichissez-vous") through the development of industry and trade, and at the improvement of the economic status of the peasantry. It included demands for better and more general education, and for a struggle against ignorance and conservatism. The positivists were strong supporters of liberal and democratic ideas; they believed in cultural progress and the power of science and education, and advocated freedom of conscience and social reform.

The ideological nucleus of the later powerful Peasant Party was formed at about the same time. Simultaneously, the rapid development of industry and trade, especially in the then Russian part of Poland, was bringing about a definite change in the relationship of social forces. The workers' political movement came into existence as an independent factor, based upon the traditions of Polish Utopian Socialism and on the new socialist ideas from the West. Despite repression and the persecution of its leaders by the Czarist authorities, the workers' movement showed remarkable vitality.

These ideological currents determined the forms of Polish intellectual life during that epoch. As in earlier periods, the outstanding men of Poland fought for democracy and progress. The foremost representative of Polish Positivism was Bolesław Prus, one of the greatest Polish novelists, whose works embody the finest features of Polish intellectual life: Europeanism, universalism, liberalism, anti-nationalism, democracy, and an unquenchable faith in human progress. These ideals were also expressed in the writings of Eliza

Orzeszkowa, the outstanding Polish woman novelist, and an original thinker, Alexander Świętochowski, and many others, whose talents were perhaps inferior, but whose ideas and courage equalled those of the greater writers.

The movement for individual freedom and social justice went hand in hand with the movement for national independence, which found its strongest support among the thousands of organized workers and peasants. The Polish Socialist Party, the leading organization of the Polish workers, and the Peasants' Party, both striving to change the economic and social system in Poland, became also the centers of the movement for national independence during the early years of the 20th century.

The foundations of the new Polish State were laid during the First World War. When Poland was finally restored, on November 11, 1918, the democratic and progressive forces were at first the most active element in the new nation's life. The first Polish Government was known as "The People's Government." The leaders of Polish intellectual life, headed by the famous novelist, Stefan Żeromski, aligned themselves with the Polish democratic movement. But later the reactionary elements, representing all the social evils which had always been fought by Poland's best sons, regained their strength. The history of modern Poland, of Poland restored to her status as a nation, is a history of the struggle between the progressive-democratic elements and the reactionaries.

The abandonment of the democratic traditions by Piłsudski and his group was of tremendous importance in national politics. The rule by the so-called "Sanacja" (the Piłsudski and Rydz-Śmigły dictatorship) represented a marked return to narrow reactionary nationalism and an ever greater leaning towards collaboration with fascist elements. But every reaction engenders opposition, especially in a nation deeply moral and steeped in the traditions of struggle for social and political justice. The progressives, representing the masses of the Polish people, rallied their forces in stubborn and dramatic struggles against the dominant fascist-totalitarian groups and tendencies, which drew their strength from the governmental apparatus. This struggle, which unfortunately failed to result in a victory for democracy, was nevertheless of immense moral importance, for it clearly demonstrated that the majority of the Polish nation refused to accede to dictatorship.

Today, in underground conspiracy, courageous and profoundly progressive ideas are maturing again, ideas which are the fruit of the thought and struggles of generations of Polish fighters for freedom, equality, and justice. Now Poland is marching towards a better future along the road blazed by Modrzewski, Staszic, Kołłątaj, Kościuszko, Mickiewicz, Prus, and Żeromski.

* * *

It has been our endeavor in this collection to give the American reader a true picture of Polish thought on moral, cultural, political, and social problems. We hope that this book will serve as convincing proof that all that is truly great and creative in Poland has ever been and is today moved by the spirit of humanism and freedom, by liberal and progressive ideals. To judge Poland merely on the basis of the foreign and internal policies of the governments which ruled her during the years preceding the present war would be grossly inaccurate and unjust, for these policies, which have received their full share of criticism, were never supported by the mass of the people.

Most of the authors whose writings are included in this book are widely recognized and accepted as outstanding contributors to Polish culture. Others, who may be of lesser caliber, nevertheless represent the same ideological trends. We also reproduce a number of historic documents and governmental decrees, as well as appeals and manifestoes of political parties, which give expression to the progressive Polish ideals.

We have attempted to be wholly objective in the selection of the material. The authors chosen represent many political camps and tendencies, although their ultimate goal is the same. Their democratic and progressive approach is the result

7

of a common humanitarian feeling towards fellow-men and fellow-nations, of a profound hatred of hypocrisy and lies, of indignation at the denial of human dignity, at inequality and social wrong.

The selection has been attended by many problems of purely technical character. We have been obliged to limit ourselves to material available in the United States and in Great Britain. Many serious omissions, especially with regard to modern writers, have been unavoidable. But even the older writers were not always available. Thus, we were obliged to omit the writings of Polish Unitarians. Often we were unable to secure the most representative works of a given author, and were therefore forced to resort to his less characteristic or less important writings. Our chief difficulty, however, has been to reduce the wealth of available material to the practical limitations of publication, which necessitated drastic editing. But despite that, and despite the omissions, we believe that this collection presents an accurate and true picture of Polish progressive political thought.

We particularly wish to beg the reader to keep in mind that the importance of ideas must be judged not only by their present value, but also in relation to their time. Ideas which today may seem commonplace, were new and often revolutionary when they were first formulated, centuries ago. In their time, the Polish writers of the 15th, 16th, and 18th centuries were revolutionary trail blazers and had to struggle to win acceptance and recognition.

* * *

In conclusion, we wish to express our deepest gratitude to all who cooperated with us in the preparation of this book. We wish to thank the contemporary authors who permitted us to reproduce portions of their work, as well as those who were unable to extend their permission because of war conditions. Particular thanks are due to Mrs. Valetta Malinowska and Dr. Bry of Rensselaer Polytechnical Institute, for their gracious permission to reproduce part of the last book of Professor Bronisław Malinowski, which has not yet been published, and to Professor Aleksander Hertz for his assistance in the selection of the texts and in their preparation. We also extend our deep appreciation to Dr. Ludwik Krzyzanowski for his editorial contributions and his careful translations, and to Mr. and Mrs. Sidney Sulkin for their valuable help in the final shaping of the English versions of the texts. We add our hearty thanks to the great number of friends who cannot here be named separately but whose generous efforts and good will were indispensable to the materialization of this book.

THE EDITORS

FIGHT FOR HUMAN RIGHTS

HISTORICAL BACKGROUND

(1370-1795)

In the 15th century, Poland under Władysław Jagiełło joined with the Grand Duchy of Lithuania in an alliance which exercised a powerful influence on the affairs of Eastern Europe. Subsequently Hungary, Bohemia, the Baltic and the Danubian countries were gathered into the Polish orbit. In 1410, a Polish victory at Grunwald struck the death blow to the German Teutonic Order. Later wars were fought with the Muscovite State for the posession of White Russia and the Ukraine.

In this period Poland's power reached its summit. Kazimierz the Great had already codified the Polish law. And an indifferent religious tolerance left the gates of the land open to all faiths. In the 16th century under Zygmunt I and Zygmunt II, political liberty grew and for a time Poland enjoyed a golden era of literature.

The 17th century brought a series of wars with various countries. Internally, new struggles rose among the aristocrats. The power of the king collapsed as the star of the gentry rose. The Jesuits had manoeuvred themselves into control of the church. Religious intolerance and economic disaster followed.

Capitalizing on Poland's internal dissension, Prussia and Russia sought to dominate Polish affairs. In 1768 a protracted rebellion broke out against Russian interference and in 1772, Russia, Prussia and Austria united for the first partitioning of Poland. However, a considerable part of Poland remained independent.

There followed an era of intense political activity among progressive Polish groups. The Constitution of May 3, 1791, was issued as the clearest documentation of the political and social reforms for which these groups had been struggling. Rejecting this Constitution, Russia, seconded by Prussia

13

once again, declared war in 1792. The upshot was the second partition of Poland, this time between Russia and Prussia. Only a small part of Poland was then left as a nominally independent state garrisoned by Russian and Prussian troops. The national uprising of 1794, led by Gen. Kościuszko, followed, but was beaten down in a few months. Thereupon, the third partition was agreed to by Russia, Prussia and Austria. This was the end of Polish independence for 123 years.

ORIGINS

EXCERPTS FROM OLD DOCUMENTS

Like the rest of Europe, Poland of the XV and XVI centuries was a state organized on the basis of distinct corporate estates each having a different social and legal status. Whereas in England and Sweden all the Estates were represented in Parliament, in Poland representatives of the gentry were practically the only ones admitted (although provisions were made granting representation to the royal cities). The gentry was a very large class of society and constituted almost ten per cent of the whole population.

The exclusively "gentry" character of Polish political life at that time developed consequences of importance. First consider the idea of equality within the Estate. All noblemen were considered legally equal, irrespective of their fortune. Another consequence was the exclusion of commoners from all political privileges exercised by the gentry. The reader is reminded that the extensive liberties and privileges quoted in this chapter were enjoyed by noblemen only. In this, Poland was in no way behind most other European countries. Nevertheless these excerpts from the old monuments of Polish law express the contemporary tendency toward liberalism and tolerance within the so-called "Gentry-Republic".

THE POLISH-LITHUANIAN UNION AND THE ADMISSION OF THE LITHUANIAN GENTRY TO POLISH CLAN TIES
(From the Act of the Union of Horodło in 1413)

".... Nor can that endure which has not its foundation upon love. For love alone diminishes not, but shines with its own light, makes an end of discord, softens the fires of hate, restores peace to the world, brings together the sundered, redresses wrongs, aids all and injures none. And whoso invokes its aid shall find peace and safety and have no fear of future ill; through it laws are made, kingdoms are ruled, cities ordered and the state of the Commonwealth attains to the highest end . . . ."

".... Let those be united to us by charity and made equal, whom the practice of religion and the identity of laws and

17

privileges has bound to us. And we promise by our immutable and solemn word that we will never desert them . . . ."

The Charter "Neminem Captivabimus"

(From a document of 1430, awarding personal immunity *"Habeas corpus"* to the landed gentry)

". . . . We will not imprison anyone without a lawful verdict . . . ."

From a 16th Century Law Book

". . . . Provided however that both the king and all the estates of the realm shall be subject to the law"

Closer Union Between Poland and Lithuania

The privilege concerning the Union of the Grand Duchy of Lithuania with the Crown (of Poland) voted by their Lordships the Spiritual and Temporal Counselors and the Deputies of the Gentry, at the Diet of Lublin, in the year of the Lord 1569.

". . . . For closer Union, common and mutual brother love, in eternal common defense of both countries, for the eternal glory of God, with eternal thanks to the glory of these two excellent nations, Poland and Lithuania . . . . we have renewed that old alliance, and agreed upon the rules hereto set forth: . . . . That the Kingdom of Poland and the Grand Duchy of Lithuania are now a body one and indivisible, a Republic one and indivisible consisting of two States and Nations, who joined to form one people".

Equality of Rights for Protestants

(From the Act of the General Confederation of Warsaw in 1573)

We, the Spiritual and Temporal Counselors, the Gentry and the other Estates of the one and indivisible Republic, from Old and New Poland, from the Grand Duchy of Lithuania, etc.—and from the Cities of the Crown (declare):

". . . . Whereas there is a great dissidence in affairs of the Christian Religion within our Country, and to prevent any sedition for this reason among the people—like what we see clearly in other Kingdoms—we promise each other, on behalf of ourselves and our descendants, for perpetuity, under oath and pledging our faith, honor and consciences, that we who are *dissidentes de religione* will keep peace between ourselves, and neither shed blood on account of differences of faith or kinds of churches, nor punish one another by confiscation of goods, deprivation of honor, imprisonment or exile . . . ."

VOICES OF HUMANISM

JAN OSTRORÓG

(1436-1501)

One of the first Polish political writers, Ostroróg projected a number of reforms concerning the treasury, the army, the courts and legislation. These are interesting when one considers the period in which they were advanced. Particularly significant is his independent attitude toward the Pope, and his demands for uniform legislation. His work, written in Latin, is entitled "Monumentum pro Reipublicae Ordinatione."

FROM THE "MONUMENTUM PRO REIPUBLICAE
ORDINATIONE"

(1475)

On the Diversity of Laws

... Such a diversity of laws is not good at all, that the nobility be judged by one, and the plebeians by another, that one is called Polish law, while the other German,* and this again varies and is persistently observed as if the Germans were exclusively the most learned men in the world. Such a mixture in one state is not compatible with reason. Therefore, let there be one law, binding for all, without discrimination among persons: for the infliction of wounds and for homicide let the same fine and criminal punishment be preserved as was customary of old. If, however, different laws be deemed necessary for plebeians and for gentle folk, for the sake of the difference of their estate, then let that one be called civil and not German, though I believe that all inhabitants of the country alike can and should govern themselves by one and the same law.

On the Necessity of Enacted Laws

Enacted Laws are necessary in order that sentences may not be passed according to the whim of a single mind but

---

* The so-called Magdeburg law.

according to the judgment of many persons. No better laws can be invented than those instituted by the Roman Senate and the famous emperors. From them should be chosen what is necessary for the courts, while certain applications may be left to the consideration of the judge. The objection that might be raised that using these laws is a sign of submissiveness is of no consequence, for they are used by others who do not on this account recognize any supremacy over themselves and are not because of it regarded as submissive to those whose laws they observe, and we likewise use the rules of Aristotle and other philosophers, though we are not submissive to any of them.

On Giving Tithes

God ordered to give tithes; He ordered, I do not deny, Aaron and the Levites, to whom He had given the spiritual law, to do so, but He did not order that they be exacted from laymen by force, as now happens, so that tithes are taken not without wrong to the donors. They were once given by the rich, not by the poor, while now poor peasants give them to those well provided and well fed who haughtily accept them. Are the words observed: I want compassion —not sacrifice? If therefore some one wishes to receive a gift, let him take it when it pleases the donor, not according to his own, but according to the donor's will.

On Electing Bishops

If the lords, bishops and the whole clergy were indeed so spiritual, I would then truly approve that no temporal authority should interfere in the election of the clergy. The king should then take care of temporal matters, and the clergy should attend to spiritual affairs as within their own province so that these powers, as is seemly, should be separate. But when the rules pertaining to the condition and instruction of the clergy are scattered over many works, how is it possible to become acquainted with them if there are neither learners nor teachers? Let antiquated custom rule. Evil is pleasant. Therefore to avoid a greater evil, the appointment of bishops by the king seems better, so that they be not only learned but amenable and so that the ill manners and ill-will of individuals may not provoke with constant hatred one estate against another.

On Payments Made to the Pope

A woeful and inhuman grievance oppresses the Polish Kingdom, otherwise completely free, in that we permit ourselves to be deceived and beguiled by the slyness of the Italians to such an extent that under the pretext of piety, which is rather a falsification of teaching into superstition, we allow such great sums of money to be sent annually to the Roman *curia*, as they call it, in the payment of an immense contribution called *sacra* or *annates*. When a new bishop is appointed in a diocese, he does not receive his consecration unless he pays the Pope in Rome several thousand ducats, though the sacred canons teach that the newly elected bishop should be consecrated and confirmed by the archbishop and the bishops. The cunning and crafty Italians arrogate this power to themselves while we yawn and fall asleep. It is well known that the German and Polish lords permitted the Apostolic See to take *annates* only for a few years with the aim that aggressors on the Christian faith be checked and the savage Turk be stopped in his attacks. And this also is certain: that these few allotted years have long since passed and that the *annates* are turned to completely different uses than those for which they were destined. Therefore this false piety should be stopped, and the Pope should not be a tyrant under the pretext of faith, but on the contrary a benign father, as the One is merciful Whose vicar on earth he proclaims himself.

ANDRZEJ FRYCZ MODRZEWSKI

(1503-1572)

A Polish political writer and moralist of the 16th century, Modrzewski was widely known in Western Europe. He wrote a number of works of which the most important are: "De poena homicidii" (1543) and "De Republica emendanda" (1551). In them he proclaimed very progressive and, for his time, unusual theories, namely, equality of all social classes before the law, enactment of uniform punishment for all for similar crimes, abolition of certain legal restrictions placed upon townsmen, alleviation of the suffering of peasants by depriving lords of the right to seize land or to bind the peasants to it forever (this bondage was called "glebae adscriptio").

FROM "ON IMPROVING THE COMMONWEALTH"

(1551)

1. The condition of laws should be such that all are enacted for the common good and weal, so that uniform rewards for virtues as well as uniform penalties for iniquities are instituted.

2. No liberties should be held so important that any one using them as a shield may avoid punishment, or receive lesser punishment. For true liberty lies in constraining evil thoughts and offenses, not in the wantonness of doing mischief as one pleases, or in meting out slighter punishment to the offenders.

3. If for the same offense a diversity of punishments were to be preserved it should not be used to give a loose to iniquities but to restrain them. Therefore the magnates, the nobility and persons holding office should be more severely punished than the poor people, the peasantry and people holding no office, and still more severely those who trespass against the office, than those who trespass against common persons.

Let, therefore, the legislator's first care be that in enacting laws he should not deviate from reason or caution, and that he should make all laws contribute (as reason dictates) to the common good and weal. For just as a medicine is praised which either helps the whole body, or if only one of its parts, cures it so that it will not injure another part, likewise that law should be praised which rewards similar virtues with similar prices, and decrees medicines and similar penalties for similar infirmities and offenses. For who would fain use such a medicine as would drive heat from the liver and bring cold to the stomach? I believe that no one, because where the stomach is cold there can be no digestion of food whatsoever, and hence the liver and other organs will also be affected. How then, can that law be praised which rewards like virtues with unlike prizes, or punishes the offense committed by various people in like manner with unlike penalties! Being too lenient with some, it gives a loose to offenses, while decreeing severe penalties for others it deprives them of the power to defend themselves from wrong. For I am speaking (by way of example) of the law by which the penalty, very severe for some, and very light for others, is decreed for homicide. What is said of this one law should be understood also for other similar ones. It came to pass in a certain county that two men, one of common, the other of noble estate, both rich and possessing sufficient land, severely wounded a man not so rich as themselves but nevertheless a nobleman. The wounded man was taken to a barber's, but as some of his wounds were mortal he died after a month or two. They who visited him out of friendly dutifulness, or they who were sent by the authorities to examine his wounds, inquired to which of those two who had beaten him he would ascribe the greater guilt. He answered that the nobleman had started the fight, but in beating both had fallen with equal force upon him, so that he did not at all know from which one of them he had received the more injurious wounds. Then the questioners vexed him saying that both those who beat him should be punished for inflicting the wounds, but that if these wounds should cause death only one of them could be punished capitally, because according to our law two cannot suffer capital punishment for one homicide. To that the wounded man replied that he had lost hope of his recovery, but that in his conscience which soon would be submitted to God's judgment, he could not with certainty decide on which one the guilt of murder should be laid since he was about to leave this world due to the wounds inflicted by both alike. When, then, the wounded man died, they sought out the man of common estate, and when he was brought before the justice he was pronounced guilty and later beheaded. For it is in the statute book that a man of common estate, if he has killed, crippled, or severely wounded a nobleman (who has given no cause for attack), will pay with his life. This, then, is the penalty which the manslayer of common estate sustained for his crime, but that nobleman is still alive and lives among people; it is said that he is to be summoned from his residence before the justice and according to the procedure of Polish law is to be punished either for the wounds or for the death with a fine. For God's sake, is not this a matter that requires for these two kinds of men two commonwealths so remote from each other that there can be no access from one to the other, so that one needs no help from the other, so that their citizens do not understand or know each other, and finally have neither water, air, nor sun in common?

For is not that strange, which is our custom, that of the people living in the same commonwealth some, for the same reason, are beheaded while others are treated leniently? In a commonwealth in which such laws obtain one cannot expect the fulfilment of the aim for which human societies exist: that all citizens may live peacefully and happily; where one is master over your life and death, while you, fearing death, must sustain injuries and humiliations, or rebukes? In such a commonwealth it is a trifle or a joke to kill you, whereas when you kill or wound another it is considered a crime.

*   *   *

All possible care should be taken that war be averted. And if it cannot be averted, what should be done? What measures should be taken in peacetime? And on organizing a defense on the border?

In order that it be not necessary ever to wage war, peace should be preserved as much as possible with all neighboring peoples, and we should never commit an act that would give them cause to conceive hostile action against us. If anything should start through some wrong done by one side or the other, care must be taken that this be decided by law or by the judgment of good people. Usually, mutual treaties are contracted between neighboring nations or lords who, as they have no judge, elect of their own good will judges from both sides to decide the dispute—either from among strangers or from among their own subjects; and these, for the duration of the trial, they free from oath (to which they are obliged), so that they may the more freely discuss and decide among themselves all laws according to justice. That such pacts should be entered into not only by people of one religion or one faith, but by people of different faiths as well, may be shown by the example of the Fathers: as when first Abraham and Isaac formed an alliance with Abimelech and confirmed it with an oath. Indeed one must seek to establish peace with all people; peace, I say, that will be stable and enduring, and that will have no impediments. For, if under the cloak of peace someone should prepare war against us, with him there is no true peace; but the longer he is allowed to delay war, the more prepared and powerful for war will he be. Therefore, in peace time one must carefully watch what these people do with whom he has dealings; in what they are engaged, with what nations they enter into councils. And if it becomes apparent that their counsels and affairs tend toward war, one must counteract this by all means, if he be only honest. And thus all materials out of which they make war necessities should be prohibited them from our country, which we may easily do by declaring that we need them ourselves. And our borders should be provided with soldiers as well as with other defenses. That these serve to frighten away the neighbors, especially those eager for looting, can be seen from the example of the Tartars who, when they hear that our soldiers are encamped on the border, remain at home and do not harass our lands. It is an old saying that occasion makes the thief. This may be applied to other things, for an evil mind is attracted not only to thievery, but to any crime by occasion. As far as possible, therefore, all causes must be removed from those whose loyalty and friendship is suspected by us.

PIOTR SKARGA POWĘSKI

(1536-1612)

Skarga was a Catholic priest and writer of the 16th century. Among his works, the "Sermons Before the Diet," addressed to Polish senators and deputies, achieved great fame. With uncommon force of oratory Skarga opposed the abuses of the magnates, their class egoism, and their neglect of the nation, defended the underprivileged and wronged peasants, threatened the nobility with grave consequences if it should continue its oppression and foretold the downfall of Poland.

FROM THE SERMONS BEFORE THE DIET

(1597)

On the Love of the Motherland

O powerful lords, o earthly gods, keep a generous and open heart for the weal of your brethren, and your peoples, and all the souls which this kingdom and its territories encompass within themselves. Do not confine and cramp your love in your homes, do not save it for personal favors, do not lock it in your chambers and treasure chests. Release its flow from you, great mountains, on the whole populace, as a river flows to the flat fields. Follow that Christian king who, having set out with his army, had painted on his banner a bird which with its blood enlivened the little birds poisoned by the snake, thus manifesting that he was prepared to die for his people, promising death unto himself and life unto them.

There are those who say: What is the use of the Kingdom and of the Commonwealth if I fare ill and do not have what I desire? It is a thief's heart that wishes riches to the detriment of others. Do not seek riches, ask the Lord for your needs, and be content with your condition, and be not squanderers or idlers, and do not seek to destroy scores of thousands of people, your brethren, for your own sake. Lord, grant that there be few such monsters, who, worse than the beasts of the field are bereft of humanity or mercy.

31

It is said that there are such who do not wish to serve the Commonwealth if they cannot expect advantage for themselves, or if they are not to be recompensed. They are indeed stupid who do not know that virtue seeks only its own decency for reward, who do not see that true rewards stem not from earthly kings but from the Monarch of the world itself. Only God is so powerful and rich and we should seek our rewards with Him . . . . Who serves his country, serves himself, for in it, as we have said before, all goodness is contained. Who will say: pay me for I protect my health, and my home, and my wife and my children; the protection itself is thy reward, why dost thou clamor? When thou eatest, drinkest, carest for thy health, dost thou seek a reward for this?

On Unjust Laws

All things require that the laws be just, useful to all, implanting virtues, and most of all fear of God, protecting God's glory and worship, and finally be well executed and disciplined. For laws which want no justice are distorted as human wrong; they are not laws but evils, for justice is the foundation of the whole Commonwealth. The kingdoms that lack it, says St. Augustine, may truly be called thiefdoms not kingdoms.

The law which serves one party or one estate and harms and injures the other should not be called law. For the laws should be universal, for the advantage of all citizens. As the head does not bid one hand to do what would harm the other, but what is useful to both, as the Apostle says: "One limb in the body has care of the other; and what one suffers all suffer with it"; so also in the Commonwealth, which is one body, nothing should help one estate that would harm another, for thus the whole body would harm itself.

Also that evil law must be mentioned which makes yeomen, freeborn men, Poles and Christians subject, and poor men slaves, as if they were bought or captured in a just war; whereby others do with them as they please, giving them no protection of their possessions or life and providing them with no court of justice to plead against their intolerable wrongs . . . . and exercising over them a supreme domination at which we ourselves shudder.*

Whether that be proper and whether there be a little justice in this law one must ask of the laws and customs, spiritual and temporal, of the whole of Christendom. If they be neither bought nor captured, if they are Poles of the same blood, not Turks or Tartars, why do they groan in slavery? Why should we use them not as hirelings but as slaves? He sits on thy soil, and if he misbehaves, drive him away from thy soil, but do not take his natural and Christian freedom away from him, or make thyself, without a judge, supreme master over his life. The ancient Christians, who when they were pagans had bought slaves, gave freedom to all, as brothers in Christ, when they released themselves from the devil's bondage through holy baptism. And we, faithful and holy Christians, forcefully coerce Poles of the same nation who have never been slaves; and when, like bartered cattle, they must flee from their misery we search for them; and when they, poor and miserable, seek their food elsewhere we exact ransom on them as Turks on prisoners. This is unheard of in the whole of Christendom. I know that not all in our country do this, but according to an evil and savage and unjust law they may do so, which God forbid, to their own damnation. How is it possible not to feel shame before all Christendom for such a law? How is it possible not to fear lest the pagans use such force and absolute domination over us as a consequence of God's vengeance?

For God's sake let us avoid this curse and misery with which the Lord threatens us through his Prophets. Abolish evil unjust laws that obstruct justice; do ye not know that their purpose is the general weal, and when they harm, they must be changed? Not only are these mentioned here which have always been evil and harmful, which never contained any justice in them, but also those which may have been good for our ancient fathers, but are harmful to us at the present time . . . .

* Skarga refers here to the peasants who were attached to the soil, i.e., they were not free to leave their village or their master's soil on which they were forced to work for one or more days during the week.

TOWARDS A GREAT REFORM

STANISŁAW KONARSKI

(1700-1773)

*One of the precursors of Poland's political and cultural renais-
sance in the second half of the 18th century, this Piarist monk,
reformer of education and literary style, was the first to dare
openly and boldly to take a stand against the "liberum veto", one
of the most harmful anomalies of the Polish parliamentary
procedure. The law stated that for the enactment of a bill the
unanimity of all deputies was required. The veto of one deputy
defeated the bill and could also make impossible further deliberations. Konarski dealt this pernicious system a decisive blow in his
work on "Effective Counsels." Konarski was also founder of the
"Collegium Nobilium" in Warsaw in 1740, the first modern,
progressive Polish school to educate the young generation in the
spirit of the enlightened ideas of the age. His "Ordinationes"
(School regulations), written for that college, are conceived in
the spirit of modern pedagogy and didactics.*

FROM "ORDINATIONES" (SCHOOL REGULATIONS)

(1753)

If it were possible to eliminate from our schools corporal
punishment this should be very desirable. Let us then at
least behave in such a way as to take care lest the schools
earn the name of "torture chambers" and "children's
shambles", and the teachers the name of floggers, whippers,
executioners and butchers. Therefore, one should follow
that important counsel urging moderation which is given
to educators by wise persons, and always observe the principles recommended by mere prudence: *viz.*, the boys should
not be flogged for negligence in their school duties or assign-
ments, etc., or even for more frequently occurring excesses,
outbursts of anger or even slight disrespect of religion in
church, for arrogant answers, improper fulfillments of some
duty, or some other offense, but solely and exclusively for
obstinacy, stubbornness and headstrongness. When one says

37

for obstinacy and headstrongness in evil, the concept of the cause is very wide and contains much in itself. But where this cause is actually absent, one should refrain from flogging, and instead appeal rather to reason, double one's watchfulness, admonish, chastise, and in general try all other means tending to the improvement of youth, namely, to the extirpation of laziness, lying or any other wickedness.

If the stubborn are not willing to better themselves, displaying an obstinate inclination for sinning, this extreme means of correction—if that is at all possible—must be applied. As this is for the boys the extreme and greatest punishment of all, it would be outright stupid and barbaric, and even sinful, to have recourse to it immediately, if there still were some hope that the boy's not too inveterate obstinacy might be broken by other means. The boy who has once received corporal punishment, may by any good and prudent teacher be kept by threats and fear for long or even for good in the fulfillment of his duties without resorting time and again to that most opprobrious and most disgraceful means. It is certain that as a result of flogging, boys most frequently become obstinate, as the basest slaves, instead of changing for the better. It is true, that there are also those who sometimes require this incentive; but prudence, moderation, religiousness, courteousness, Christian love, and finally the very sense of humaneness, as well as our education which places us above the coarse and uncouth commonalty, all loudly proclaim that one must not treat harshly creatures still weak and inclined to evil, and that this remedy should not be used otherwise than as physicians apply poison and iron.

* * *

. . . . Servants should never be maltreated, either by the use of coarse speech or by the least display of violence. The surest sign of an evil or cruel disposition at any time of life is found when a man's own servants do not like him and he has become hateful to them. Not to be as tyrants or abusers to those who serve them, but to stand rather in the relation of a father to children—let that be the ideal of our youth!

Students in their time of life do well to consider obedience the fairest of virtues, knowing that on it depends the government of the human race. They will never experience in college such rigor as the soldier must bear . . . . where men suffer the direst discomforts, know hunger and the loss of liberty or even life, in order to carry out commands when given. No excuse from any call is possible. So, too, does every walk of life have its own discipline to which men and women should be submitted when young; for those who have not learned thus to subordinate their wills to others fall in later life into the worst of evils.

Well born lads should refrain from the practices of deceitfulness into which youth so easily falls; as from the worst disgrace, the deepest shame, and the gravest evil. For lying is the proof of a false, perverted and unworthy nature, and whosoever falls into this loathsome habit loses his reputation for the whole of life. He will never get free from it. . . . A youth of good character and honest spirit will always tell the truth even though he be afraid of what it entails; for lying is worse than losing a good name. He will prefer to suffer rather than compromise his own credit and the Divine patience . . . .

One of the greatest benefits of the school should be the habit engendered in the student of reading good books: books treating of life, history, public questions, books about literature and the sciences. Reading alone can make men learned and great in their nation, and those who take good books for their tutors need no others . . . . It is also clear that when one leaves school the only way to make up for time ill-used there is by reading. And what hope is there that he who does not form a love for books while at school will find time for them, when out in the world and facing so many distractions? Whoever while young learns to love books will certainly not forsake them the rest of his days.

Since it is our special purpose in this college to incline men to what is good more by persuasion than by any other method, we exhort now, and shall continue to do so, all well born students in residence, that they permit those into whose care they are entrusted to rule them by clemency, and never to have recourse to means which will grieve both themselves and their teachers. They may be sure that such means are no less painful to their elders than to themselves. Let them hold to the good by their own sense of courtesy and that inborn instinct which they have from their fathers! Let them hate evildoing, not for fear of punishment, but for love of the good.

The youth should have often in mind their country for which they were born; learning from earliest days to love her, and not disappointing the hopes she entertains of them. They should school themselves in good habits and a life worthy of great sons of their nations. They should keep ever before their eyes the name and honor of their own families, whose ornament and strength they must become. Above all they should ground themselves in the love of our Holy Faith, for which their fathers shed their blood: as also, in godly fear, in Christian duties and excellence, without which no one can be of use either to himself or to the commonwealth.

We do not wish that students should find the studies in the college a burden, or too severe a business. If the truth be told there is nothing so hard that it does not become easy, if only one gets under it!

FROM "OF EFFECTIVE COUNCILS"

(1760-1763)

That we Poles should consider ourselves wiser and more prudent than all the human race, than any ancient or modern commonwealth, would be an unheard of presumption which would only make us ridiculous before the world. Let us govern ourselves like sensible people, as the rest of the race does! Have done with pretences that we are better than others! The argument that things are one sort abroad and another in Poland has so little sense as to be no argument at all. For the God of nature did not search for a different clay or a different model when he made the Poles, from what he used for Englishmen, Swiss, Belgians, etc.; and if the unanimity chimera* had taken root in those nations, the same disorder and helplessness would obtain with these as with us!

---

* Allusion is made to the Polish Sejm custom, Liberum Veto.

STANISŁAW STASZIC

Staszic was one of the most erudite and independent minds of his epoch. His activities were carried on during an era of conflict between obsolete reaction and new democratic trends. Staszic was one of the leading intellects of the reform movement of the Diet, which conducted its session continuously for four years (1788-1792). He was also one of the spiritual authors of the Constitution of May 3rd.

FROM "MANKIND"

(1780-1820)

Justice and Freedom

Freedom which is not based on justice is an empty word full of delusions. The greatest tyrants of mankind cried most loudly of freedom. The Greeks and Romans, most zealous followers of freedom, wrote and declaimed about it most of all; yet these same Greeks and Romans were the greatest violators of mankind. Inhabiting one or several cities, they held in subjection millions of helots, men who were slaves, men reduced to the level of animals. Englishmen, proud of their own freedom, oppressed millions of men who led a miserable existence and died in cruel labor to satisfy the insatiable greed of the East India Company, a group of oligarchs, who, to preserve their sovereign rights and therefore to maintain the slave trade, dismembered India and drove mankind from one war to another. The German and Polish nobility, who compared freedom to precious gold, were exclusively autocratic and gazed with indifference upon millions of men in their own countries who were forced to exist without freedom, without land, without honor of birth, without justice or rights. Similarly the boyars, in other countries, bending and groaning under a despotic rule, nevertheless consider themselves almighty and free on their own lands and in turn oppress their serfs. When all freedom and the rights of independent nations were violated in the case of Poland, we could observe in

1814 that those with the greatest guilt were the most vociferous in calling upon freedom. When they disrupted the council at Chatillon, in a treaty signed in Chaumont (on March 1, 1814)* they declared most solemnly before the world that they were motivated only by a desire to restore the former relations between the European nations and the governments, relations based on equal rights of nations and on just laws. Their solemn proclamations announced that during the period of universal peace in Europe, it was their wish to raise and guarantee once again, the rights and freedom of all violated nations; that they desired to prevent states from augmenting their power by means of provinces torn from kingdoms of the old Europe; that they wished to maintain the immemorial balance in order that the ancient nations of Europe might regain once more their independence, their political rights and their nationality; for these ancient nations could not be altered or incorporated within a nation alien to them however many centuries of foreign rule they were subjected to, and to surrender and annex them was a violation of all rights of nations and could not assure the balance of power nor the freedom of Europe. Nevertheless, these same proclaimers of the independence, freedom and progress of nations repeated their violations of 1772, 1775, 1795.* In the conception of an epoch of constitutional societies true freedom should mean universal justice for all. This aim, toward which the endeavors and strivings of such societies are directed, is clear and distinct; it is easily understood by all men of common sense.

Let all men beware of losing themselves in egoism and self regard, beware of fraud and words that conveniently serve the heartless selfishness, beware of freedom and progress without justice. Let all men improve and foster the true spirit of citizenship within national societies, in order to establish and guarantee universal and equal justice for all.

---

* This relates to the Councils of the European powers, after the fall of Napoleon. In 1815, as a result of these deliberations, the Congress Kingdom of Poland came into being, comprising a very small part of the lands of the former Commonwealth.

* Reference to the policies of Russia, Prussia and Austria toward Poland.

HUGO KOŁŁĄTAJ

(1750-1812)

*Hugo Kołłątaj was the real framer of the Constitution of May
3rd (q. v.). Following its proclamation he was Crown Under-
Chancellor and Minister. He wrote profusely urging the Poles to
wipe out class distinction, and to do away with internal anarchy
through the creation of a strong constitutional government. The
socio-political and moral rebirth of Poland toward the end of
the XVIII century, at a moment when she was being partitioned
among Russia, Austria, and Prussia, is largely the work of
Kołłątaj.*

FROM "LETTERS BY AN ANONYM"

(1788)

We know full well that the worker on the estates of the
gentry became a possession of the manor-house and by an
incomprehensible violation of humanity ceased to be an
individual, contrary to the obvious law of nature. Given
over into the custody of the lord, left in his legal, if one
may say so, bondage, regarded as no better than cattle, he
experienced the kind of fate to which only a land-owner's
prejudices, education, greed and passion could expose him.
Finally, sold into the hands of the Jew,* submerged in
drunkenness, uneducated, he grew slothful in servitude and
misery, happy only insofar as his landowner was good. If
by anything, then it is by the state of our servitude that we
can judge what Polish freedom is: for who will convince
me that a man knowing and loving its prerogatives, expressing indignation at violence and lawlessness, will look with
cold indifference upon the servitude of a man similar to
himself? This is known only too well by virtuous landowners, by the benevolent friends of humanity, and we do
not consider that servitude was formerly so widespread in

---

* Reference to the village tavern-keepers, the Jews, who were also usurers.

44

Poland as it is widespread in later days; for aside from the royal and church estates,† in which the freedom of the people is not infringed upon by law, we have countless estates, we have entire provinces where the husbandman possesses land under contract, acquires it by purchase and pays the agreed rental rate or works off the amount. Basing ourselves on the practice of good landowners, let us reflect, pray, on the goodness of the laws of Kazimierz* and the iniquity of later statutes.

Whoever follows the spirit of the law will not find it difficult to notice the evident contradictions we are in the habit of exhibiting relative to the servitude of the people. Let us reflect for a moment that all of us, as many as are borne by the Polish earth, rich or poor, are the subjects of the Republic. It is Poland which wields the supreme power over us, whose laws govern us, whose will commands us, whose power protects us, whose might curbs and punishes us. Through what prejudice can we remove the lowest beggar from this highest power? Through what presumption can we arrogate unto ourselves the sovereign and independent rule over the poor farmer, and how can the free man, contrary to his feelings, dare to be the despot over another and violate that law which he prizes in himself more than the pupil of his eye? If one human being cannot be the subject of both Peter and Paul, he can certainly not be the subject of both the Republic and a private citizen; what then is the difference between a gentleman and a peasant that the spirit of the law clearly indicates to us? Namely, that the gentleman, subject to the Republic, may own permanent estates in all the provinces of Poland while the peasant, subject of the Republic, may not own them, that the gentleman, at liberty to own permanent estates, as the lawful owner, may administer them as he pleases under the protection of the law, while the peasant, having no permanent estate anywhere in Poland, may enjoy them only in

---

† Holdings of the Crown and the Church in which the lot of the peasants was a better one.

* Kazimierz the Great, King of Poland (1333-1370).

accordance with the conditions he has accepted from the owner: either by socage or by payment of rent.

O truth! Most merciful gift from Heaven! If ever your residence among people established the happiness of nations, enter today into the hearts of free Poles, enlighten their minds and inspire them with a magnificent attachment to freedom! May this earth, which Providence allotted to human freedom, no longer suffer the meanest slave in its bosom! May the rich man and the great man do homage to all-seeing Providence, respecting humanity in the poorest peasant! May he come to realize that all his splendor and luxury are the gift of the peasant's miserable hand, that all his magnificence shines with the sweat of the poor! This bloody sweat, mingled with tears and oppression, laid down such a great class distinction, awakened the arrogance of the estates to such an extent, that we finally almost forgot that we are people of a similar nature and subject to the same misery. The moans of the oppressed are said to bring down great plagues upon our nation, surrendering us to shameful degradation and to dependence on others in payment for the great degradation which human nature suffers in our legislation. The third estate does not require great sacrifices of us. It has no need of empty democracy, it merely demands natural justice, civil justice. Let us return to it what we sacrilegiously took away from it, violating divine and human law, let us return to it the freedom of its person and of its hands. If we do this, this industrious folk—the folk that feeds us and that gives fertility to our lands— will raise the standard of living and will multiply our wealth; it will love the Fatherland and will consider it truly its own, instead of, as today, feeling no different from animals in relation to it.

FROM "THE POLITICAL LAW OF THE POLISH NATION"

(1793)

Prudence, the most noble quality of the human mind, will probably cause you to reflect that the time has not yet come to reveal the truth in its entirety to the Polish nation. But this same prudence never permits such despairing thoughts: its service in legislation is needed only to find the means of presenting people with the truth and not to conceal the truth from them until the right moment or to break the laws of justice and humanity because of prejudices. There is no time, or excuse for a time, at which it would be becoming to infringe upon the rights of man or to refuse to restore the rights that have been taken away! The nation in which man is unhappy cannot be termed unfettered; the country in which man is a slave cannot be free! Thus, no legislation should pass over the rights of man in silence, no society may sacrifice people for people! Such prudence would be called either injustice or fear! For, to say that the uneducated people may not have their rights fully restored is to speak against the rules of fairness and prudence. Let anyone seeking to place the yoke of servitude upon an uneducated man go back to his own heart, let him think whether if fate had placed him among the common people he would permit his natural rights to be taken away from him, let him answer whether he would tolerate being deprived of the security of his person and his goods. Or can we say that the gentry, to which Polish laws assured not only freedom but equality in governing, is universally enlightened? .... That prudence which refuses to restore the rights of man to an individual on the ground that he is not educated, would be as hard and unjust as that which would deprive the poverty-stricken gentleman of his civil liberties for this very same reason.

It is true that Poland is not alone in committing this injustice. The Muscovite Empire, Bohemia and certain French and Spanish provinces have maintained the same violent attitude toward the common people. The French islands, the Dutch and the English colonies mete out much worse treatment to the Negroes, these unfortunate citizens of two worlds. But can deep-rooted prejudices and the injustice of other countries justify the violation of the laws of nature?

47

Who is the subject of one's land? How is he to be regarded in the order of birth, in which Providence wanted everyone to be equal? Whether he be white or a black slave, or whether he moan under the violence of unjust laws or of chains, he is a human being and in no way differs from us!

The misery of human beings grows in proportion to their enslavement. A republic cannot suffer the special rule of individuals; in a monarchy there is only one sovereign but in a feudal aristocracy almost every peasant has his own despot. What kind of a government do we desire in our country? Do we want a genuine republic or an oligarchy? Do we want to restore freedom to Poland or only to a few families ruling over the rest of the slaves? Let us do as we wish; nature itself will take vengeance on us for such an obvious injustice! The common people will then be, as they have been heretofore, the property of the squires but the gentry will, without fail, be common people and the same sophisms which we use today, contrary to our own heart, to drown out the voice of truth, will serve our greedy neighbors to make slaves of us.

As for granting freedom to our peasants and restoring their liberty before the law, this was necessarily the principle of the social contract,* which can in no way violate the natural rights of man. No one is in a position to renounce this right or to get rid of it and no government may accept such a renunciation from anyone, even if it is offered of free will—because an individual's entire moral behavior depends on personal freedom. An enslaved human being is incapable of good or evil, he is not worthy of reward and does not deserve punishment, for in such a condition all his actions are determined—and hence cannot be included in a decent community.

Freedom alone will guarantee his moral behavior, from freedom stems the authority of civil and criminal legislation and on it are based all descriptions and contracts. Whoever is not free can assume no responsibilities and no duties, for he is a powerless and dispensable being, And how was it

---

* In keeping with his times, Kołłątaj was a fervent believer in the social contract (Locke, Rousseau).

48

possible to require that a wise law-maker not abolish such shameful abuse and leave a human being, who has common beginnings with others like him, in the category of cattle? Such a social contract is forbidden by common sense, prohibited by the Christian religion, precluded by the general welfare of nations, for it would amount to a violation of natural rights, be a crime against such a sacred religion, and would cover us with shame in the eyes of enlightened nations. In the face of such weighty and just reasons of our law-giver, the interest of personal gains should be silenced; indeed these become unworthy as soon as they are predicated on the violation of the holy rights of nature and of religion; an interest of this type could be inspired only by the bad habits of barbarism and the want of education. We shall probably say that the peasantry is not prepared to accept such great beneficence. And was it not up to us, who became rich through his blood-sweat, who cemented our great estates through his tears, was it not up to us to see that the peasant was ready? The Koenigsberg philosopher* gave an exhaustive answer by means of an irrefutable objection. Either enslavement, says Kant, disposes people to enlightenment: therefore they must be already fully enlightened, and having remained for so long in this disgraceful state, are worthy of having their freedom restored,—or through enslavement (which seems more likely to me) they could not as yet be enlightened, therefore their freedom should be restored so that they might become worthy of the enlightenment befitting their station. It was the duty of the wise law-maker to restore the rights proper to man; the government's duty is so to guide the people that it may acknowledge its own happiness and not abuse that of others. A good government has more effective means to carry this out than have individuals; it can prevent all abuses, it can enlighten the people in proportion to its needs; the law will protect it from oppression and will keep it within the bounds of accepted duties. This must not be doubted for a moment, for what citizen, even the most influential, cannot be kept

---

* Immanuel Kant (1724-1804), permanent resident of Koenigsberg.

within these bounds? This is all the more true of the poor
man, living by the toil of his hands and having no benefits
from nature save the forces of his own person which must
serve to meet all the demands of life. It is in vain that
many complain that by losing possession of another's person
our income would suffer, as if the labor of a bond-servant
could bring us greater gains than an agreement with a free-
man based on mutual needs; let us admit, rather, that these
supposed gains conceal an obvious injustice which has been
practiced for so long by greedy and cruel landowners. For
those to whom pity has spoken in behalf of these poor
people are well aware how much the peasant's upkeep costs
them. The land workers of good and just masters will not
even feel the change from a state of legal bondage; but
wicked and unjust masters will find themselves compelled
not to abuse the rights of the common people if they do not
wish to see their lands and property laid waste. It is not
only now that humanity is taking the side of this most
worthwhile class; there have been who have long spoken in
its behalf to the stubborn usurpers of its liberties. Warnings
did not help; the whole nation now bears the shame that
this justice which we ourselves were unable to call forth,
has been rendered to our people only by the universal law-
giver of Europe . . . .

FROM "TO THE ILLUSTRIOUS DEPUTATION FOR THE FRAM-
ING OF A CONSTITUTION"

(1791)

. . . . Would it not be better to educate the common people
first, to prepare them intelligently to accept the holy gift
of freedom? It would not be better, I answer. Indeed, he
would be the harshest law-maker who would await the education of the masses before restoring their freedom. There
is nothing worse in human nature than an educated slave:
he then feels the entire weight of the injustice pressing upon
him and thinking of nothing else than of restoring to himself his natural rights, devotes his whole intelligence to

planning vengeance upon him who has heretofore unfairly held his inheritance and this fires his heart to embolden it to achieve the height of revenge. Let no one be surprised by the cruelty of the masses, about which he happens to have read or heard, for the fruit born of oppression and enslavement must surpass in venom and cruelty anything rapacious and death-dealing that we can imagine. Let us hasten to restore to the people what nature assured them; the educated will restore it by themselves and the ignorant will serve as the tool of the hypocrite and the despot to strip us of our liberties; the less we are willing to remedy the situation in today's revolution, the more certain we may be that either we or our progeny will become the victims of the despair and vengeance of the masses . . . .

POLISH CONSTITUTION

(1791)

FROM "CONSTITUTION OF MAY THIRD 1791"

The Polish Constitution of May 3rd, 1791 was a bold attempt to reorganize a gentry Poland in the spirit of the Constitution of the United States and the French Declaration of the Rights of Man and Citizen. It abolished certain weaknesses which had until now paralyzed the state. The "liberum veto" was annulled, the crown (worn at that time by Stanisław Poniatowski) was made hereditary; nobles were subjected to taxation; and varieties of religious faith were allowed.

But the new Constitution was never applied. For, in 1972, Catherine of Russia invaded Poland, abolished the constitution and invited Prussia and Austria to join her in partitioning the land.

. . . . Valuing above life and personal happiness the political existence, external independence and internal freedom of the Nation we have resolved upon the present Constitution . . . .

We recognize all royal cities in the lands of the Commonwealth as free.

We allow to the citizens of such cities the hereditary possession of the land in the cities occupied by them, of their houses, villages and territories wherever such now legally belong to the cities.

Guided by justice, humanity and Christian duties, as well as by our own well conceived interests, we take the peasants, whose labor is the most abundant source of the national wealth, who constitute the most numerous population on the nation and therefore the country's greatest strength, under the protection of the law and of the national government, resolving that from now on any liberties, grants, or contracts whatsoever authentically agreed upon by the landlord with the peasants of his estates, whether these grants and contracts be made with the communities or with each village inhabitant individually, shall constitute a common and mutual obligation, in accordance with the true meaning of the terms and the description contained in such grants and contracts, and shall be protected by the national government . . . .

In human society all authority originates from the will of the nation. In order therefore that the integrity of the country, civil liberties and the order of society may be forever equally maintained, three powers should, and by virtue of the present law shall forever, constitute the government of the Polish nation: these are, the legislative power vested in the assembled estates, the supreme executive authority vested in the King and the Guardianship,* and the judicial power vested in the jurisdictions established or to be established for that purpose.

The happiness of nations depends on just laws; the effects of laws depend on their execution . . . . Having therefore insured to the free Polish nation the power of making laws for itself and watching over all executive power, as well as of electing officers to the magistracies, we entrust the supreme power of the enforcement of the laws to the King and his Council, which Council shall be called the Guardianship of the Laws . . . .

The judicial power shall be exercised neither by the legislative power nor by the King, but by the magistracies established and elected for that purpose . . . .

The nation must act in its own defense and for the preservation of its integrity. Therefore all citizens are defenders of the integrity and liberties of the nation. The army is nothing but the defensive power selected and organized from the general strength of the nation. The nation owes to its army a debt of respect for its complete devotion to the defense of the nation. The army owes to the nation the defense of its frontiers and of the general peace; in a word it must be the nation's most powerful shield . . . .

---

* Council of Ministers.

ALLIANCE WITH PROGRESSIVE EUROPE

HISTORICAL BACKGROUND

(1795-1863)

After the partition of Poland in 1795 several attempts were made to recover independence. A Polish legion, formed by Polish refugee officers in France fought under Napoleon in many campaigns in Italy. A campaign in the French West Indies brought disaster to the Legion. However, remnants of this legion found their way into the army of the Duchy of Warsaw. This was a French vassal state composed by Napoleon (in 1807) of fragments of Polish territory.

The Duchy of Warsaw was administered by Poles and had a Polish army, though its legal institutions were mainly French. When Napoleon was defeated certain areas of the Duchy were returned to Prussia. The Congress of Vienna in 1815 granted the rest of the Duchy a quasi-independent status and it was called the Congress Kingdom.

This Kingdom was the center of Polish activities up to the reestablishment of Poland's independence in 1918.

Although the Congress Kingdom enjoyed internal independence to a great extent and maintained an army of its own, the Emperor of Russia was the king of Poland, and the Congress Kingdom took no part in international affairs. In 1830 an insurrection initiated by Polish cadets and intellectuals drove the Russian troops from Poland. Attempts to appease the Russian government failed, the Czar demanded unconditional surrender of the Poles, and war broke out. The Polish government was not characterized by a very revolutionary mind and failed to put to use its well organized economic and administrative apparatus. Accordingly the Polish army was not reinforced by a general mobilization and the Russians succeeded in storming the Polish capital (September, 1831). There followed a great emigration which transferred the center of Polish intellectual life to France for the next thirty years.

In conquered Poland the Poles struggled for many years to defend their administrative autonomy. Russia moved consistently toward the abolishment of all separate Polish institutions.

In 1863 young Poles were subjected to compulsory military service in the Russian army. The January insurrection was a direct result of this. For about two years isolated skirmishes were fought between Polish guerrillas and Russian military forces. The majority of the peasants, however, refused to join the uprising and the insurrection failed.

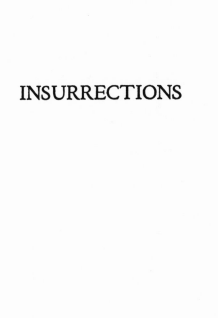

INSURRECTIONS

TADEUSZ KOŚCIUSZKO

(1746-1817)

Kościuszko fought under George Washington in the American Revolution of 1776. Later in 1794, he led an Insurrection against Russia for the independence of Poland. Reared in the liberal and progressive environment of the Polish Age of Enlightenment, Kościuszko understood the necessity of emancipating the Polish peasants if freedom was to be regained for Poland. But in 1794, Kościuszko's Insurrection was smashed and the following year the third Treaty of Partition blotted the country from the map.

FROM "THE POŁANIEC MANIFESTO"

(May 7, 1794)

All Civil-Military Orderly Commissions are to announce to the people:

That according to the law they remain under the protection of the national government.

That every peasant is free and that he is allowed to move freely from place to place, provided he notifies the Orderly Commission of the province whither he goes, and provided he pays all his outstanding debts and national taxes.

That the peasants shall have relief from labor, so that he who has worked five or six days in the week, shall be freed for two days in the week; he who has worked three or four days, shall be freed for one day; he who has worked two days, shall be freed for one day. Moreover, if both man and wife have performed statute-labor relief will apply to both. Such a release shall last for the duration of the insurrection, until in due time the legislative authority shall make a permanent arrangement in that matter.

The local authorities shall take care that the farms of those who serve in the army of the Commonwealth shall not fall into decay and that the soil which is the source of our wealth shall no lie fallow; the manors as well as the communities shall apply themselves to it.

From those who are called to the general levy, as long as they remain under arms, no statute-labor shall be exacted, but shall begin after their return home.

The possession of the·land held with the duties attached to it, according to the aforesaid relief, shall not be taken away by the landlord from any peasant unless he has previously pleaded before the local overseer and proved that the peasant has not fulfilled his duties.

To be better able to keep order and to secure the results of these directions the Orderly Commission shall divide their *voivodships*, provinces or counties into supervision districts, so that each district shall comprise a thousand, or at the most twelve hundred farmers. They shall name each district after the main village or township and encompass it within such a circuit that dispatches may be sent easily.

In each district they shall appoint a supervisor, an able and honorable man who will receive complaints from the peasants concerning their grievances and from the manor in cases of the peasants' disobedience and insubordination. It shall be his duty to settle disputes, and if the parties should not be content, to refer them to the Orderly Commission.

Issued at the Camp of Połaniec, May 7, 1794

TADEUSZ KOŚCIUSZKO

TESTAMENT*

(1798)

I, Thaddeus Kościuszko, being just in my departure from America, do hereby declare and direct that should I make no other testamentary disposition of my property in the United States, hereby authorize my friend Thomas Jefferson to employ the whole thereof in purchasing negroes from among his own as any others and giving them liberty in my name, in giving them an education in trades or otherwise, and in having them instructed for their new condition in the duties of morality which may make them good neighbors,

---

* The text is the original English.

good fathers or mothers, husbands or wives, and in their duties as citizens, teaching them to be defenders of their liberty and country and of the good order of Society and in whatsoever may make them happy and useful, and I make the said Thomas Jefferson my executor of this.

T. KOŚCIUSZKO

5th day of May, 1798

FROM "THE MANIFESTO OF THE DEMOCRATIC SOCIETY"

(1836)

The Democratic Society, whose manifesto is printed below, in part, was founded by Polish émigrés in Paris after the failure of the November Rising of 1830-31. It brought together all Polish progressive and sincerely democratic elements, kept in close touch with Western European democratic movements and prepared the ground for the future democratic reorganization of Poland. Although it was composed mainly of members of the gentry, it broke completely with the gentry caste system. It proclaimed the sovereignty of the people, and promised equality and freedom for all citizens of the Commonwealth irrespective of origin and creed.

*　　*　　*

. . . . For almost half a century European humanity has been developing a new destiny on the ruins of the old order, has been seeking new conditions of social life. This tendency is manifested today in the whole intellectual and political world, in all endeavors and movements of the peoples, in the very concessions of governments which are unable to offer efficacious resistance to the demands of those who strive for emanicipation. The most enlightened protagonists of the old order, the most timid and the boldest opponents of it, men stationed on the highest as well as the lowest rungs of the social ladder, all alike foresee or demand democracy, that is, abolition of privilege and the rule of equality.

This equality, in ancient times the vital base of the social order of the Slavs, subsequently developed and expanded by the ruling class in Poland, today so strongly evoked by the light and necessity of our age and announcing the complete happiness of mankind is the cardinal, unalterable, national principle of our Society, the symbol of its unity, the common belief of all its members. We are deeply convinced that a social order based on usurpation in which

64

some enjoy all the advantages attached to social life while others are forced to sustain only the burdens of that life, is the sole cause of the misfortune of our homeland and of all mankind. As long as such an order, violating natural justice, persists, the internal struggle will continue between the oppressed and their oppressors, between the mass condemned to ignorance, misery and slavery and the small groups which have seized all advantages of social life for themselves. Amid such anarchy a free and harmonious development of national forces cannot take place. Mankind has understood this. Therefore the right to equality, so far only existent in thought, must be carried out in reality.

From that universal, infallible conscience of mankind as well as from the national thought we derive our faith.

All men, as beings of one and the same nature, have equal rights and equal obligations; all are brethren, all are children of one father—God; all are members of one family—mankind.

Every man is entitled to seek his own happiness, to satisfy all his physical, mental and moral needs; to develop and perfect all his faculties; to share equally, according to his work and abilities, in all advantages of social life.

It is also every man's duty to seek the happiness of others, to contribute to the satisfaction of their needs and to the development of their faculties, limiting his own advantage by the happiness of others and of the community, and to help to carry the public burden in proportion to the advantages derived from social life.

Privilege, by whatever name it may be called, is a breach of common obligations, or an usurpation of some right, and consequently the denial of equality and a violation of nature.

Without equality there is no freedom; for where some are not allowed to do what others may do, there must be slavery on the one hand, despotism on the other, and anarchy in the whole community.

Without equality there is no brotherhood; for where some cast off their obligations and transfer them to others, there must be egoism on the one hand, and mental and moral abasement on the other, and mutual hatred among the members of the whole community.

The right of man has its source in his individual nature, in freedom; obligation is derived from social nature, from brotherhood.

Between rights and obligations there must be harmony. Where individuals are everything and society nothing, there is anarchy; whereas where society absorbs individualism there must be despotism. Neither anarchy nor despotism is the nature of societies. They are only its two extremes.

Society, faithful to its duties, insures equal advantages to all members, lends each one equal assistance in the satisfaction of his physical, mental and moral needs; it concedes the right of possessing land or any other property only to work; it develops the faculties of its members through public and uniform education accessible to all, and through the unrestricted freedom of expressing one's thoughts, and does not restrict freedom of conscience by persecution and intolerance; by means of free development and nurture of the national forces it purifies its members of egoism and ignorance, and leads not only individual, separate parts of the nation but the whole of it on the road of continuous progress toward perfection.

Society cannot even begin to fulfill these duties under a system based on privilege or any other anti-social element; for the inevitable consequence of such elements is an unequal distribution of the advantages and burdens of social life; dividing men into masters and subjects, they bring power, riches and education to some, and subjection, poverty and ignorance to others. The lot and future of such a society does not depend on itself, but on a ruling class, on a handful of privileged people. It is obvious that any such form which violates the universal principle of equality is contrary to nature, justice and truth.

Everything for the people, by the people; this is the most general principle of democracy comprising both its purpose and form. Everything for the people, for all, is the purpose;

everything by the people, by all, is the form. In the form based on equality, all have a common interest; therefore there are no dissensions, there is unity. This unity is manifested everywhere; it creates general harmony and gives strength which makes possible the fulfillment of the national mission among other societies. It is only in democracy that the sovereignty of the people ceases to be a delusion . . . .

Societies organized in this fashion can, in the harmonious striving to attain the common, general goal, completely fulfill their particular missions. There is only one way to attain that goal; continuous and simultaneous self-improvement in the physical, mental and moral order. This improvement, depending on the harmonious development of all national forces, cannot take place if all members composing each society do not improve; and the whole mass cannot improve if all men do not fulfill their duties under the law, if the general principle of equality is violated by any privilege.

Consequently, equality contains all conditions of individual and social happiness; without it neither individual man, society, nor mankind can fulfill their missions.

Equality introduces into life two great, omnipotent feelings: brotherhood and freedom. The love of mankind possesses an enchanting power; that power daily increases. Freedom is also an indestructible force which seizes ever growing masses. The love of mankind, and freedom having united their forces, will shatter the old world of privileges; the same love and freedom will by their united efforts build a new world of equality.

Thus do we understand the principles for whose realization mankind is striving today. It is on them that we base the future regeneration of Polish society, it is in their spirit that we work for the achievement of its independent existence.

An independent Poland and a democratic Poland is the aim of our society.

Not one portion, not one fragment of the great nation, but the whole Poland circumscribed by the pre-partition boundaries is able to maintain its circumscribed existence, to fulfill its mission . . . .

The reborn, independent Poland will be democratic. All, irrespective of faith and origin, will receive mental, political and social emancipation; a new order, comprising property, labor, industry, education and all social relations, based on the principles of equality, will take the place of anarchy which until now has been dubbed law by the usurpers . . . .

Only an independent and democratic Poland is able to fulfill her mission, to break the alliance of absolutism, to destroy its pernicious influence on the civilization of the West, to spread democratic ideas among the Slavs, today serving as tools of subjugation, to unite them with that idea, and by her virtues, by her purity and strength of spirit give rise to the universal emancipation of the European peoples. For the revival of her independence Poland has within herself immense forces that until now have not been stirred by any conscientious or sincere voice. This is a power, untouched as yet, dreadful to external and internal foes alike. Through it Poland will rise.

The Polish people, deprived of all rights, oppressed by ignorance, misery and servitude, continues to till the land, wrested from it centuries ago, and sweats and bleeds for the benefit of others; to this day in the old provinces seized by Moscow the peasants are sold together with the land as property inseparable from it. Humanity, suffering and insulted in them, calls for justice. The domestic oppressors were deaf to that voice. During the recent struggle for independence, abusing the sacred name of love and country, they sought to feed the starving people with the mere sound of words, they urged them to shed their blood for a country which for so many centuries has rewarded their labor with contempt, abasement and misery; they clamored for the people to rise and destroy the invaders—they who themselves were the invaders of the people's rights! Only a weak echo answered their hypocritical clamorings—and we fell!

If this terrifying lesson, bought at the price of so many bloody sacrifices, is not to be lost; if a new rising is not to be a sad repetition of former risings; the first call to arms must be the emancipation of the peasants, returning to them unconditional possession of the land wrested from them, the restoration of their rights, the summoning of all without discrimination of creed or origin to the enjoyment of independent existence. Only such an application of conscientious, sincere, unequivocal justice can develop in the whole oppressed mass the feeling of true sacrifice and imbue it with the conviction that a nation of twenty million is able to break and destroy the coalition of all Europe, as it was recently destroyed by republican France . . . .

For the reestablishment of her independence on democratic principles Poland also has national elements within herself. The democratic idea, first spread through the whole nation, later developed and improved in the gentry class, may again be easily implanted in the people, who, despite long bondage and oppression have preserved unobliterated vestiges of the ancient popular rule.

But together with her own forces Poland has natural allies; while the sanguinary struggle against the enemy was still in progress, each of her victories was cheered and admired by Europe; and we, representatives of the subjugated nation's misfortunes and hopes, have found hospitality and a kind haven amidst general sympathy. The peoples of Europe have allied themselves with the immortal spirit of Poland, and on the same grave where absolutism concluded its infernal union, they have tendered each other fraternal hands. Our enemy has become their enemy, and their foes our foes. Therefore, convinced that former national hatreds have completely disappeared, we believe in the sincere collaboration of these peoples in the spirit of brotherhood and the common need of emancipation.

Cabinet negotiations will not restore Poland, nor will monarchial wars administer justice to the people. However, our Homeland is so dear to us, we are so grieved by its wounds, that we will not neglect to make use of any event, any favorable circumstance. We shall therefore embrace everything that may in any way be useful to our cause, that is able to facilitate and bring nearer the attainment of the main goal.

This is the conscientious, sincere, unequivocal exposition of our principles, aims and means. We shall sacrifice all our lives to their realization. We have sworn before our country and humanity not to rest until Poland regains her independence and establishes her existence on democratic principles. This pledge, sworn with youthful enthusiasm, we shall carry out with manly perseverance. We are not discouraged by the immensity of the task, we shall not be intimidated by adversities; because the justice which we demand, the truth which we proclaim, are omnipotent . . . .

FROM THE PROCLAMATION OF THE ORGANIZATION "POLISH PEOPLE, COMMUNITY GRUDZIĄDZ"

(1835)

Unlike the Polish emigration in France which, after the Rising of 1830-31, was composed mainly of members of the nobility, the Polish emigrants in England were mostly workers and peasants who had fought in that rising. Imprisoned by the Prussians, they had managed to escape to England. Here they organized the "Polish People, Community Grudziądz", named after the fortress in which most of them had been held prisoner.

This was the first Polish independence organization with a socialist character. One of its first leaders was Stanisław Gabriel Worcell.

The "Polish People" was dissolved in 1846 when news of a rising in Poland and the so called "Cracow Manifesto" reached England. The majority of the members then tried to return to Poland to take part in the rising.

*　　*　　*

We deem each man's own strength to be his primary, most sacred possession; and the right to apply that strength to whatever work he may choose as well as the right to profit by the fruits of his labor we deem to be his natural right, God-given and inviolable. But here, as in the exercise of any other rights, there exists a limiting condition: namely, that to other people belong the same natural rights of work and existence. Any transgression of this condition, this fundament of social equilibrium, any employment of one's own strength and work to the detriment of the strength, work or existence of another, results in violence and injustice, and consequently the rights to the fruits of such labor are forfeited.

In the present social organization, many rights to profits allegedly gained by one's own labor, but contaminated by monopoly or violence, ought to have been forfeited . . . .

71

We desire that property, as the social form through which the external world is turned to man's advantage, given by society as a guarantee of man's existence as a link uniting its individual members into one society, shall not belong to them but to the whole group, the association, which, fulfilling the obligation appropriate to that right, will in turn have to supply or equip each member with the means of livelihood, that is, first with education and then with the tools of work which for some is land, for others workshops, offices, etc.

We desire that this equipment shall be effected on the basis of the administration of local assemblies and that it shall constitute, so to speak, a capital equal for all, applying every one to the work chosen by him; its choice shall be left to the one equipped, but this he will have the right to do only once, cases foreseen by the law and independent of his will excepted.

We desire that, being in this way sons of their country and brothers among themselves, all its inhabitants shall with their lives repay it for their lives taken from it, and that they shall replace their egoistic aims by a spirit of sacrifice, brotherhood and social unity.

We desire government agencies to establish banks in all parts of the country which will lend or give credit and take the place of the present monopolistic private banks, factory owners, etc., which will give to those requiring them the necessary means to do business and will supersede the powers of individual people. We desire moreover that the freedom of industrial and business corporations, etc., shall bring people together in groups based on cooperation which will spread ever more and more.

We therefore desire that the arts, sciences, industry directed toward social aims shall continue to produce the same amount of profits, but more moral ones than hitherto; and that they all shall tend toward the social and intellectual development of the social body under the supervising influence of one administration controlled by the people, but active, strong and centralized.

FROM THE MANIFESTOES OF THE NATIONAL GOVERNMENT OF 1863

(1863)

In the year 1863 an armed uprising against Russian rule in Poland spread through the so-called Congress Kingdom. The secret National Government which proclaimed that outbreak, wished to attract the peasant masses to it, Polish, Lithuanian, and Ruthenian (Ukrainian and White Ruthenian) alike, with the intention of converting the struggle for political independence into a great peasant mass movement. On the first day of the revolt a decree was published abolishing serfdom and emancipating the peasants. Soon afterwards the National Government issued appeals to the Lithuanian and Ruthenian groups calling both peoples to the struggle. Although the uprising, as in earlier cases, was suppressed, the decrees of the National Government set forth directions which later emancipation movements were to follow. Most important of these was the realization of the necessity of linking the cause of the peasants with any struggle for national freedom.

* * *

Whereas, the emancipation of the peasants has so far in spite of the general desire of the nation, and due to the obstacles put in this way by the aggressor government, not been effected; moreover,

Whereas, the acquisition by farmers of lands which heretofore they have held by right of rents, statute labor or other obligations diminishes the property of those who have hitherto been the owners.

The Central National Committee, acting as the Provisional National Government, resolves and decrees that:

Art. 1. All landed property which any farmer has held hitherto by right of statute labor, rent or by any other right, together with gardens, houses and farm buildings, as well as the rights and privileges attached thereto, shall become from the date of the present decree the exclusive and hereditary property of the hitherto holder without any obligations, tributes, statutes, labor or rent whatsoever, with only the

73

condition that taxes due from it be paid and the appropriate national services be rendered.

Art. 2. The hitherto owners of the land ceded to the farmers shall receive indemnities corresponding to its value from national funds, through the state debt.

Art. 3. The principles for defining the amount of the appraisal of the land and the kind of the credit to be instituted shall be indicated in separate decrees.

Art. 4. All ukases, and rescripts issued by the aggressor government concerning so-called peasant relations are abolished and therefore binding to no one.

Art. 5. The present decree shall apply to private properties and to government, donative, ecclesiastic and any other properties.

Art. 6. The Central National Committee, acting as the Provisional National Government, charges the military and country chiefs with the promulgation and execution of the present decree.

Issued in Warsaw, January 22, 1863

TO OUR RUTHENIAN BROTHERS!

The banner of insurrection has been planted on the soil of Poland. The struggle for the independence and liberty of Poland, Lithuania and Ruthenia has already been begun by the youth of Warsaw who resist the violence of the Muscovite conscription. Masses of the people hasten from all directions to the national standards, and many a blow has already been dealt by weapons wrested from the very hands of the enemy and by the scythes of the peasants. The insurrection spreads and gathers strength, for its watchword is the liberty and happiness of the nation, and its first act shall bring justice to the numerous peasant class. Through the decree of emancipation issued by the National Government we have won millions of new citizens in the whole area of the Commonwealth who, despite differences of faith and language, shall enjoy equal rights in the free determination of their fate.

Ruthenian brothers! Your land, which for so many centuries has shared good fortune and bad with the rest of the Commonwealth, must today also reverberate with the cry of freedom! Blood spilled on your soil, on your fields will bring victory to the insurrection. The Czarist armies will meet the grave under your cairns, and your scythes united with the Lithuanian and Polish scythes will achieve independence and liberty for Poland, Lithuania, and Ruthenia.

We shall mold a guarantee of victory out of unity, endurance and stubborn, intrepid and decisive struggle. Ruthenians, we summon you to the struggle! Your negligence, your hesitation, may postpone the moment of general happiness. Do not be guilty of impeding the regeneration of our common homeland.

We are faced by a strong foe, but the Czar's bayonets and guns, his frauds and deceptions which seek to incite the peasants against the insurrection which gives them liberty, property and citizenship, his intrigues which aim to disrupt the brotherhood of the peoples of the Commonwealth, will splinter and fall before the banner of justice which we carry.

To arms, to arms, we call you, brothers, and the first act of your insurrection shall be the immediate emancipation of the peasants!

Issued in Warsaw, February 5, 1863

UNDAUNTED SPIRITS

MAURYCY MOCHNACKI

(1804-1834)

Mochnacki was a literary critic and publicist in the period of the Polish November Rising of 1830-1831. The Rising was started by a group of cadets and young men, and the national government was formed of well-known and respected men representing various shades of political opinion, who fought off the Russians for almost a year. When finally they were defeated, the last traces of Polish freedom were erased. Congress Poland was abolished and the state was completely absorbed into Russia. Mochnacki together with other writers, fled to Paris, which became the intellectual capital of the Poles for many generations. There, before he died, he completed an exhaustive history of the 1830 Uprising.

FROM "TO BE OR NOT TO BE"

(1831)

From now on this fragment of Shakespeare's verse is to be the motto of our Patriotic Society. We have also adopted it as the motto of our newspaper. These words genuinely comprehend our cause, and the principle of our policy. Why?

In its boldness, its perils and its immensity the Polish rising is unsurpassed. There has never been a riddle more involved than the question of our existence. Here in the center of Europe is a great nation that crumbles because of the weakness of its constitutions, crumbles because of the numerous defects of its social system. It was not because of traitors that we crumbled, not because we disagreed among ourselves, not because of the insidious schemes that Moscow paid to have woven around us, not at all; these were but the consequences of an evil that lay much deeper. We crumbled because with us not the majority but the minority has always been the nation. We perished because the social revolution in no way changed this disproportion. This evil was deeply rooted: Kościuszko took up arms in the cause of the insurrection, whereas, he should have fought in the cause of social revolution, as Kołłątaj counselled. The French, English, Belgian revolutions aimed, to a large extent at internal improvement: They bore the characteristic of a domestic dispute, a family misunderstanding. Discussions and bloodshed did not bring about the fall of France and England. On the contrary, England on the sea, and France on the continent, owe their supremacy to social revolutions. As with convulsive emotions or accelerated blood circulations or even extreme paroxysms in the human body, so with nations: wherever the wrath of heaven has visited itself upon nations their material strength has multiplied, their patrimony has expanded, their intellectual culture has spread, their wealth and riches grown. Such revolutions, like a thunderstorm at the close of a sultry day, rarefy the condensed atmosphere of peoples . . . .

There are certain moments in history when the doubt rises whether a social or eccentric revolution will save the nation. In Kościuszko's time there was no such doubt.

He knew very well that in Poland the minority was the nation and the majority nothing; he knew that all evil sprang from this disproportion. Why, then, did he not change it? Why, then, to save the whole did he not sacrifice a part? Kościuszko was confronted with the following syllogism: "In order to crush the Russian yoke, proper material forces are necessary; the proper forces are contained in the masses; consequently the masses must be stirred, they must be given new rights, a new meaning. Granting these rights constitutes the essence of social revolution". Consequently, to develop the maximum forces necessary to liberate the nation from the foreign yoke, from external oppression, Kościuszko should have given the revolution a social insurrectionist character.

This idea frequently occurred to Kościuszko; but he was constantly seized with fright at the very thought of a social commotion. This evil reduced us to nought. Out of consideration for the minority, Kościuszko did not wish to give the nation over to the majority. He did not succeed in winning the interest of the masses; millions watched indifferently as the country fell. So far as they were concerned only the names of the oppressors were being changed. The people did not care who ruled.

Those who believe in diplomatics live from day to day in hope, in expectation. They do not believe in social commotions. They are terrified by the noise of the people, they are terrified by the rising of the masses. They fear this as they do a stormy sea, a pestilence, a flood, a fire. But if there is no other means, what then? Those who do not believe in diplomatics place their entire hope in power and right. They call the masses to life to defeat the enemy; they find in a social upheaval the force necessary to spring the insurrection. . . .

History has left us this truth; that the strength with which a nation meets an external enemy is in direct proportion to its internal, material and moral strength. To increase the former it is necessary to multiply and intensify the latter.

ADAM MICKIEWICZ

(1798-1855)

Greatest of Polish poets, by some regarded as the greatest among Slavonic poets, Mickiewicz was in various periods of his life active in social and political spheres. In his youth he organized the students of Wilno University into societies based on principles of enlightened liberalism. After the failure of the Polish rising against Russia in 1831 he published a periodical abroad called "The Polish Pilgrim," which concerned itself with problems of the liberation of Poland. In 1848, after the outbreak of the revolution in Italy, he organized a Polish Legion in Rome to fight against Austria; later in Paris he headed an international editorial committee which published a revolutionary paper in French, "The Tribune of Peoples". In 1855 he went to Turkey and formed a new Polish Legion to fight with the Turkish army against Russia in the Crimean War.

The following articles are from the "Polish Pilgrim" and the "Tribune of Peoples."

THE TENDENCIES OF THE PEOPLES OF EUROPE

(1833)

It has justly been said that the spirit of the age, that the mass of peoples possessed by that spirit, puts a riddle to government and statesmen and like a Sphinx devours those who do not know its solution. How many persons have been devoured, how many heads threatened since the time of the French Revolution! The riddle on which so much depends seems always to become so much more involved and obscure that there must be some common error in the methods that have been used to solve it. If the striving of the masses of the people is called the spirit of the age, why do proud statesmen detach their thought from these masses and, instead of observing the general trend, shut themselves up with their own reason? If the spirit of the age is the spirit of the future, why do they seek to clothe this future, like a growing youth, in old, worn-out, children's dresses and

82

wonder that such a dress tears and shreds? If, finally, the feeling of the whole people, the heart of the whole people, speaks through the spirit of the age, how can one measure this feeling by personal calculation? If scholars had a little more political humility and were willing to observe what goes on around them, if they collected and summed up the conversations of the people, its clamorings, its prayers, they would perhaps learn more than from books and newspapers. The sounds that issue from the mouth of the people are a great petition which the spirit of the age in all humility submits to the cabinets, the houses of parliament and the schools, before it attacks them with stones and bayonets from the pavements. Before the eruption of a volcano it is enough to observe the water in the wells, the smoke in the crevices of the mountain to foresee the danger; woe to those who then sit down to read up on the theory of volcanoes!

What is today the first, foremost, most vivid desire of peoples? We do not hesitate to say that it is the desire of reaching an understanding, uniting, combining their interests; without this it would be impossible to comprehend the general will, just as without calling together the members of a stock corporation it is impossible to guess their desires. Let us draw attention to a few symptoms which clearly show this great tendency of the spirit of the age.

During the French Revolution the memory of the brotherhood of nations, disrupted by the governments, was revived. In the Napoleonic wars a dim presentment of European unity was more and more distinctly manifested in the fact that the people's parties joined hands with the French. But after the fall of Napoleon a political epoch is discernible. Who does not remember how after the outbreak of war in Greece collections for the insurgents were made, how young men hastened from everywhere to join their ranks? The revolutions in Naples and in Spain were also looked upon with favor. Often important discussions of local parliaments were silenced upon the arrival of news from the Levant or from Madrid. From Gibraltar to Moscow one could find homes making merry or in mourning at the news of the triumphs or defeats of the knighthood of freedom. This feeling of sympathy was not deduced directly from any theory, it was not referred to in any constitution. On the contrary, the French sophists argued that a constitutional king had the right to overthrow the constitution in neighboring countries. The sophists did not rejoice or laugh because no article prescribed it. What does this prove? It proves that none of the constitutions of that time expressed the needs of the age.

When after the July Revolution riots broke out in various sections, the People everywhere first attacked custom houses, frontier offices, passport offices. This attack was not caused, as some think, by revenge, for the extortions of the toll-collectors, because the toll-collectors mostly annoy merchants and travelers who do not do much in revolutions; it was the result of the premonition of a greater and more extensive reform. The people felt instinctively that these customs and frontiers were contrary to the current tendency. Indeed, can there be anything more disgraceful than the old prejudice that a line drawn by the finger of kings through one country, often through one town, is to divide the inhabitants, even relatives, into natives and foreigners, into natural enemies? Things have gone so far that every European going from one place to another not only loses all political and civil rights, but is beforehand, as it were, suspected of theft and must provide himself with descriptions and certificates. This custom has stunned many otherwise honest people; many cannot comprehend how in America, even in England one may do without such restrictions.

We shall content ourselves with enumerating those two symptoms, leaving it to the future to trace others. Perhaps they will explain why Napoleon has evoked and continues to evoke such great sympathy in France, and even in Italy and Germany. Napoleon broke and overthrew the old governments which, like hot-houses, previously helped the growth of nations and now oppress and choke them. Napoleon felt that the cause of freedom is a European cause and that all Europe should be involved in it. Perhaps Europe expects such men today, too.

ABOUT THE GREAT MAN OF THE FUTURE

(1833)

It was our general national complaint that we did not find in our revolution* a man who could guess the will of the masses and satisfy their expectations. Poland has clamored for such a man, has expected him until now and anticipates him in the future. This future great man, the expected national Messiah, whence will he come, by what is he to be recognized? There is no agreement on this point. Our countrymen imagine him in various shapes, with various attributes. He naturally appears to all with sword in hand; but some provide him with a guillotine, others with a genealogical tree, still others with a scroll of protocols. Possessed with that feeling of national expectation, J. U. Niemcewicz† hopes that some new Pisistratus, Cromwell, Caesar or Napoleon will save us.

But in the history of nations nothing repeats itself; nothing new happens in the old way, by old means. All the men mentioned here were fully original and none imitated the other in any way. We shall constantly repeat to our countrymen who prepare themselves to be dictators, or at least commanders-in-chief, that they should not deceive themselves by imitation, that they should not look for principles of conduct in Machiavelli, in the memoirs of Caesar, the French Revolution or Napoleon. This much may be said with certainty, that our future great-man-warrior will not resemble any of those who went before.

If we may continue our surmise, the spirit of the Polish nation indicates that no Pisistratus or Cromwell type will strike root in our soil. There is in the Polish nation a great, profound, universal sense of noble-mindedness, honesty and

---

* The Polish Rising of 1830-31 against Czarist Russia.

† Polish poet, novelist, political leader of the close of the XVIII and beginning of the XIX centuries. Stayed several years in the United States and wrote one of the first biographies of Washington.

sincerity. A schemer and a cheat will never win popularity in Poland. Even in Europe public opinion speaks more and more strongly in that spirit. One name popular in Europe, generally esteemed, found no opposition: the name of Washington. Napoleon himself often repeated that if it were in his power he would like to become Washington. With us Kościuszko's name was and is so great. It seems that the first condition of the future great man must be this nobility of character, this cordiality, this good-heartedness that won Kościuszko and Washington the love of their contemporaries and the respect of posterity. Great military and political talents can mature in the present state of the national atmosphere only when planted in such a soil.

Our faith in the national spirit, our trust in the hearts of the Polish people cause us not to fear among us any authority *de facto*, provided it is not imposed by foreigners or foreign theorists. We are waiting for that *de facto* authority and promise to obey it. Therefore the *Pilgrim*,* in its article on the insurrectionist constitution, concedes great attributes to this authority, contrary to all constitutions. Indeed, to what constitutions should we appeal? We rather appeal to the moral conviction that among us an indolent or unworthy hand will not seize power, and if it ever held it, it was not by the will of the masses of the nation, not *de facto*, but on the basis of old articles and enactments of constitutions imposed on us. It has been brought against the *Pilgrim* that in conceding to the authority the power of life and property over the citizens, it legitimatizes robbery and plunder. We call the history of the Rising in the provinces to witness: no laws, no forms were preserved there, and yet no one accused the leaders of the Rising of robberies, no one held them guilty of pillage. On the contrary, the commanders often refused to take the great sums voluntarily offered them by the citizens. The national spirit tempered the authority and insured obedience; in due time this spirit would express itself in laws whose contents and composition we are unable to foresee.

---

* Periodical published by Mickiewicz in Paris in 1833-34

FROM THE "TRIBUNE OF THE PEOPLES"
OUR PROGRAM

The condition of Europe is such that it is impossible that in the future any nation will be able to proceed along the road of progress in isolation from others unless it wishes to expose itself to ruin and thus threaten injury to the general cause.

The enemies of the people in Europe continue to act in solidarity; they confirm this solidarity by action at every step. More conscious of their common danger than anyone else, they have united themselves as never before. Their tactics consist of using all their government forces against each nationality that separately seeks liberation, and thus suppressing one after another and one through the other. Their plans, formed long ago, become evident when carried into effect; they are based on accurate data, according to which all the selfish interests of governments as well as of the individuals that exercise influence on them were calculated and the degree of their ambition, which is the motive prompting them all, was estimated.

 . . . . We are founding a European people's organ, *The Tribune of Peoples*. Determined to proclaim and defend the rights of France, provided they are in accord with the interest of the people's cause in Europe, we summon all nations to come to that tribune, each with its free word.

A group of foreigners who in their homelands have won popularity by their word as well as by their efforts and sacrifices fraternally lends us their collaboration. Through them we shall have exact and accurate information on what concerns their countries. As men of the February Revolution we are also in full agreement with the tendencies of the Great Revolution and the Napoleonic period as far as their realization is concerned, because Napoleon actually put the revolutionary principles into effect when as an armed missionary he experienced the republican phase of his life.

The moment the First Consul abandoned this principle in order to negotiate with the old world and put the crown on his head a series of misfortunes began from which the people still suffer today. In spite of this it is still the revolutionary Napoleon, who in the eyes of the people is the representative of the Great Revolution because he defended its ideas most perseveringly and most effectively. On the other hand those who came after him became traitors on the very day they assumed power.

We shall seek the frontiers of the Republic even beyond the confines of Napoleon's power; we shall regard as reactionaries all those who, adopting the republican principle, measure its external activity according to their selfish interests, or who, admiring the spirit of action and strength of the Napoleonic epoch, would nevertheless like to exclude from it the spirit of sacrifice and republican expansion.

France, as we conceive her, is that very spirit which became the people and was embodied in the republican form.

That means that we shall defend the present Constitution, that we shall cooperate as best we can to accelerate its evolution toward a republic with all its consequences.

This is as far as internal affairs are concerned. With regard to foreign countries we shall courageously deal with matters directly concerning us: Italy, Poland, Germany, Denmark, Spain, the Slavonic countries, Hungary, the Danubian provinces.

Both internally and externally we shall be guided by the principles of Christian polity and the solidarity of peoples. In relation to the parties which struggle for power in Europe, in France and in the National Convention we shall always support those men who, faithful to the progressive instinct of the masses, will work to build a social order concordant with the new needs of the people. Only on this condition shall we recognize them as the true political representation of the people's interest in the whole world, the only true interest of France.

INTERNATIONAL BROTHERHOOD

(1849)

What significance is attributed among us to the sacramental word *brotherhood*, placed in the official emblem of the Republic? The kings call each other brother. They have a right to give themselves this beautiful name. They need not shrink from the sacrifice that the duty of brotherhood imposes upon them. They place it above any secondary considerations of territorial or commercial policy. When the rescue of the royal person of their brother Louis XVI was at stake, the monarchs of Prussia and Austria, England and Spain, Catholics, schismatics or Lutherans, forgot their political quarrels, united all together in the family interest against the French nation and did not cease fighting against it until they had restored their cousin to the possession of what they considered his property. Even today we see how much effort is spent by the king of Prussia to recall his brother, the Grand Duke of Baden, from exile.

At the first intelligence of the victories of the Hungarians,* the Russian emperor publicly declared that he took it upon himself to save his Austrian brother, even if it meant sacrificing his last thaler and his last soldier. The Russian emperor kept his word. We are convinced that any other monarch would do the same in a similar case. The kings set an example that the peoples should eagerly imitate. The sons of the earth are wiser than those who claim to be sons of light.

The war that for fifty years has continued to disturb the peace of Europe is a war of families: a war between the great royal family, one and indivisible, and the people, dispersed members of the great European family. Victory favors those who better fulfill their duty of brotherhood. The French people have a deep sense of that duty and displayed it enthusiastically in the days of February. If this sense was not manifested in actions, the responsibility for

---

* In 1848.

it rests on the politicians to whom the people then entrusted power. Some of these men did not understand the significance of the new dogma of solidarity, others exploited it in the interests of their parties. Thus public opinion was corrupted, a fact that later became the cause of the unfortunate result of the manifestation of the 13th of June. The aim of this manifestation was to draw the attention of the French people to the danger of its brother, the Italian people. There is nothing more legal and more human. And yet the manifestation did not achieve its purpose.

The government feared it, the people mistrusted it; one recalled with terror and grief the consequences of the manifestation organized a year before in behalf of Poland.

Then the French people rose united; it wanted only one thing, it wanted to show the sovereign assembly of its representatives that it was ready to fulfill its duty of brotherhood to Poland. It expected that the Assembly, having made a moral review of the large army of the new World which was now animated by such sacred enthusiasm, would sense its omnipotence in the face of the old world and would have the courage to speak the salutary word. The people wanted only this. But the partisans, who placed themselves at the head of the Parisian people, instead of following these noble instincts, believed that it would be better politics to seize the occasion to change—what? the system of government? No—only the composition of the government, the personnel of the rulers! They compromised the principle of international brotherhood and for long retarded its triumph.

And yet, sooner or later, this principle is bound to triumph.

JOACHIM LELEWEL
(1786-1861)

Most important Polish historian of the XIX century, professor at the University of Warsaw and the University of Wilno, member of the National Government in 1831, member of French, Belgian and Russian scientific institutions, Joachim Lelewel was one of the founders and theoreticians of modern democratic Polish ideology. After the failure of the Polish insurrection of 1831, he left the country to live first in Paris, then for many years in Belgium, the scene of his far-reaching scientific and political activities. He published numerous monographs in Polish and French treating of the Middle Ages as well as of more recent times. Renowned for his extraordinary erudition, he placed Polish historiography on scientifically exact foundations.

FROM "THE REGENERATION OF POLAND WILL COME ABOUT AS SOON AS ITS FORCES ARE WELL DIRECTED."

(1844)

It is said that a city is not raised with a single stroke; good weather does not favor the masons and carpenters every day, and if they use bricks, beams or other materials of inferior quality, their construction will not sustain for long but will crumble before it is completed. This is what has happened thus far in the reconstruction of Poland; poor materials were used, the wrong elements employed. No one dared or desired to improve the lot of the people, something which could have made them understand that they were fighting for their own sake. This element then was not of perfect quality. But, instead of evoking their own strength, those who wished to rebuild their country, roamed the world, forming legions subservient to foreign conquerors. Do not blame the refugees who emigrated after the nation's fall thus to avoid Siberia and imprisonment;* but curse those who abandoned their families with the intent of joining the émigré legions which

---

* Reference is made to the Polish political emigration after the unsuccessful rising of 1831.

† The participation of the Poles in the French Foreign Legion and Napoleonic Wars.

were to fight at Santo Domingo, at Algiers, in Spain,† where
they were decimated several times over before the opportunity presented itself of returning to their native land. You
may be sure that the number of your brothers who will
return disabled is large enough without multiplying it. Those
who reach manhood on their own soil should remain at home
and take up arms at the opportune moment, for Poland will
never be reestablished save within the confines of her own
territory. Let others continue to count on foreign support.
Woe to the people that recovers existence through the inter-
position of another; it will never be free or independent;
it will remain submissive, subjugated. Indeed, experience
has proven that nothing contributes so much to failure as
too great a reliance on diplomatic assistance. Where is the
monarch who will sincerely champion a people? And if
there were such, he would constitute only a bad element in
the construction; he would build nothing but a duchy of
Warsaw,* a Czarist kingdom†—clay hovels that would
tumble into the mud at the first storm, at the first rains.
Some such structures have already issued from imperial or
Czarist hands. What then would issue from Austrian hands,
if they were allowed to carry out what several leaders have
imagined to the misfortune of the nation? It would mean
an Austrian king over a part of Poland, a garrison in white
uniforms, special permission from Vienna to speak and
write Polish, a privileged censorship, for the more fiery
spirits a sojourn in the damp dungeons of Munkacs,‡ a
paternal discipline administered by the heel of the shoe, the
shame of state submission, an oppressive apportionment of
taxes by states, degradation and enslavement; these were
the bitter fruits planted by the obstinate individuals who
placed their salvation in Austria. The future lot of Poland
rests neither in diplomacy nor the support of foreign cabinets but in the uprising of the peoples and in their emancipation. Poland will find better elements for reconstruction

---

* The Grand Duchy of Warsaw set up by Napoleon in 1807.

† The Congress Kingdom set up by the Congress of Vienna in 1815, bound to
Russia by a personal union.

‡ A prison fortress in Hungary.

on her own soil, in her own faculties, and the first people to revolt and to fight for her freedom will be the natural friends of Poland. She will not ask their support, but their fraternity and alliance; thus can such people be of service to the Polish nation, just as the latter can be reciprocally useful to them. Time prepares everything. Forty years in the life of nations is, I repeat, but a brief space. Hence, the painful action of regeneration requires years. You are growing up, my friends, and it is possible that you will reach maturity in an epoch of the greatest excitement, which will demand your service. Think about it and train yourselves so that you may be useful children to your country, more enlightened and more logical than those who have previously committed so many mistakes. Reflect upon what I have said to you, and if my words are true, if on rereading them you find them correct and good, act accordingly. You will then sweeten the bitterness of exile for me, convincing me that through this little work I have once more been able to render a service to the national cause. Remember the past, preserve the serenity of your spirit and repeat the song of your fathers; for Poland will not perish so long as you are alive.

SPIRIT OF THE PHOENIX

HISTORICAL BACKGROUND
(1863-1918)

The collapse of the Insurrection of 1863 signaled the beginning of a long period of Polish suffering. In the section of the land dominated by Czarist Russia, Polish land estates were confiscated, Polish institutions abolished, schools were converted to Russian. At the same time this part of Poland was being rapidly industrialized. A new social class—the city bourgeoisie began to play a more important part in Polish life. This group together with the landed gentry enjoyed the favor of Russia and was prosperous. Meanwhile the socialist and peasant movements were born. These parties emphasized the necessity of an independent Poland and opposed any compromise with Russia.

In 1905 the all-Russian revolution broke out. In Poland this outbreak was marked by sharp differences between nationalistic and socialistic groups. The revolution was put down and Polish independence parties were forced underground. Joseph Pilsudski became the leader of the independence movement. Pilsudski's basic policy was the creation of a Polish army which would be prepared to take military action against Russia.

In the meantime Galicia—in Austrian occupied Poland —became the center of Polish political and social life. Here Austria had been compelled to grant the Poles autonomy, their own schools and freedom of the press. After 1905 Pilsudski fled to Galicia where he began to organize the future Polish army.

In the Prussian part of Poland a strong attempt to Germanize the Poles was made by the occupying authorities. Persecution was general. In contrast to Galicia, where industry was still undeveloped, the Prussian part of Poland was agriculturally well organized and therefore economically better off. The Poles in this section were mainly conservative. As in all of Poland they were strongly anti-German.

97

DEMOCRACY FOR EVERY DAY

KAROL LIBELT
(1807-1875)

A student of idealistic philosophy and esthetics, Libelt often made himself heard in public affairs as well. He was a member of the lively intellectual movement which sprang into being in the first half of the XIX century in the section of Poland which at that time was under Prussian domination.

FROM "POLITICAL FEUILLETON"
(1846)

A people which does not know how to govern itself needs a governing power; but to prevent the supreme power from degenerating into arbitrariness, a constitution is necessary.

.... From autocracy or absolutism stem servitude, misery, and the degradation of millions of people;—the human mind resists the idea that the fate of millions should be dependent upon the mistakes and caprices of one man ....

.... The millions that constitute the populations of the nations never did and never can align themselves with the ideas of one man. Were he even a second Napoleon and should he actually realize his ideas by force of arms, the machine constructed by him would fall apart as soon as the bayonet were replaced,—for humanity is not machine geared by the will of one man, but a living spirit ....

FROM "ON CIVIL COURAGE"
(1843)

Freedom of the press

Freedom of the press is a representation of the spirit; it is the constitutional right of the spirit resulting from its inherent freedom. Where one is forbidden to print his thoughts, speaking is also forbidden—which should logically lead to the prohibition of thought on certain subjects. Such violence can never be done to the spirit, for it exceeds the influence of human power over the spirit, which can be neither shackled nor imprisoned. Thus, only the spoken and the written word can be reproved. It is only when thought manifests itself that it becomes the object of censure and restraint. Nevertheless, the right of the spirit to find expression by means of the spoken and the written word is an innate impulse of the spirit, a natural law which man can abuse just as he can all the other laws, but of which he cannot be deprived simply on the ground that such abuse is feared. Therefore, one must in this case, as in every other, grant freedom of action to the individual spirit and designate penalties for transgressions. This indicates the need of a law relating to the press which would, on the one hand, insure universal freedom for the revelation of thoughts in print and which would, on the other hand, protect society from abuses. Violations would have to be passed upon by a jury and justice would be meted out by a judge.

There is also a purely legal consideration which supports this point of view. An original idea like an original invention is the property of the author, and no one has the right to appropriate it arbitrarily or to destroy it. And the question as to whether this property of the author's might endanger society can be decided only by a legal trial and verdict.

Censorship, which places at the disposal of a censor the most sacred right of author's property and the equally sacred right of freedom of spirit, violates this rule. Those three chief mandates of all censorship, namely, that nothing against the government, religion or morality should appear in writing—how difficult to interpret them equitably in each single instance! The timid censor prefers to be on the safe side, to incur the wrath of the author rather than that of the government, and so mercilessly he strikes out the most brilliant thoughts, thoughts that he has neither sufficiently probed nor adequately appraised. The impossibility of relying on the censor's whim is best demonstrated by the police regulation which stipulates that even censored books and newspapers may be banned and confiscated—which again takes place in accordance, with the arbitrary views of the higher police power. Against the background of such arbitrariness, there is no security for publishers' and authors' property, for contracted agreements, for literary companies and speculations, because no law and no court of justice grants such guarantees.

From the standpoint of science, censorship fetters the development of the philosophic and critical spirit whenever the latter comes down from the realm of pure abstraction and inspects the real phenomena of the world. For it is impossible not to touch upon principles of government, religion and morality in this connection and not to pay attention to the spiritual forces which cannot, by their very nature, stand still, but should proceed forward. These are fundamental laws underlying the social life of nations; but precisely because nations advance through education in the most essential aspects of their development, they cannot remain true to the same conceptions and ideas forever.

Nations as well as individuals go through a period of infancy, youth and maturity. In the first phase, it is possible to forgive the ruling power when it treats the nation like a child, from whose hand an object must be removed lest it do itself harm. When adolescent forces are growing up, a nation will strain and fume at censorship decrees that rein in its soaring thoughts just as a high spirited horse will strain at the bit. But when the nation comes of age in its intelligence, it becomes improper, impolitic, and even dangerous to use the rod and to introduce the hampering bridle of censorship—as was demonstrated twelve years ago by the July Ordinances.* Censorship can last only for a certain time, only until the nation's intelligence achieves maturity. To wrestle with it, when it has come of age, is a very unequal struggle and liberty always emerges the victor. Intelligence without liberty is like life without breathing:

---

* Allusion is made to the July revolt in France in 1830.

where it is stuffy, the chest expands and seeks to breathe at all cost. The invention of printing caused as great a reform in the forces of science and ideas as the invention of powder occasioned in the physical force of knighthood and armed might. Printing is the heavy artillery of thought, it blasts the rocks of superstition and habit; it screams among opinion like a grenade in midair and wherever it strikes, it bursts, destroying and shattering. The press is a powerful mortar that carries the shells of thought in all directions while its roar resounds to the four corners of the world.

That is exactly why, says the censor, I extinguish your lighted tinder-boxes whenever the foundation and walls of the social structure are the target of your missiles, because you would blow them into the air. To this we would reply: bring out, rather, a second battery and let the cannon be silenced. Truth is ammunition, intelligence the gun maker. It will be seen on which side they both are. Falsity will soon run out of powder and its shots will for the most part either exceed or miss their mark. The might of the spirit and of truth is immovable and the gates of hell will be of no avail against them.

Censorship is the law of the fist (*Faustrecht*). It could have been put into practice in the days of knighthood and the middle ages, but today, it cannot hold its own in the face of the mature conception of right. The question as to whether we are still in the stage of the law of the fist as regards intelligence is another matter, the analysis of which does not belong here. Governments should be careful, however, not to err in their chronology by peering at the birth certificates of their peoples and counting their years.

To tell his government the truth and to tell it decently and publicly through the medium of print and the press, so that every one else to whom the national cause is of interest might form an opinion concerning it, should not only be permitted to each citizen of the state but indeed, it should be his sacred duty. What of it, if we learn about politics through the study of states sunk in antiquity? The autopsy of the corpse will enlighten the physician but it will be of no help to the dead man, it will not bring him back to life. While the patient was still alive, consultations should have been held, a diagnosis made, and evil warded off. So also in the governing of each nation, as Jean Paul states, sick bulletins should be issued to forestall autopsy bulletins. It is good to take apart the political body of Rome and Athens, but it is far better and more useful to make observations on the living regimen of a nation.

True love of country and of motherland, true attachment to the cause and to the government is evidenced, therefore, not in passing over evil in silence or in indifference to what is happening, but in zeal for public affairs as well as in the proper but courageous and open declaration of one's views. If censorship does not allow this to take place, it sins against the general welfare and the government deprives itself in this wise of the most effective remedies. Memorable in this connection are the words of Napoleon, who, after his abdication in Fontainebleau, was looking through the newspapers and publications, freed from imperial censorship, and exclaimed: "If they had only told me one hundredth of all this three years ago, my throne would still be standing today."

BOLESŁAW PRUS

(1847-1912)

Bolesław Prus was the foremost novelist during Poland's era of positivism. His role in Polish life may be compared to the role of Dickens in England. Like that writer he was a superb story teller with a fine sensibility and a sunny humor. He was popular throughout Poland as a wise and witty, compassionate and unyielding champion of democratic rights. Though he stemmed from the gentry, he had declared war on reaction and injustice at the very start of his career. Besides many novels, among which "The Doll", "The Emancipators", and "Pharaoh" are the most famous, he published countless feuilletons, articles, columns and sketches.

PATRIOTISM

(1886)

There are individuals and even publications that with an inconceivable thoughtlessness, inform society that under such and such circumstances, it will cease to enjoy their sympathies . . . . We know of no situation in which this or that citizen might have the right to threaten society with indifference and we have no intention of weeping if those who so conceive their responsibilities carry out their threat.

There was a time when the word "patriotism" meant singing (in low voices of course) certain melodies,* sighing over certain misfortunes, and a deliberate enthusiasm about everything pertaining to us, whether simply our distaste for work and order, our haughtiness towards our inferiors or our humility towards our betters, etc. It is obvious that so sterile and unhealthy a patriotism had to be subjected to criticism and that there had to spring into being a party that marveled at these "Polish" traits which rendered us ridiculous and which were harmful to us.

---

* Reference is made to patriotic melodies banned by the Czarist régime.

Unfortunately, people and parties never stop half way, but carry through to the end—and often enough wind up in some absurdity. Exactly this befell certain social critics. Just as they began by spouting sentimental patriotism in the name of science and pan-human ideals, so now they wish to crush out of it the very things that are necessary for science and pan-human ideals.

Historical patriotism takes pleasure in meditating upon the days when Boleslaw the Great* drove frontier posts into the Elbe and the Oder, and industriously seeks out documents proving that Berlin was founded on Slavonic soil. Current patriotism, on the other hand, discovers with horror that since the days of Boleslaw the Germans have already reached the middle of the Vistula; it strives to halt their advance and forestall further colonization on the last remnants of our land. The one contemplates with delight the sumptuous mantles depicted in the canvases of Matejko,† the other seeks shoes and untorn coats for the real, unpictured people of our land. The one dreams of ancestors who were victorious at Vienna‡ and Samosierra,¶ the other trembles with the fear that poverty will destroy the military prowess of our sons. The sympathies of the one extend, true to history, only to a handful of the wealthy and the educated, the other extends its sympathies to the millions of poor and uncultured without whom there exists, not a nation, but simply a precarious system of castes. The one proclaims loudly that, regardless of circumstances, it will be loyal only to those to whom it has been bound by its thousands of years of civilization, the other repeats the peasant proverb: "May the merciful Lord help him who desires the good."

The question is not which of these two patriotisms is loftier. The "current" one is certainly practical and, above

---

* King of Poland, 992-1025, creator of the medieval power of the Polish state, the frontiers of which he expanded considerably.

† Illustrious Polish painter of the XIX century, specializing in the portrayal of historical scenes.

‡ Under Jan Sobieski of Poland, in 1683.

¶ The Polish legions in Napoleon Bonaparte's army during the Spanish War.

all, protective. In peasant Warmia* only the "current" brand exists, in Galicia† the "historical" holds sway—and what a difference in results . . . Nor is this all. In Eastern Galicia current patriotism predominates and there we behold a multitude of peasant shops and publications: during vacations the youth traverse the country in all directions seeking acquaintance with the practical life; song-books are published, choral groups are organized. In Western Galicia, thanks to the preponderance of historical feelings and views, the abyss between peasant and intelligentsia has widened: the peasantry wastes away physically, the enlightened classes bicker over inept projects for statues, while the high dignitaries obstruct the development of education.

"Too much of a thing, etc."‡ And who knows whether the reason why we have become annoying to Europe (which, alas, is the case) is not that we always speak of our misfortunes and of others' guilt. Perhaps if we began to speak of the misfortunes of others and of our own guilt, our voice would acquire a new force, so mighty that everyone would pause to listen . . . .

Polish society is not the Christ of nations as its poets have maintained¶ nor is it so evil and incompetent as its enemies claim it to be. It is a society in part regenerating itself, and in the main young, not having as yet discovered its new civilizational road. Its inflexible hatred of the German testifies to the power dormant within it; the rest is in the hand of God, Who, even in Greenland, never fails to send a joyous summer after winter and six months of night.

We are a very young society, which causes each one of us to have slightly too much faith in his own convictions and slightly too little respect for the conviction of others . . . . In our religious feelings, in our national sympathies, in our political opinions, in our evaluations of people and events, not only do we speak but we act as if we (1) were infallible, (2) enjoyed a monopoly on "the whole truth". And

---

* A section of East Prussia inhabited by Polish peasants.
† A section of Poland then under Austrian domination.
‡ A Polish proverb which concludes thus: " . . . . is not wanted even by pigs."
¶ An idea proclaimed by the poets of the Romantic Period. It may be encountered in Mickiewicz, in Słowacki, in Krasiński.

yet—the humblest truth is a forest in which man sees only a part of the path, and not always clearly at that.

THE JEWISH LITTLE QUESTION

Strictly speaking, there can, in my estimation, be no Jewish question, but only a Jewish little question, just as there exist the peasant, the industrial, the gentry and the colonizing little questions and just as there exist the little questions of ignorance, poverty, bigotry, incompetence, dishonesty, gullibility, etc. There are very many such little questions. They plague various countries and they group themselves into social questions.

I would term the Jewish little question a question if I could believe, as do some of my colleagues, that the Jews are a power. Unfortunately, as far as I can see, the Jews in no wise constitute a power except possibly insofar as they are rather numerous and their proletariat is multiplying rather swiftly.

There are some who think that the Jews are the sole capitalists among us, hence a financial force. I, on the contrary, regard their vast majority as poor men, the poorest among the poor. There are those who accuse them of unusual solidarity, which I again find amusing, because, as far as I know, the faith not only is divided into classes filled with mutual hatred and scorn, but also has a reactionary and a progressive party and even, it would seem, religious sects. Finally, there are those who are fearful of Jewish mental prowess which, though it doubtless exists, represents no danger for our race.

It may be that this view is erroneous. In any case, it would have to be refuted by facts. And until this happens, I believe and shall continue to believe that Jews fill us with apprehension and aversion only because we know absolutely nothing about them and because we make no effort to get to know them.

We laugh at the French, who have no conception of geography or the ethnography of European peoples; how much more ridiculous are we ourselves, who do not study the customs, religion, and life of almost a million of our fellow-citizens who will sooner or later be fused with us into a uniform society.

What then lies at the base of the Jewish little question? Is it the religion or the nationality of the Jews? Certainly not. The Jews are not a nationality,* and no one has any intention of depriving them of their religion. But there are other factors apart from these: ignorance and caste spirit. Let me draw the attention of those who like to use their intellectual endowments to the fact that ignorance and a caste spirit do not alone form the foundation of Jewish separatism. We must sorrowfully admit that in our beautiful country, ignorance reigns supreme from the basements to the rooftops. Equally ignorant are the peasants who waste their time in the taverns and at the fairs, and the fine gentlemen who are bored in the theatres, in the trains or in their offices. The same drab impression is conveyed by the illiterate churl as by the man who knows his letters but who feels a distance for books or even for certain scientific and social theories. Thus the Chasside* Jews, with their superstitions, their backwardness and belief in miraculous rabbis are not a glaring exception. Indeed, I should even say that, in this respect they are very good conservative citizens.

As for the Jewish caste spirit—dear Lord! where is there no caste spirit? Is it so long ago that the gentleman was ashamed to learn a trade or to engage in commerce? And how many officials are there today who would give their daughter in marriage to a locksmith or a carpenter? The Jews do not like the Christians to open stores—but are our farmers or cobblers so willing to have Jews as neighbors or competitors?

To these two chief and common ingredients: ignorance and caste spirit, let us add Yiddish, the long black coat, and early marriages, let us sugar all this over with poverty,

---

* This was written at a period when Jewish national aspirations were just beginning to awaken. Prus, like many other progressive writers of his day, denied the national character of Jewish tendencies, proclaiming the slogan of the assimilation of Jews into Polish culture.

* An extremely fanatic and conservative trend of Mosaism.

responsible for swindling and usury, and we shall have a whole cake known as the Jewish question. It is unsavory true; but I cannot believe that it will not one day collapse under the pressure of education and progressive ideas.

Since I have gone so far, let me go a little farther. What is the explanation for the difference between my views and those of my anti-Semitic colleagues? It is twofold. Whenever the question of the relationship of Jews to Christians comes to the fore, my anti-Semitic colleagues think only of the faults of the Jews and of the virtues of the Christians. I do otherwise. I know that both groups have their failings and their good points, and since they are both part of the same society, in my heart I concede equal rights to these and to those. It can't be helped—I simply have the psychic constitution that cares more for the whole and less for classes and individuals.

In the second place, my anti-Semitic colleagues and friends look solely at the Jewish present: I, however, take into consideration the past and the future. The past teaches me that the demoralization of the Jewish proletariat was brought about equally by Jews and Christians,—and that, therefore, it is impossible to hold only the Jews responsible for their present mistakes. The present teaches me that once the Jews became educated and were accepted by society, they became good citizens—which in turn leaves me with the blissful hope that in the future the same thing will hold true for the masses. Those who do not possess this confidence, who do not believe that some day the world will be better, may revile me, nay, they may even proclaim that the majority of our press is friendly towards Jews because it is dependent on them . . . .

To those who . . . . know no nobler thought than dependence, I offer a bit of advice, namely: that they place a rope around their neck, for it is not worth living and working for universal contempt in a world such as they see through the spectacles of pessimism.

ELIZA ORZESZKOWA

(1842-1910)

Eliza Orzeszkowa belonged to the same generation of writers as Swiętochowski and Prus and shared many of their opinions. Her numerous novels reached to the bottom of human misery, representing the abysmal conditions in which peasants and Jews were forced to exist. In pamphlets and articles she attacked a wide variety of social and moral evils.

THE JEWS AND THE JEWISH QUESTION

If we lived in the blessed times in which every social complication was cut through by the sword and burned through by the fire, we would be inclined to proceed with the Jews in the same way as once the Spaniards did in relation to the Moors; that is we would like to burn the half of them and expel the other half from the country. Unfortunately for those who have committed a gross anachronism by being born into the world in the 19th century burning, expelling or any kind of extermination is today nothing but old junk reduced to ashes in the purifying fire of civilization. These ashes still fill people's eyes with dust and poison the moral atmosphere, but as instruments for solving problems they have completely gone out of use. This is the result of having science explain the conception of justice and allowing it to mitigate old customs. It is also the result of accumulated experiences which plainly proved that wherever Spaniards oppressed and exterminated Moors the Moors fared badly, but the Spaniards fared worse. Horrified by shameful and injurious acts of violence and persecution what should we do, and how should we do it in view of the conditions of our life?

Obviously we ought to look for ways of removing difficulties and dangers in a peaceful way, by means of reason,
good will, moral, spiritual and economic improvements.
Concerning the Jewish question we have been looking for
such means for quite some time, and for more than a decade
very diligently, but our search has one capital fault: we do
not define accurately the objective for which we are to put
into practice the theories we have invented. We say:
enlighten, improve, assimilate, unite—but our knowledge
of those who are to be enlightened, improved, assimilated
and united by us may for many reasons be called childish.
What do we know about the Jews? From what point of view
do we look at them? On what foundations do we base our
opinions about them? These questions force a smile to our
lips, because they bring to mind hundreds and thousands of
statements and opinions about Jews, which seem to compete
with each other for first place in the sphere of childishness
and human superficialities. A cheat, an exploiter, a fanatic
when he belongs to the mass of the ignorant and poor; boast-
ful, arrogant and vainglorious when he has become rich—
such is the Jew according to the conceptions generally established with us. What! and nothing more? Do we not look
in this social group of human beings for any other features and characteristics? Perceiving the features enumerated above, do we not ask ourselves: whence did they
come? What historical and social factors created them?
Was nature when creating the Jews really so very capri-
cious that she marked one tribe with a stain from which all
other tribes are free? We do not look for anything and we
do not ask for anything. We behave worse than the poorest
novelist who well knows that he cannot cover the paper
with patches of soot. Of a work of imagination we demand
that the man in it be what he is in nature: a being very
complicated and many-sided, explained by the influences of
life and the world. In reality, however, we agree that in the
book of humanity, and especially on the page of our country, nature has painted great spots of soot.

I venture to state that, excluding a small group of really
courageous writers and citizens, our judgments about the

Jews are superficial, wrongly motivated and unenlightened, that they are influenced not only by motives of an emotional nature, but also by prejudice and superstitions derived directly from the treasury of medieval fairy tales.

It seems to me, however, that if we wish to endow certain objects with forms and colors, it is necessary to start with an accurate, impartial examination of those objects. Proceeding differently we risk certain errors, wasting our work and bungling the cause. Therefore, before starting the examination of the Jewish question and the means, by which both sides, *i.e.*, Jews and Christians, should solve it, let us look for a moment at the Jews themselves, at their defects and qualities; let us look without those dark glasses with which the differences of race and creed and ancient habits cover our eyes, whenever we turn them in this direction. Taking the dark glasses from our eyes we also take the clamps of bigotry from our minds, that most terrible enemy of independent thought.

Among the ignorant masses of our people and among the ignorant masses of the Jewish population it is our duty to sow what the past centuries have not sown, civic conceptions. Feelings and tendencies do not exist in them for they cannot yet exist, but they will come, they must come together with the training for participation in civic rights and dignities. Both these social groups have only very recently thrown off the burden of humiliation that has weighed upon them for so long. Only very recently have the sanctuaries of intellectual light been thrown open to them. Two decades cannot destroy the work of several centuries. It is not hatred that is needed here, or malediction, or contempt. On the contrary, philosophical indulgence, benevolent help, patient waiting for the results of long work are needed. In relation to the Jews this work is in one sense easier and in another more difficult than in relation to the peasants. It is facilitated by the mental alertness of the Jews, their versatility and their more frequent and more numerous contact with the enlightened classes in the sphere of various business. It is rendered difficult by differences of language, creed, religious fanaticism on both sides, but above all by ill-disposed and scornful prejudice, developed through centuries, which has been almost completely given up by the enlightened classes with regard to the peasants, but which has continued in them with regard to the Jews, perhaps with less intensity than before, but still very strongly. We have the right and even the duty to perceive in Jews any lack of civic feelings and tendencies; we have the right to demand from those among them who can understand these things that they help us plant these ideas among those who still do not understand them; we have the right to fight against any peculiarities which, by setting a wall between them and education, may prevent them from acquiring a knowledge and love of civic duties. But we have no right to condemn Jews as such, not acquiring what has long been denied them (but by no means them alone); we have no right to declare that a Jew, as such, cannot be a good citizen of the country; we have no right to believe that nature capriciously produced a monster-people and offered it to us as a gift.

. . . . Finally and above all let us believe, as other nations do, in the great beneficent power of the light kindled by science and in all the intellectual and social results of it. Under this light, the terrible metamorphoses which turn virtues and qualities into offenses and faults will disperse like bad dreams. Under this light will disappear the empty roads and the overcrowded roads which bring here the silence of death and there the suffocating pressure of life. By this light the eyes which today look only to the ground will be able to look upward and those which are accustomed to look too much into the clouds will see that often horizontal earthly roads lead to lofty ideals. For the quicker kindling of this light the Jews can be very helpful to us. They possess not only the financial abilities ascribed to them, but also other attributes that make them zealous cultivators of learning whenever the key of fanatic exclusions does not lock the gates of its sanctuaries before them.

. . . . What should and can we Christians do for the solution of the Jewish question? As to theory, we must not rack our brains to invent it. It was invented by the greatest statesmen of our past. The literature of the Four Year Parliament*, the writings of Czacki, Staszic, Butrymowicz,† the activity of Marquis Wielopolski,‡ testify that we have a tendency which is already a hundred years old toward complete and absolute equality of rights for the Jews. Whoever is against it today deviates from our best tradition. It is not necessary to develop widely the arguments supporting these theories. They are the credo of every really enlightened man. For the less or only seemingly enlightened people they may be expressed in a few sentences. The deprivation of any rights whatsoever takes from the consciences of those whom it touches their corresponding duties and consequently, as time elapses, makes them increasingly less capable of fulfilling their duties. Exclusion from rights induces people to evade the law and consequently spreads dishonesty, hypocrisy and cunningness. Pushing people from one road makes them crowd other roads and consequently causes physical misery and one-sided development of abilities. Humiliation provokes the violent desire of elevation without choice of means. Segregation, contempt, injury of any kind, awake mutual underestimation and hatred, and the strongest intellectual and moral aberrations. Finally, above all the practical considerations rises the idea of justice, the magnificent creatrix of all good human feelings and deeds, the idea of equality of men among themselves in the light of their rights and duties, the cornerstone of civilization. Remove that stone and the whole structure of the modern world will fall to pieces; from learning and art to the lowest human works and destinies everything will fall into decline and rottenness. The nations which have most deeply absorbed this idea and are able to best realize it are the happiest and noblest. Those that lack it most tremble most on their foundations and carry the most poisons within themselves. I repeat: these conceptions are neither new with us nor rare.

---

* The Parliament of the Polish Commonwealth 1788-1792, culminating in the adoption of the Constitution of May 3rd, very liberal and progressive for its day.

† Polish political writers and leaders at the close of the 18th century.

‡ Prominent Polish statesman, governor, under the Russian Czar Alexander II, in the Polish Congress Kingdom in 1861-1863.

The absolute equality of the rights of Jews with those of other classes of the population appears before us today in the same light in which the equality of right for townsfolk appeared to the statesmen, deliberating in the four year Parliament. The dearest names of our past and the experiences known to it, the most eloquent voices and the most violent needs of our present summon us in that direction. All works for all, all social dignities for all, all ways, aims and tools for all, and most important all sources of education for all, this is the prayer which morning and night we must send to heaven; this is the plea we must make on earth as well to those who do not yet grasp it and to those in whose power lies the ability to transfer it from our lips to actuality.

ALEKSANDER ŚWIĘTOCHOWSKI

(1849-1938)

*For many years Świętochowski was editor of the weekly
"Prawda" (Truth), the fighting organ of the XIX century positivists. Here Świętochowski wrote his programmatic articles under
the pseudonym "Messenger of Truth." Rejecting romanticism in
literature, life and politics, he proposed a plan of "organic work,"
that is slow economic and cultural evolution which would replace
the revolutionary outbursts and risings so frequent in Poland.
This evolution was to proceed on the liberal and democratic model
of Western Europe.*

*Świętochowski's history of the Polish peasants is a basic work
on that subject.*

FROM "POLITICAL DIRECTIONS"

(1882)

If—leaving out of consideration the conscious or unconscious deception of the general public with fairy tales about
the enchanted princess who is soon to awaken from her
death-like sleep and break the evil spell of her oppressors
—we examine the prudent political directions, purged of
all fantastic admixtures, which our people have, we shall
notice winding through them one common thread, namely,
the principle of regeneration through the progress of civilization and a decided break with the tradition of armed
risings.* How widely that idea is considered as a result of
our experiences, may be seen by its simultaneous appearance
on the standards of camps utterly opposed to each other. The
ultramontane, aristocratic party of the so-called Galician
Stańczyks,† permeated with refined legitimism, has joined

---

* Allusion to the numerous Polish risings.
† Popular name of the Cracow Conservatives who published their political creed in
Stańczyk's Portfolio. Stańczyk was the court fool of King Sigismund the Old (1506-1548),
and is the embodiment of bitter irony.

in that symbol with the freethinking and democratic elements of our people. Among these factions there is a series of profound differences in the comprehension of that political rule, though it is formally the same in both . . . .

If the conditions of which human thought dreams for the distant future were already a reality for the people; if they could already discard the warlike equipment with which they insure themselves against each other; if they were able to develop their material and spiritual resources without fear for their lives and could satisfy their needs—the mere loss of their own political institutions would, from the liberal standpoint, not seem a misfortune to us at all. For the happiness of the people, in our opinion, is not strictly dependent on their power and independence but on their participation in universal civilization as well as on their advancement of their own civilization. We all know of nations completely independent and yet half-dead, backward and by no means prosperous. If some expected but unfulfilled ideal of a people hovers before our eyes it is not a threatening armor-clad state, but a system of conditions allowing all individuals to develop naturally, work peacefully and manifest their desires universally. What does everyone of us, taken individually, demand? Is it soldiers, battles, victories, conquests, parliaments, representatives, ministers, in a word a political apparatus? No, everyone dreams only of being able to live happily, in conformity with the laws of his personal and collective nature. The former apparatus is by itself able to dazzle only minds that pursue glittering appearances, and nations would indeed have long ago ceased striving for it if it did not serve them as a shield in their struggle for existence. It is a fatal characteristic of the present organization of Europe that it has based international relations exclusively on physical power and often does not create conditions of safe existence for the weaker peoples. The states present the picture of trains speeding toward each other on the same track while the engineers strive to apply the brakes but cannot prevent the collision and smashup. Is it strange that those sitting in the coaches long for a train of their own and would renounce it if they were not obliged to make dangerous journeys? If, therefore, small nations, deprived of a political frame, regret not having it or want to have it it is rather the result of their desire to preserve their domestic life than to acquire external power. Let us shield that life sufficiently and political dreams will disappear from it. From us—as we have said—necessity has removed them.* Fate has circumscribed all our desires and hopes by civilizational work. Are we condemned within this scope to slow extinction, or can we maintain ourselves and, at least to a certain extent, develop our innate forces? We choose the latter hypothesis. In spite of the preponderance of physical factors the struggle of a nation for life is not only a series of armed clashes but also a chain of spiritual conflicts to which ultimate victory always belongs. In Europe we actually see independent states, quite inconsequential ones from the point of view of civilization, which were brought into being by a concurrence of favorable circumstances; but the same chance, the same diplomatic caprice or subterfuge that created them may destroy them just as easily. Even in political calculation only educated nations count. Therefore, we should not only strengthen ourselves, improve our minds, develop a brave character and cultivate the pure feeling of love for our country, but also—as much as the dependence of our collective work in its conditions permits—constantly breathe the fresh air of the progress of general human thought, refresh our organism with the blood generated by it and strain all its creative energy. So far we have usually trusted a worn-out atmosphere, deprived of nutritious elements—because of this our heart beats too slowly, and our mind moves too heavily. We must open more windows on Europe and permit its currents to blow through our sultry house. Let us not say that health is only inside, and pestilence beyond. True, we were born in it, brought up in it, have experienced joy and grief, happiness and despair in it, and deposited the treasures of our native civilization in it, but let us not suffocate voluntarily if we want to live. Like primitive peoples

---

* I.e, the partitions of Poland.

who frighten away new ideas that dim the brightness of their traditions, or, like children, we place glistening tinsel in the corners to brighten up the dusk of our house. We do not readily drink from the wells of pure knowledge, untroubled by prejudices, and we prefer our native bogs under the steps of our chapels. Nay, let us not despise any, even the most muddy, native spring, but let us clean each of slime. Amid a hail of reproaches this very task has been undertaken by the progressive party which even today sees numerous fruits of its efforts. Certainly it is not alone in its work for the general good, but it will be no boast on its behalf to say that it has infused an energy into the people, brought many ideas to it from Europe, immunized the general public to the clerical epidemic and accelerated its intellectual liberation. Its activity is the sowing in recent years of the seed of the future.

The social class on which it based its main hopes for the happiness of all—the peasants—belong to it also. This ignorant, unconscious mass appears more and more in our life as a powerful element of our national development. It would be a childish exaggeration to declare that our progressives are its representatives, but it is certain that they defend its interests. This union is by no means artificial. Free thought must be democratic everywhere, for it replaces privileges with equal rights, nobility with merit, and luxury with labor. Moreover, our nation, which experienced its history onesidedly, as a privileged class, which was considerably late in emancipating others, contains in its relations many anachronisms and in its conceptions many prejudices. Its sentiment has remained gentry-like, requiring domination for some and servitude for others. Leaving aside the superannuated justice and validity of such a division, we must observe that it would impoverish the existing forces and would not produce new ones. First, we are a small nation, therefore each invalidated or undeveloped element is a painful loss in the struggle for existence; second, even if we should absolve the classes which have in the past monopolized civic rights from the guilt of bringing the country to ruin, we still must confess that they themselves would not be equal to the task of lifting the nation. The Polish gentry has definitely spoken its last word, the peasants have not spoken it yet. We entertain the hope that when they increase in wealth and acquire a better education, they will exercise a deep and advantageous influence on the country's future. The progressive party hopes to obtain the greatest amount of precious metal from this ore.

If we can no longer be enticed by the laurels of our kings such as Chrobry and Batory,* this does not at all mean that we should be condemned only to the defense of our own home and be stopped completely from moving beyond its boundaries. Every nation that is not in the process of dying out, but which lives and progresses, must be imperialistic if not by way of arms, then by civilization. We are far from intending to apotheosize our fate, however, we should indicate a propitious aspect of its destinies. It opens before us a wide field of industrial and commercial conquests of which we have so far not taken sufficient advantage and in which we may win surer victories than those in which we placed all our trust until now. Let us not expect anything from political revolutions, wars, treaties, the shifting favors of foreigners, but let us trust only our own vitality. Let us occupy all vacant positions, let us penetrate all gaps, let us strike roots wherever we find propitious soil. To kneel at the grave and weep or to protect it from being exhumed by some hyena is all right as an effusion of despair, but not as a manifestation of energy. Let us place around this grave cradles of new life, let us draw with their radii ever wider circles of influence, let us spread our civilization far and wide—this is a program of reasonable and efficacious activities, the more so, as the state, a part of which we form, opens wide scope in many directions. Such, in our opinion, are the main current political directions which we could barely indicate here but whose completion we leave to the perspicacity of the careful reader. They are contained in the following conclusions: Dreams of regaining external independence must today bow before endeavors for domestic

---

* Polish kings victorious in many wars. Bolesław Chrobry (Brave), 992-1025, Stefan Batory, 1574-1586.

independence. This independence can result only from the strengthening of our intellectual and material resources, from a general national development linked with universal progress, and from the nation's democratization calling to action its dormant and immature elements. Only such power, such constant intensity of energy, such progressive movement can maintain the vitality of the nation and insure its growth.

JAN BAUDOUIN DE COURTENAY

(1845-1929)

Descendant of a French family which had lived in Poland for many centuries, Baudouin de Courtenay was a profound linguistic scholar, well known in Europe. He was professor successively at the universities of Dorpat, St. Petersburg, Cracow, and Warsaw. Besides his linguistic works from which sprang the so-called "school of Baudouin," he is known for many pamphlets and articles concerning social and national problems.

ADDRESS AT THE OPENING OF THE AUTONOMISTS'* CONGRESS IN ST. PETERSBURG

(November 19, 1905)

Before proceeding to a discussion of the problems which interest us I suggest, gentlemen, that we perform a rather painful operation on ourselves.

We shall be obliged to cut off or suppress in ourselves a part of our own ego, that part which is fed either by the conviction of the superiority of our own nationality and beliefs over others, or by the striving for preponderance and domination of our own nationality and our own beliefs over others.

Personally I find myself in the fortunate position of not at all having to remove such an organ from my physical constitution. For I rid myself of all national and confessional prejudices long ago and belong to that widely condemned group of people *Sans foi et sans nationalité* (without faith and nationality). I make no discriminations among

---

* The Autonomists advocated the necessity of a reform in Russia by granting autonomy to the nationalities forming part of the immense Empire.

the various nationalities or social groups and treat them all in the same impartial way. On the other hand, I have always defended those who were wronged and persecuted. In Kazan I defended the Tartars when they suffered persecution at the hands of the Russians. In Dorpat I defended the Estonians and Letts against the Germans, and subsequently all of them against the Russianizers.

I could by no means approve the attempts made by the Poles in Galicia against the rights of the Ruthenians or Ukrainians. In the Congress Kingdom and in the Western Country† I must protest against the Russianizers and the converters to Orthodoxy.

If, at any time, the Great Russians and the adherents of the Orthodox faith were to suffer persecution, I would, as a matter of course, take a stab against their oppressors. My un-nationalism and undenominationalism, more strictly speaking, my extra-nationalism and extra-denominationalism and the equal treatment resulting from them of all nationalities and other social groups do not display any merit whatsoever. Merit is only involved in the case of persons who cannot obtain international justice without the painful operation I have mentioned.

We have not gathered here because of a sudden brotherly love for each other. Avowals of love should be eliminated once and for all . . . . There is no reason that we should love each other. If, however, there is no mutual love among us, we may have mutual interests.

Besides our community of interests other motives of the simplest elementary justice are admissible. People must suffer all too frequently and too much from elemental disasters: therefore one at least should not consciously increase and multiply human sufferings. When we endeavor to remove or at least restrict the elemental disasters inflicted by the forces of nature, as well as by the unbridled passions of irresponsible criminal neighbors, we are guided above all by selfish feelings. First, we want to create personal security

† Name given in Russia to those provinces of old Poland which did not form part of the Congress Kingdom.

for ourselves, under the condition of certain concessions to other people, which constitutes the essence of any sensible freedom.

Second, we experience satisfaction from the consciousness that we have given advantages and contributed to the common wealth. It will not make a mistake when I express the supposition that these very feelings induced many of us to gather at the Congress and to deliberate about our common needs.

In the list of nationalities which consented to participate in the Congress the principle of logic is lacking. Three principles have been confused here. The Finns, as citizens of what is properly speaking a separate state united with Russia by a purely federal union, could be invited by us only as guest advisers. Finland offers us an excellent model of how two nationalities, differing so much with respect to language as the Finns and the Swedes, can live in harmony with each other and form a single political and economic entity.

Subsequently, within the boundaries of the Russian Empire proper, we enumerated some nationalities according to the language peculiar to them. With respect to language the Armenians, Georgians, Estonians, Letts, Lithuanians, Poles, Ukrainians, and White Ruthenians differ from each other. The isolation of the Jews into separate groups is based primarily on their community of religion, in contradistinction to the so-called Christians.

The separation of the cultural and social groups united by Islam or Mohammedanism should have the same denominational foundation. Indeed, such a standpoint is necessary where on the one hand one continues committing wrongs against the Jews, while on the other, one emphasizes and exploits for the purpose of criminal agitation the confessional differences between the Jews and Christians, as well as between Moslems and Christians. As far as the White Ruthenians are concerned, it is rather difficult to regard our fellow members appearing under that name as being representatives of a nationality to the same extent to which the representatives of other nationalities can regard themselves as such. The White Ruthenians have among us merely their advocates who, nevertheless, are their completely devoted representatives and defenders of their cultural interests. Besides the nationalities enumerated in the original invitation we are happy to see in our midst the representatives of some Moslem nationalities. Strangely striking is the absence from among us of representatives of the German nationality which plays a prominent role in Russia. It is just this outstanding role of the Russian Germans that was the cause of their absence. Among democrats there is no place for fundamental aristocrats who do not recognize national equality and who claim the right to dominate "underlings" who speak other languages. Undoubtedly, among the Russian Germans there are also just men who do not endeavor to oppress others: but the vast majority of them look with contempt on non-Germans, while some are even ready to support the former autocracy in order to preserve their privileged position. When the Russian Germans admit their error and look with a gracious eye on the plebeian nationalities, they will be *eo ipso* included in the Association of Autonomists.

BETWEEN GERMANY AND RUSSIA

OSWALD BALZER

(1852-1933)

In 1897 the renowned German historian Theodore Mommsen, published an article in one of the Vienna dailies, warning Austria against the Slavs. He particularly attacked the Poles and the Czechs who, he declared, were bringing barbarism and ignorance into the Austrian Empire. Balzer, Professor of Polish law at the University of Lwow and a distinguished scholar who had never engaged in politics of any kind, struck back at the German historian in a brilliant open letter. Today, in the face of German barbarism, Prof. Balzer's letter takes on a timely significance.

FROM "SLAVIC AND GERMAN CULTURE"

(1897)

"Raum für alle hat die Erde"—SCHILLER

The Slavs whom you have in mind and who supposedly intend to establish in Austria a reign of barbarism and ignorance are mainly large groups of Western Slavs, especially the Czechs and the Poles. Before going on I might point out here that even the groups of Southern Slavs who are part of the (Austrian) Empire have in the main belonged to the realm of Western Civilization for centuries. However, to simplify matters, I shall confine myself to Western Slavic nations; I hope you will accept this limitation inasmuch as it was only these Slavs that your letter seemed to have in mind.

There were two external elements which contributed to the civilization of Western Slavs: Christianity and the lay Western Culture. Thus, our Slavic civilization is not completely indigenous; it has been permeated with foreign elements though these were neither exclusively nor slavishly accepted. The third factor at work was the native genius which modified the other elements according to its own needs and peculiarities and united them into an organic whole. German civilization had exactly the same origins and character: it, too, grew out of Christianity and the Western lay culture as received by the Germans at their birth and as later transformed by them in their own national way. Neither of the tribes is, therefore, the creator of a completely original culture; both started out on borrowed capital and it is doubtful whether either has any right to claim superiority on that account. The sole difference lies in the fact that while the Germans availed themselves directly of the ancient civilization we profited additionally by whatever developments they subsequently added to it. On that particular account the Germans merit the gratitude of the Slavs, which we do not mean to deny—but on the same account let the Germans be consistent and not accuse us of lacking in culture. Such accusation could be justified only if we had been unable and unwilling to reap the fruits of the civilization we found at our historical inception.

In the period of our growth and up to the present day we have profited in many ways by the achievements of German culture, though not by them alone, for in the meantime the powerful Latin civilizations had developed and we did not remain strangers to them. The same is true of Germany itself. It is a well known fact that the development of urban life, which was to play so vital a role in the economic and social growth of Germany and, accordingly, in the intellectual life of that country, was based on Lombardian models. The great spiritual rebirth of the nation, which occurred at the close of the Middle Ages and at the beginning of modern times, brought about the study of old as well as of newly discovered treasures of ancient literature and art; yet even this Renaissance did not spring up in Germany itself but was brought there from Italy. In the 17th and 18th centuries petty German rulers were not the only ones to model their courts on French patterns— German literature, which in the 17th century could not produce a Moliere or a Corneille, and in the 18th century could not boast of a Voltaire or a Montesquieu, fed freely on French examples. Surely you remember, sir, what opinion was held on that subject by Frederick II. And in the field of material culture—to quote but one instance let me remind you how unattainable, for years and even to this day, has been the standard of perfection set by French artistic industry, and how much Germany owes France in its own recent achievements in that field. Yet, I should like to see the countenance of any German, were a Frenchman or an Italian on that account to fling in his face the derisive accusation that he comes of a low grade civilization, let alone that he is utterly lacking in culture.

How are we to determine whether the Slavs took part in the development of culture or whether they were at all capable of so doing? Let me remind you, sir, of a few facts. Here is one, fairly typical: of the first two universities founded in Central Europe one was built in Prague and the other in Cracow—the two capitals of Western Slavs. True, it is commonly said that the Prague University was German, but it is yet to be proved that it was so in the Middle Ages. Education in those days was thoroughly cosmopolitan. Among the professors there were Germans as well as Czechs —for that matter, Italians and Frenchmen too—so it was not the Germans alone who carried the torch of knowledge. The University was founded by a prince who, though elected King of Rome, was at the same time hereditary King of the Czechs, and he was not one to subordinate the welfare of the Czechs to that of the Germans. Indeed he was jokingly called "the father of the Czech Nation and arch stepfather of the Holy Roman Empire of the German Nation". The Czech character of the university became so apparent at the beginning of the 15th century that German professors began to leave it in droves. And the greatest personality produced by the Prague University in the Middle Ages— a man far exceeding in stature the common rank and file of professors—was a Slav by origin and name, Jan Hus. But let us proceed with our review. In the 15th century we find Długosz in Poland, writing his great history. In spite of the legendary yarn he wove around the prehistoric origins of his nation, as was the custom in those days, in spite of his obvious partiality in the presentation of contemporary events, he surpassed by far, both in scope and in his broad outlook on historical matters, the narrow attitudes of the Central European chroniclers of his times. Germans would be hard put to it to mention a single name among their own Middle Age chroniclers fit to be placed alongside that of Dtugosz. In the 16th century in Poland we see the genius of Copernicus rising over the whole of Europe; and may we recall that Copernicus studied astronomy at a Polish university and under the expert tutelage of a Polish professor. The same century boasts of two other illustrious names: that of the statesman Modrzewski and that of the great poet Kochanowski. In the 18th century the Czechs produced an educational reformer renowned throughout the civilized world—Komensky, and in the present century the Western Slavic nations have contributed to the world of science such names as: Palacky, Safarik, Śniadecki, Szujski and Kalinka; to the world of poetry: Mickiewicz, Słowacki, Krasiński, Neruda, Halek, Vrchlicki and Sienkiewicz; to other fields of art: Grottger, Matejko, Siemiradzki and Chopin. Here are but a few of the names I could mention; but they will serve our purpose, for some of them are so great that many a pseudo-great who cries that Slaves have no culture at all would do well to remember his place as compared with them.

If the nations who claim a monopoly on culture and civilization had had the good fortune to be able to count these men among their own, without a doubt they would have placed them among their most prominent national figures. One fact should be emphasized, namely, a large number of those pioneers of civilization not merely Slavonic but European, appeared in the last century, at a time when the national progress of Western Slavs was hampered from every direction, as for that matter it still is today. The cultural impulses and abilities of these nations must indeed have been indomitable if, in spite of all these handicaps, they were able to contribute as much as they did to the progress of civilization. For all these great men, quick or dead, bear ample witness to the fact that their nations are civilized, they are living refutations of the malicious accusation of barbarism; barbarism could never have contributed what those men have contributed to the common treasure of civilization.

To go back, I wish to make it quite clear that I have not the slightest intention of concealing the historical faults of the Western Slavonic nations. The faults most often mentioned, sometimes with undue emphasis, refer to the social and political structures of these nations: the privileges of the upper classes, the subjugation and degradation of the lower classes, the weakness of the government's authority and its inability to maintain a strong political organization. I am ready to admit that this was true in certain historical periods. But I would not dream of insulting you, sir, an expert historian, by explaining at length that such momentary weaknesses and even downfalls may occur in the lifespan of any nation which has contributed and may still contribute to the progress of civilization, and that such downfalls are not necessarily final but may be followed by periods of Renaissance. And I need not remind you, sir, that many of those deplorable phenomena were not peculiar to Slavonic nations alone, that we find them elsewhere among people who consider themselves leaders of civilization. The privileges of the upper classes were not abolished throughout Europe until the French Revolution; at that time the Czech state had for almost three centuries been without its independence, and Poland was just being partitioned. In certain small states belonging to the German Empire serfdom was abolished only at the end of the 18th century. At the same time, though her fall was imminent, Poland, for all her weakness, announced the complete equality of all citizens in the Constitution of May 3rd, 1791.* On the other hand there was never a Polish or Czech ruler who would sell human flesh, leasing whole detachments of his army to foreign powers for money, as did certain German princes as late as the end of the 18th century. German residents in Polish cities were allowed to use their own language in official documents as long as they wished to do so; when

* Cfr. p. 53.

they adopted the Polish tongue it was of their own accord, without special laws and without the coercion of the Poles. German children were taught in primary schools in German: their language was not systematically eliminated from the curriculum. The ill famed *Liberum Veto*—the right of minorities to break up parliaments,—was partly restricted by Poles themselves in 1768, and completely abolished in 1791, and there is not a single Pole today who does not condemn that practice; yet now, at the end of the 19th century it has been revived in its essential form by those very people who advance the theory of the cultural inferiority of the Slavs. . . .

Not only did these Slavs strive to develop culture within their own borders, they also were forced to defend it against attacks from the east.

They gave their lives for it, whenever the necessity arose. On the battlefields of Lignica died a Polish prince whose task had been not simply to defend his own country but to save the whole of Central Europe from the Tartar flood that threatened it. And when in 1683 a Polish king came to the rescue of besieged Vienna he was nobly fulfilling his duty to the entire Western civilization. From the 14th century to the 18th century Poland, in constant and ever renewed conflicts with the Tartars and Turks, lived through a glorious epic of its own, and not once did the Western world come to its aid, though this Western world was willing enough to give generous help to a German Order when the latter was fighting with Poland . . . .

What is more, Western Slavs were eager to carry Western culture into lands where it had not yet penetrated; they were conscious of its importance, conscious of the obligations and duties they had assumed upon entering the orbit of Western civilization. Heathen Poland received Christianity from the Czechs; the son of the first Christian ruler of Poland, as far back as the end of the 10th century, sponsored the propagation of the faith among pagan Prussians; and he found a zealous executive for plan in the person of a saintly Czech bishop who was himself a descendant of Slavonic princes.

The Germans and the Slavs embarked upon their respective cultural tasks under totally different conditions. The young German states were rising at a time when the rotten structure of the old Roman Empire was crumbling, and when its direct heir, the Eastern Roman Empire was too feeble to assume any serious undertaking. It had already been defeated once by the barbaric tribes of Visigoths on the battlefields of Adrianople, and the later victories of Belisarius and Narses were to have only a temporary effect. The ancient culture which has engendered the German civilization was not represented by a large and powerful state which, on the strength of its cultural superiority could attempt to subdue the newcomers politically and nationally. Beginners as they were, the Germans became at once independent; there was no one to hamper them, no one to dominate them; they were free to develop Western Civilization as they pleased, and, indeed, for a while they developed it single-handed. This was their good luck, not their merit. The Slavs, on the other hand, found themselves in totally different conditions at the start of their cultural development. They were not building on the ruins of an old order; it was from their own lands which they had settled many centuries before (or had occupied after the German tribes had voluntarily left) that the Slavs wished to, and in fact did, join the orbit of Western civilization. Next to them they have always had the powerful and civilized German nation with its older cultural past. Thus emerged, I would say not two different civilizations, for both are founded on the same basis, but two cultural centers, each focusing the efforts of its respective people. The trouble was that "the older brother" wanted to focus all in one center and for that reason immediately extended his tutelage over the "younger brother"; he was determined to draw him into the sphere of his influence, and if possible, conquer him and incorporate him into his own possessions. And, as we know, he was ready to do it by hook or by crook. Perhaps, on purely formal ground, German actions may be justified with regard to some of the Slavic tribes; the Cis-Elbean Slavs, for instance, were obdurate pagans, and paganism was the negation of culture; culture, therefore, had to be introduced by force. But how can one justify the German attempts against those Slavic nations which, once they embraced the principles of Christianity and Western culture, openly adhered to them and signified a willingness to cooperate in them? Even these, however, the Germans would not spare. The Czech King Venceslas I, who laid down his life for Christianity and Western culture, was the first to be subjugated by the Reich; the Polish King Bolesław the Brave, who converted Prussians and helped the Germans in their conquest of the heathen Cis-Elbean Slavs, was forced into a long and bitter war with Germany to preserve his nation's independence. Were those Slavic people, simply on account of their cultural youth, incapable of progress without outside supervision? When the Germans themselves emerged from barbarism they pursued their cultural apprenticeship unaided and would undoubtedly have resented any similar unsolicited control. Yet they were able to produce a great civilization. Perhaps, then, the Slavs lacked the necessary ability? But we have demonstrated in the preceding paragraph that they did not. In fact, it was precisely those Slavic nations which escaped total German subjugation, like the Czechs, who were but loosely bound to Germany, and the Poles, who early established their absolute independence, that were most successful in achieving a higher degree of civilization; other Slavic tribes such as the (Western) Serbs, for instance, who fully enjoyed the advantages of the German rule, show little progress. German guardianship and interference were, therefore, both unrequisite and inexcusable, and, from the standpoint of cultural progress, indifferent, since, without them, civilization would have progressed just as well, if not better.

Besides, did cultural motives actually play the leading part in Germany's attempts at domination? Here is a small but very significant fact recorded by a German chronicler. When a section of the Elbean Slavs, defeated by the Germans, finally accepted both Christianity and German rule, and it seemed that from that time forward everything would proceed according to the desires of the culture-missionary, quite unexpectedly the tribe reverted to paganism. Christianity, in the minds of these simple people had become identified with the German rule, and they renounced it because they were sick of the Saxon greed ("avaritia"). As we see, besides sponsoring the great cause of civilization, these missionaries also pursued certain private ends which they did not even take the trouble to conceal.

But far more significant and illuminating than this little incident, are other facts which show that even when the Slavs had progressed considerably along the road of civilization, and were determined to carry Western ideals further East, thus serving the very principle of which Germans consider themselves the most faithful exponents, the same Germans not only did not help them but in many cases threw obstacles in their path . . . .

None of us Slavs would make the slightest objection if Germans were to praise this, that, or the other of their actions as a great achievement, as a triumph of wise and foresighted diplomacy, as a victory of the valiant German arms and spirit. All we ask is, do not wrap all this in the cloak of special services rendered to culture and civilization. For the great majority of German tribes the interests of culture always coincided with political motives, and incidentally, political interests took precedent over cultural ones. For the sake of political gains they were ready to carry Western civilization to the Slavic East but they did not hesitate to abandon the cause whenever it interfered with these selfish political aims. Their primary motive was to conquer and Germanize, not to civilize, yet they identified culture with their own state; they believed and even attempted to convince the world that the road to civilization leads through Germany and that other people should consider themselves fortunate if allowed to travel that way to the upper strata of civilization.

They declared themselves the guardians of all nations which embarked upon the great task of civilization later than they did, never asking whether such guardianship was welcome or not, forgetful of the fact that those nations had been endowed by God with abilities equal to their own and were therefore perfectly capable of working independently for the cause of civilization. This assumption on the part of the Germans has greatly obscured and distorted their own judgment in the matter. It was not by chance that a modern, undoubtedly brilliant German historian, faced with the problem of choosing the most momentous event in German history, picked the Germanization of a part of the Slavic East. By his choice he has defined, though unconsciously and in defiance of his own purpose, the real essence and value of the historical progress of Germany. There is nothing to prove that those Germanized Slavic tribes were incapable of developing a high degree of culture of their own if left to their own devices, as other Slavic nations had gone when not hampered by German domination. From the point of view of civilization as a whole, therefore, the value of this event chosen by the German professor as most momentous is highly dubious, though it still remains a great political and national gain. If such is the greatest service the Germans have rendered civilization we have no reason to envy them their achievements.

So, let us call a spade a spade, that cry of distress which came from your lips, sir, was not caused by any peril that actually threatened civilization, it was a cry of despair at the sight of a slipping German supremacy. Why not call things by their proper name instead of clothing them in a travesty of culture? Not only truth but the Germans themselves will benefit by it. For the accusation of barbarism thrown in the face of the Slavs, would, if true, prove the greatest charge brought against the Germans in the face of God and humanity. In most cases where Germans supposedly brought culture to the Slavs the latter were made to pay for it by the renunciation of their supreme possession— their nationality; and whenever Slavs were unwilling to pay this price the Germans hampered their spontaneous cultural growth, and prevented civilization from spreading further —despite their self exaltation as culture's most faithful servants. Those Slavic nations which did not lose their nationality and yet succeeded in acquiring a culture did so against Germany's will. And so today the Germans call them uncivilized and barbarous. If this were true, whose fault would it be?

Slavs have no desire to "Slavonize" the sites where Mozart and Grillparzer lie buried. History proves that they did not "Slavonize" German lands, it proves only that the Germans Germanized Slavonic territories. All that the Slavs ask is that the sites where once Premysl Ottokar sat on his throne, where once Jan Napomucen died a martyr's death, where now stand the tombs of Palacky and Safarik, remain Slavic as they have been for fourteen centuries. It is no man's right to take this away from them in the name of culture, for they are willing and able to work for that culture of their own accord without foreign interference or guidance. German culture is not the first or last or only way to achieve perfection. As peer to peer, Slavs will gladly work along with the Germans lifting bricks for the great building of human civilization and from this all mankind will surely benefit.

In your open letter, sir, you mention with fully justified national pride the glorious name of Schiller. We Slavs, sir, admire Schiller no less than you and other Germans do: we revere in him not only a great German but also a great and noble beacon on the path of civilization. And it is not only his grave that we worship: we worship the high ideals to which his great soul gave utterance. And if only the Germans would not limit themselves to perfunctory worship of his tombstone, perhaps the profound words of the poet which I have put at the head of this letter would induce them to examine their conscience and revise once and for all their attitude toward the Slavs.

ALEKSANDER LEDNICKI

(1866-1934)

Before the first World War Aleksander Lednicki lived in Moscow where he played an important role in the life of pre-Bolshevist Russia. Member of the Russian Duma (Parliament), where he represented a constitutionally democratic party called "Cadet," he distinguished himself as an uncompromising opponent of the autocratic system of the czars. During the first World War he headed Polish democratic groups in the struggle for independence.

Lednicki's opinion on Russo-Polish relationship is expressed in the following excerpts from one of his addresses of 1917. Poland's enemy was Russian absolutism and imperialism, he declared, it was not the Russian nation. The same thought was voiced much earlier by Adam Mickiewicz.

FROM A SPEECH ABOUT RUSSIA AND POLAND

(1917)

A century and a half has gone by since a great historic injury was perpetrated which was to becloud the European horizon for many years. To redeem it many generations had to spill their blood. The partition of Poland took place at the dawn of the great era when nations began to free themselves in the name of the sacred ideals of liberty, equality, and brotherhood.

We Poles can say with pride that in this heroic and unforgettable struggle for freedom our two national heroes took part—Kościuszko and Pułaski. In America there came into being the United States, the first and most powerful democratic republic in the world. In the west of Europe the brilliant morning star of the great French Revolution was rising —of the Revolution which was to destroy the old system of oppressive absolutism. In Poland the Constitution of May 3rd brought new courage and filled all hearts with the hope that the strength of the nation would be regenerated. In the meantime the three most powerful representatives of the system of absolutism, fearing lest it be overthrown, tore to pieces the living body of the Polish nation—that republican nation which fought to the last for its right to life and liberty. The Republic was shattered, and thus was also stamped out the breeding place of liberty. The rule of absolutism over the peoples of Europe was perpetuated for many years.

Thenceforward the Polish question and the history of Poland's struggles for independence were inseparably intertwined with the great struggle of nations for freedom wherever that struggle broke out. Our nation took part in all revolutions, and for the Poles every battle for freedom was a harbinger of resurrection, reunion, and Polish independence.

Russia's participation in the dismemberment of Poland served those cultural ties which up to the Partitions had united two peoples in spite of friction and wars. The Partitions destroyed the possibility of continued harmonious and brotherly community between two peoples racially akin, and a period of separation set in . . . .

But Poland's struggles for independence were never directed against the Russian nation, and whenever the Russian nation fought for its own liberty it strove at the same time for liberation of Poland. The spiritual union between the two peoples, severed by the policies of the Czars, kept asserting itself in the struggles of the Decembrists, in the Polish Revolution of 1831 when the Polish standards proclaimed the uprising as a struggle "for Your Freedom and Ours". It asserted itself in the Russian Narodnaya Vola and in the popular movements of the first years of our own century . . . .

. . . . The Polish nation was more than once the object of various political combinations and intrigues, but the Polish problem was never solved by them.

The Polish problem was not solved by the Grand Duchy of Warsaw which Napoleon established in 1807, and which hardly survived till 1815; nor was it solved when, after the Congress in Vienna, the Kingdom of Poland was set up and united artificially to absolutist Russia. Each attempt led invariably to self-destruction in mutual conflict. The Uprising of 1831, the repeal of the Constitution of 1815, the Organic Statute of 1832, the plans of Wielopolski,* the Uprising of 1863, the abolition of separate judicial procedure, the establishment in 1869 of a Russian University at Warsaw to replace the former Chief School (Szkoła Główna), the introduction of Russian law-courts, the closing of the Bank of Poland in 1886, etc.,—all these things created a vast series of legal, political, and financial problems and complications. They created in the course of time a tangled and chaotic legacy difficult to remove . . . .

---

* See footnote p. 130

POLITICAL INDEPENDENCE AND
SOCIAL EMANCIPATION

LUDWIK WARYŃSKI

(1856-1889)

*Ludwik Waryński was one of the founders and leaders of the
Proletariat, organized in 1882 as the first socialist party on Polish
soil. Its program and tendencies were a composite of the theory of
Marx and the practice of the Russian revolutionary party "Narodnaya Wola". The Czarist government, setting out systematically to
destroy the party and its influence, arrested a number of the
leaders and organizers. Their case was tried for one full month
and on December 23, 1885, the defendants were found guilty and
sentenced. Four were executed, and the rest condemned to many
years of prison, hard labor or exile. For a long time the activities
of the Polish socialist party were throttled, and it did not again
acquire strength until after 1892.*

*Waryński, sentenced to a long prison term, died in 1889 in the
fortress of Schluesselburg.*

*The trial of the Proletariat gave great impetus to the develop-
ment of the workers' movement in Poland. For the first time the
socialist program had been openly and clearly stated in a court-
room for all the public to hear and, at that, by men who possessed
the courage to advocate it in the face of certain death. We quote
below excerpts from Waryński's speech.*

FROM SPEECHES AT THE TRIAL

(1885)

. . . . There can be no question of my guilt or that of any
of us. We fought for our beliefs; we are justified in the light
of our own consciences and in the face of the people whose
cause we served. I am indifferent to the details of charges
brought against me and I will not waste time in refuting
them. My purpose is to give a true picture of our aims and
activities which are placed in a false light by the prosecution.
We are not sectarians or dreamers divorced from reality,
as the prosecution and even the defense would have it . . . .

Profound thinkers have made the most shattering criticism of the social system as it stands today; and it is they

who point out the seedlings of a better structure pushing through the soil of present conditions. Parliaments and even despotic governments have introduced in a legislative manner reforms which are absolutely contrary to the prevalent conception of private property. The concentration of land in government hands which has taken place in European countries, the assumption of control by various states, the general introduction of industrial laws, are all actions which characterize our times and bring closer the triumph of new social structure. We do not ignore these facts, we see clearly their importance and usefulness to our cause. But at the same time we are convinced that the liberation of the working class from the oppression to which it is subject should be the task of the workers themselves. Even those palliative measures with which the present governments try to prevent disaster are affected by the pressure of the workers' movement . . . . There is no government completely independent of the social classes which compose the state. The influence of these classes on the structure of the State is directly proportioned to their political development and organization. Until now the privileged classes, the bourgeoisie and the nobility have held the upper hand in this respect. It is time for the working class to step into the political arena and pit its own organization against other organizations, and in the name of pure ideals, lead a crusade against the present social structure. Such is the fight of the workers' party under the banner of socialism. The workers' party counterbalances other social classes and stems reactionary tendencies. While aiming at radical changes in the social structure, it is content at present to prepare the ground . . . .

Our aim has been to beget a workers' movement and to organize a workers' party in Poland . . . . We have organized the working class in its fight against the present order. We have not organized a revolution but we have organized *for* a revolution. We know that the ever-mounting social antagonisms and the ever-swelling wounds on the social organism will inevitably lead to a cataclysm. And we know the terror and the devastation that follow when the masses, driven by poverty to the last limits of despair, burst their shackles and turn on the existing order. It is precisely for that reason that we consider it our duty to prepare the workers for the revolution, to make their rise a conscious one, tempered and disciplined by organization, and to give them a clear program of ends and means. Can our activity truthfully be called a conspiracy aimed at violent extirpation of the present political, economic and social order?

I will answer with a simile. Imagine, if you will, gentlemen of the jury, a mountain stream flowing from the Alps into a nearby lake; the current of this stream carries with it grains of sand as well as the pebbles that lie along its bed. Some day this gravel will cover the bottom of the lake and make it shallow. In a glass of water dipped from this stream there will be found an infinitely small particle of the sand that has filled the lake. Yet it would be impossible to ascribe to this one glass of water, which is but an infinitesimal fraction of the force that has been active over a great period of time the result which could be brought about only by the phenomenon as a whole.

We are not above history, we are subject to its laws. We look upon the revolution toward which we aim as upon the end result in the development of historical and social conditions. We foresee it and do our best not to meet it unprepared . . . .

* * *

Gentlemen of the jury! The drama that has lasted for nearly a month is drawing to a close . . . . When you retire to your chamber to consider the verdict, remember that political trials clarify and determine the attitude of the government toward the convictions and parties that exist within the country. The present moment is of historical importance. Upon your verdict will depend the future direction of our movement, its character. Remember the responsibility that rests upon you, remember also, that you, too, will have to face the verdict of history!

AIMS OF THE POLISH SOCIALIST PARTY

The so-called Paris Program of the Polish Socialist Party was adopted at the organizing Congress in Paris, November 21, 1892. One of the leading theorists and publicists of the Polish Labor Movement, Feliks Perl (Res), compares the Paris Program with the manifesto of the "Democratic Society" and the manifesto of the "Polish People". He writes: "Polish Socialism has realized what it is, what it must be: THE IDEA OF THE WORKING CLASS IN A SUBJUGATED NATION."

The Polish Socialist Party, as the political organization of the Polish labor class, struggling for liberation from the yoke of capitalism, strives above all to overthrow the present political slavery and to obtain power for the proletariat. In this striving its aim is: *An independent Democratic Republic*, based on the following principles:

POLITICAL

1. Direct, universal and secret suffrage, a people's legislation conceived as both sanctional and initiative;

2. Complete equality of the rights of the nationalities forming part of the Republic on the basis of voluntary federation;

3. Community and provincial self-government with the election of administrative officers;

4. Equality of all citizens irrespective of sex, race, nationality or creed;

5. Complete freedom of speech, press, meeting and association;

6. Free court procedure, election of judges, and responsibility of officers before the court;

7. Free, obligatory, universal, complete education; students are to be supplied with means of livelihood by the state;

8. Abolition of a stable army; general arming of the people;

9. Progressive income and property tax; similar inheritance tax; abolition of all taxes on food and other prime necessities.

ECONOMIC

1. Labor legislation:

a. An eight-hour working day, regular thirty-six hour interruption every week;

b. Minimum wages;

c. Equal pay for women and men for equal work;

d. Prohibition of work for children up to fourteen years of age; limitation of the work of juveniles (from fourteen to sixteen) to six hours per day;

e. Prohibition of night work as a matter of principle;

f. Factory hygiene;

g. State insurance in case of accident, unemployment, sickness and old age;

h. Factory inspectorate elected by the workers themselves;

i. Labor exchanges and workers' secretariat;

j. Complete freedom of workers' strikes;

2. Gradual nationalization of land, instruments of production and means of communication.

BOLESŁAW LIMANOWSKI

(1835-1935)

Historian, sociologist, and politician, Limanowski devoted his long life to the deals of freedom, equality and justice. He fought in the insurrection of 1863, and later spent many years abroad as a political refugee. When finally he returned to settle in the Austrian dominated section of Poland his writings had already begun to exercise a powerful influence over the minds of the Polish youth of the day. Very early in life he had acquired a socialistic point of view to which he remained faithful until his death. When Poland became independent Limanowski, though an old man, did not withdraw from active political life; from 1922 till 1935 he occupied a seat in the Polish Senate, elected by workmen's votes. He was constantly to be found on the side of the oppressed in the struggle against chauvinism and injustice.

FROM "THE NATION AND THE STATE"

(1906)

.... It would be best if each nation could have its own homestead, its own hearth, its own republic. But in that case would not the great and wealthy nations oppress and abuse the smaller, poorer ones? It seems possible, indeed highly probable, that they would. To prevent this the nations would have to create a Central International Representation, vested with executive powers and rights, something in the line of the European Parliament proposed by Gladstone. In fact, what is to keep them from uniting in one common republic according to the ancient Polish principle: "Equal with equal, free with free?"

.... The Manifesto issued at the Slavic Congress in Prague in 1848 is of tremendous historic importance: here was stated the great principle of equal rights for all nations regardless of their political size and power. It demanded a universal congress, not simply of state representatives, but of representatives of all European peoples, a congress which would arbitrate and clarify all international relations. "We are convinced," it declared, "that free nations will reach an agreement more easily than diplomats paid by kings and princes."

This last declaration may be considered optimistic. Nationalists firmly maintain that it is so. Under the pressure of numerical growth or merely the fundamental desire to attain the greatest possible prosperity, every nation naturally seeks to augment its possessions. National selfishness is a fundamental law, they argue. Therefore, all nations which impede or obstruct the extension of a particular state's frontiers must be weakened, subjugated, brushed aside, annihilated. It is clear that the policy of such people is one of aggression and conquest. And for that reason the appellation "nationalists" is misleading—they should be called "imperialists". Gone are the days, however, when importunate tribes were simply wiped out or murdered; today the policy of denationalization has been widely adopted. This is a policy which restricts the number of nationalities within a state to one. It is based on the old conquest principle—the principle of privilege. To safeguard the privileged position of state nationality many conditions are required: a strong, centralized government, a police force, an army, a bureaucracy—in fact, the whole apparatus of the ancient state. Subsidized by capitalists and forced to take into account the growing preponderance of democratic convictions, Nationalists, or rather Imperialists, as they are called in England, are enthusiastic advocates of colonial expansion and national exclusiveness; and they seek to depict in brilliant colors the great material advantages which such a government policy will bring to the working people.

. . . . Socialists who have at heart the interests of all people in their country, and not merely those of a privileged minority, must oppose such a state policy. Under the banner of universal justice they denounce national selfishness which sanctifies violence, exploitation and robbery. Fate is fickle: *"hodie mihi, cras tibi";* a nation oppressed today may tomorrow become the oppressor. The serfdom of men has been

153

abolished, it is high time to abolish the serfdom of nations. All nations, large or small, should have equal rights. Let them unite in political and economic unions as they consider best and most profitable for themselves. Universal suffrage, in absolute freedom, must be the basis of a new order.

.... It may be expected that once universal suffrage has become the political basis for inter-state relation Europe will before long be transformed into a Union of federated national states, with a Supreme Court to settle international differences and with executive powers to carry out the decisions and ordinances of the Union. Then war in Europe will have become unnecessary and impossible.

.... It is not unlikely that just as the toll bars have disappeared from within European countries, so some day will the customs houses disappear from their frontiers in a united, republican and democratic Europe.

Only then will state borders lose their significance and controversies concerning them cease to exist.

JÓZEF PIŁSUDSKI

(1867-1935)

In his youth a member of the Polish Socialist Party, Piłsudski organized the revolutionary fight against the czarist régime and, during the Great War, created the Polish Legions which were the nucleus of the future Polish army. He was the first chief of the reborn Polish state, Minister of War in various cabinets, Inspector General of the armed forces, Marshal of Poland, and finally, after the coup d'état of May 1926, the real, although not nominal dictator.

Following are excerpts from his writings dating from the period when there could be no question concerning his democratic convictions.

PROCLAMATION UPON THE ENTRY OF POLISH TROOPS INTO THE CONGRESS KINGDOM

(August 12, 1914)

The decisive hour has struck! Poland has ceased to be a slave. She wishes to determine her own fate, she wishes to build her own future, throwing her own armed force into the scale of events. Regiments of the Polish army have crossed into the territory of the Congress Kingdom, taking it over on behalf of its true, real, sole owner— the Polish people, who rendered it fertile and enriched it with their blood.* I take it over in the name of the Supreme Power of the National Government. To the entire Nation we bring emancipation from its claims, and to its individual components the conditions for normal development.

From this day let the whole Nation unite into one camp under the direction of the National Government. Outside

---

* These words demonstrate the real, original intentions of the creator of the Polish Legions during the World War. Unfortunately, he as well as his men swiftly forgot these ideals. In the reborn Poland governed by them, it was by no means the Polish people who were the "true, real, sole owner."

this camp will remain only the traitors, with whom we know how to deal without quarter.

JOZEF PIŁSUDSKI
Commander-in-Chief of the Polish Army

*   *   *

ON PATRIOTISM

(1901)

Lithuania* has long been the scene of a fierce nationalist battle. In the course of this struggle, her fields and woods have become steeped in the blood of her sons, persecution and privileges constantly rain down upon her, while her people are torn by nationalist strife and squabbles. Under such conditions patriotic slogans and feelings must of necessity play an important social role. Thus, every thinking man must study this tumult and conflict and evolve a sane judgment in matters of such vital concern to the country while it is the duty of every faction and political party to take a definite stand on this point.

In our times, when there is no brotherhood among nations, just as there is none among men, we generally encounter two types of patriotism—imperialistic and defensive. There is a close casual relationship between the two, for just as there is no victor without the defeated, so there can be no defense against aggression without aggression. The former, imperialistic patriotism, is currently the political slogan in the majority of the great European powers. It has at its command millions of bayonets, cannon; thousands of apologists in the shape of ministers, journalists and scholars; billions in money, sweated out of the working people. It impels nations to fratricidal warfare, conquers countries, and, spider-like, sucks the life out of them. If, however, we study it attentively, we shall notice that the mainspring of this chauvinistic spirit that is now enveloping the whole world is not true patriotism, a sentiment of love and of devotion

---

* Prior to the first World War, Lithuania was a part of the Russian Empire. The author has in mind the former Lithuanian Grand Duchy, embracing a much greater area than present day Lithuania. The ethnic composition of this territory was varied (Lithuanians, Poles, White Russians, Jews and others).

to one's country. At the bottom of this current lurks the reptile which gnaws at contemporary society, a society based on the misery and the exploitation of the working people. The bourgeoisie—mistress of our present-day world—is, in every country, constantly engaged in competitive warfare with the bourgeoisie of other states and nations. In order to exist and develop, it must have the widest markets for its products, it must, in the face of the neighbors' competition, fence off the invaded markets with duties, tariffs and privileges. The more powerful, the larger a state is, the greater its export market, the more easily does it come to the defense of its industry and commerce and compel other countries to grant appropriate concessions to its products. Hence, the growth of a colonial policy, hence the conversion of the world into a military camp. To continue, a state is all the more strong as it is more uniform and united. In invaded countries, therefore, government extends its grip over the human soul in an effort to recast it in the victor's mold; the conquered peoples have the victor's religion and language forced upon them; privileges are established for the newcomers and for those who can be bought; those who refuse to submit are subjected to persecution. Before the fire of chauvinism the bourgeoisie turns another roast as well. Capitalism divides the world into exploited and exploiters and provokes conflict between them. This fight embraces increasingly wider circles of the working people and constitutes an increasingly greater menace to the rule of the bourgeoisie. National chauvinism sets one nation against another, unites that which is falling apart under the influence of class warfare, and checks the disintegration of rotting society. In the manner of despots, the bourgeoisie attempts to conceal the filth of exploitation and the vastness of human misery under the bedraggled rag of national greatness, a rag stained with the blood and tears of martyred and subjugated nations.

Such is imperialistic patriotism in Europe. Russian chauvinism, with which we have long had to contend here in Lithuania, does not differ fundamentally from the European variety. It, too, is predicated upon the exploitation of the conquered country and the profit of the aggressors. The difference lies, in the first place, in the fact that this trend is not directed by the bourgeoisie, but by the barbarous czardom, which seeks to prop up the tottering political system, throwing to its people—as one throws bones to attacking dogs—conquered countries to chew upon; in the second place, instead of sending out the inanimate European products of which Russia does not have an exportable supply, the Czarist régime floods the conquered markets with human commodities—thousands of hungry and loot-thirsty bureaucrats.

Imperialistic patriotism is so inconsistent with the most elementary sense of justice, it so poisons the moral atmosphere of the aggressors and the life of the subjugated, that every decent person must, regardless of his convictions, declare himself against it. There can be no division of opinion on this score among the Socialists. They must battle it to the bitter end, they must tear off its mask, revealing how much injury and mud is concealed behind it.

To close the subject of imperialistic patriotism, let us also mention Polish chauvinism. It does not, to be sure, have a state machine at its disposal, and being itself persecuted and fettered by privilege laws, it represents no greater danger to anyone. Basing itself, however, on a certain ascendancy that it possesses by virtue of its cultural and economic superiority, it occasionally betrays hostility towards Lithuanians. It is a known fact that priests often engage in Polonizing activity. This is countenanced by the bishops and prelates who frequently send to Lithuanian parishes priests who do not know a single word of the language of their parishioners. It is also no secret that a certain section of the Polish intelligentsia looks with ill will upon the development of Lithuanian culture and even seeks to incite the Polish people to enmity toward its neighbors.

IGNACY DASZYŃSKI

(1866-1936)

One of the founders of the Socialist movement in the Austrian-dominated section of Poland, Daszyński was the first Polish Socialist deputy to the Austrian Parliament. He carried on an inflexible fight against the gentry who controlled almost all Polish life in Austrian-dominated Poland. And it was he who undermined the power of the nobility in Polish political life.

In independent Poland he was leader of the Polish labor movement, Deputy-Premier of the Government of National Defense during the Russo-Polish war in 1920, and later speaker of the Sejm.

FROM "THE POLICY OF THE PROLETARIAT"

(1907)

In our present condition the idea of Poland's independence is the most revolutionary idea, the least deceptive idea and the idea that best comprises both aims of the present revolution: to overthrow Czardom and establish a constitutional parliament in Warsaw.

A democratic Polish republic, created by the revolutionary proletariat, is in the present conditions the highest possible degree of development. It means the creation of our own state machinery under the direct authority, or at least the direct influence and control of the proletariat. We do not overestimate the omnipotence of the modern state, particularly in view of the political abdication of the Polish bourgeoisie. But the Polish parliament and government in Warsaw would have to be under such preponderant influence of the freshly victorious Socialist organizations, that the whole state machinery would have to consider at once the chief interests of the people. What this means in a country "administered" in such a terrible, barbaric, thievish way as the Congress Kingdom, will be appreciated only by one who knows the secrets of the rule of the Russian officials. Starting with schools and ending with protective labor legislation, the present Russian rule is one crime, one violence and savage unreason, worthy of a government of spies, professional thieves and murderers. The bureaucratic centralism that leaves all decisions about our fate to the grafters in the Petersburg offices, the innumerable chicaneries of the local authorities perpetrated always from the point of view of the Russianizing policy of oppression and constant suspicion of a Polish "revolt," finally the outburst of the savage horde of officials brought from the East and regarding us as conquered colonies where the "native" is a man without rights, all this would have to yield to a different government machinery dependent on the democratic institutions of a people's legislation and of people's control. The proletariat would fight against our own bourgeoisie without having, in addition, to deal with a foreign yoke. Its every victorious step in that struggle would become established in the form of institutions and laws made at home, and controlled at home. The most important political function is directness of participation in legislation, control and administration. In such republics as, for example, Switzerland this directness leads to the confirmation or rejection of laws by popular vote (referendum) and to the election of all more important officials by the entire population. In the bourgeois system, based on exploitation, this highest political form may render immense services in every respect to the people in its class struggle.

Placing the independence of Poland at the head of revolutionary demands will force the Polish proletariat to take stock of its own forces. I would regard this as one of the most important changes. For hitherto too many of us have always counted on "something" that may or is bound to happen somewhere and have constantly listened to outside events and remote commands. This was called "elementalism", "coordination", etc., but at the bottom of all these combinations there lay always the lack of responsibility for the whole revolutionary policy, and concern only for some part of it, for carrying out an order without often realizing whether the order was necessary and advantageous for our revolution. A clear and distinct formulation of the demand of an independent Poland would force us in the nearest future to bear greater responsibility.

LUDWIK KRZYWICKI

(1859-1941)

Krzywicki was the author of a great number of scientific works, among them "Primitive Society and Vital Statistics", which is his best known book in America. Krzywicki was founder and president of the Institute of Social Economy, an independent research institution which took a large part in the study of Poland's basic social problems. But above all, he was an outstanding educator who exercised a powerful influence on several generations of Polish youth. During the present war he did not leave Warsaw; in the days of siege, he was wounded by a bomb fragment and died soon after.

FROM "SOCIAL PSYCHOLOGY"

(1900)

In the last decade the term "class selfishness" became generally accepted.

Together with it the view spread that in their activity the social classes were guided solely by considerations of material interest.

Without having submitted this statement to a more detailed analysis many construed it in the entirely distorted sense that every representative of a defined social class is a perfect egotist having in view his own personal interests.

The facts of life are the only proper criterion for the appraisal of such general statements.

These facts give eloquent evidence that in their actions men are not only guided by motives of sordid interest, but also—for the moment let us leave out of consideration the intensity of this factor—yield to impulses of a more ideal nature that induce them to devotion and sacrifice for more general aims. Among the group commonly quoted as the extreme example of class selfishness, namely among the French royalists of the end of the past century, there were

162

many enthusiasts who laid down their property and even their lives on the altar of their convictions. Whatever they were guided by in their public activity, at any rate in their conduct it was often impossible to detect individual selfishness. On the contrary, the historian is struck by the great self-denial among the defenders of the "old régime". The enthusiast of royalism lost sight of the most fundamental interests of his "ego", offered his wealth in the defense of what he considered just, and when it came to offering his blood he did not recoil even before such a sacrifice, more anxious lest he dishonor his name by disgraceful conduct than to save himself.

The opinion that the representatives of the different social classes are guided in their public conduct solely and with full consciousness by considerations of their own interest, is false, or rather not so much false as a superficial formulation of a very fundamental symptom. What matters in the establishment of the fact that class selfishness is the great motive of social life is not so much the individual actions of some person, or its moral value as the ultimate resultant of many individual activities, as the integration of these separate actions in group activity. The very expression "class selfishness" indicates that the interestedness inherent in that selfishness reaches beyond the sphere of separate individualities and brings with it group aims unable to exist without a bond of a broader nature. Class selfishness presupposes the presence of collective activity, and in such activity sacrifice on the part of individual members of the class group is not only a useful but also an indispensable action.

Thus the question arises how persons distinguished by readiness to sacrifice and who in general lack a sense of their own personal interests, can at the same time be advocates of class interest; and still more, why from among disinterested persons most often come the extremist advocates of class selfishness.

* * *

Each one of us is brought up and matures in defined conditions, horizons and ideals. From the earliest years of life we are exposed to the influence of our environment which moulds us emotionally and mentally after its pattern, endows us with sympathies and dislikes peculiar to it, makes us look on the whole social bond from a strictly defined standpoint. We learn contempt for some things, respect for others; we are stirred by the echo of certain watchwords, we become accustomed to listening to theoretical explanations that formulate the results of what, without our knowing it, has been suggested by our environment or which we have experienced in our lifetime. If we took the trouble of confronting the statements of so-called economy with the patterns amid which a great businessman happened to live, it would prove that, in the main, they are only a summary of what he himself experienced from day to day. He invested capital in his business; he spent part of it for machines and auxiliary means, he used a part to purchase materials, out of the rest he paid wages to his employees and workers. All these expenses figure in his account book with the same importance, and if they differ in anything from each other it is only quantitatively and never qualitatively. None of them contains in its name anything on the basis of which it could be regarded more than others as the source of income. The businessman cannot regard any one of them as a value creating power *i.e.*, one that brings forth income by its cooperation. This income is derived from his ability to exploit the market situation, from the fact that he sold his goods at a higher price than he had spent on their production. Whoever will more closely consider the social environment of the businessman, his calculations and expectations, particularly his attitude to the market, will agree that his opinions on the valuable powers in production, the origin of profit, etc., must be what they are. And as it cannot be expected that everyone should deeply engage in an analysis of economic conditions or be at once convinced by theories negating his daily, though superficial, experience, the conclusions resulting from daily empiricism become the articles of his social creed: such an empiricist, possibly a humane and kind man, will regard as agitators all those who do not see sources of income in the happy configurations of market conditions, but deduce them from the conditions of production, and declare that the heading of the account books are not synonymous with their value since human labor is the source of value.

The gentry of the close of the 18th century was in the same situation.

Its whole environment, all traditions left from the past, distinctly told it that it was different, more perfect, more refined than the common people. The opposition of the terms *gentilhomme* and *vilain*, originally denoting a man of high birth and a townsman, and later a gentleman and a villain, is an excellent proof of that subjectivism. The gentleman could prove his descent from his ancestors, and when and where they died in the defense of the country, sacrificing their lives for others who ploughed, traded or were engaged in handicrafts. With his mother's milk he imbibed admiration for the heroes of the past whose remains were later to be thrown into the gutter in 1794, and for tradition and history in general in which he found the names of his ancestors. He loved the institutions created by them and supported by their blood and activity. From childhood he became accustomed to care for what he called his and his family's honor, and at the same time look upon the peasant who, wronged, humbly stooped to his master's feet, as a creature possessing no nobler feelings in his heart. Well bred and refined in his intercourse he saw in the church a specimen of lower order. Consequently he believed that he was created to enjoy his social rights, while the *vilain* was created for labor bought, incidentally, with the blood of fallen gentlemen. In the goodness of his heart he sometimes dreamed of paternal protection of the peasant people, and that "the masters take their handmaidens by the hand" and together form one song in one procession, "one song, but two choirs". Thus a young man of noble origin grew up in an environment that, if he possessed more ideal impulses in his soul, made an ideologist out of him, but an ideologist of a queer class type. He ardently felt some things, breathed with enthusiasm for certain ideals, was ready at any moment to support with his own property and blood the cause of what he loved and considered just. But after a deeper analysis his ideals prove to be nothing but the formulation of a state of things in which he, the master, would forever remain the master, while the peasant would be the serf; in which even if, as a kind and gracious master, he would take his hand-maidens by the hand, he would nevertheless sing in a different chorus. He gazed intently at the ideological halo peculiar to his environment, unconscious that this was the reflection of his environment and interests. Fighting for what he loved, he did not see that he was fighting for the perpetuation of his class interest. And let us add, the more sincere an ideologist he was and the more humane toward the common people, the more painfully was he affected in case of a quarrel by the conduct of the "ungrateful", and the more severely did he punish all "agitation". In the last analysis whatever were his motives, the result of his activity had a strong class character.

Class selfishness may be unconscious of its own motives and may be accompanied by extreme readiness for sacrifice. This combination often occurs in a very characteristic form. I consider, for example, Arnold Toynbee, who undoubtedly belongs among those who occupy a meritorious place in the history of the humanitarian trends of our time. An ardent apostle of learning he gave his wealth for work in the social vineyard, especially for spreading among the masses nobler knowledge about life and nature. And yet he was a fervent advocate of the principles of extreme Manchester policy; when at a lecture which he delivered against the theory of Henry George, shouts of dissatisfaction were heard, he knelt down amid the excited crowd imploring its forgiveness for the selfishness of his ancestors and promising by his own repentance and activity to atone for their offences, and simultaneously begging that the listeners should not let themselves be led astray by such misleading doctrines as the nationalization of land.

Class prejudices, the horizons of the environment, feelings of sympathy and hatred kindled under their influence, motives, often unwitting, of interest, all these create in the human ego a combination of stimuli dominating it and driving man on a definite road. His social consciousness is the product of the class substratum; as whatever exists in the environment is reflected in a mirror.

Of course, we do not claim that every representative of a class is an ideologist. On the contrary, in the class group some are guided solely by their own, personal, perfectly realized interests. Perhaps they even form a very considerable part of the whole. But let us add that they are seldom found among the leaders standing at the head of their class. To occupy such a position enthusiasm and faith are necessary, and these qualities can be found only among the ideological enthusiasts. Class selfishness is a powerful motive of historical conflicts; in the form of religious dogma as in the sectarian movements of medieval Europe, it reaches extreme intensity, but it possesses such loftiness only because it draws upon the feeling that it is based on genuine conviction and moral assumptions.

EDWARD ABRAMOWSKI
(1868-1918)

Edward Abramowski belongs beside Freud and Janet among the orginators of the psychology of the subconscious; as a sociologist, he may be considered one of the precursors of modern humanism. But Abramowski was also a theorist of the cooperative movement in Poland. Through social cooperation rooted in the principle of free will, Abramowski like Kropotkin, visualized a social rehabilitation consummated in the spirit of democracy and social justice. In his social works he defended the concept of ethical anarchy, opposed the sovereignty of the state, and advocated the theory of the free will of social groups. Abramowski exerted a great influence on progressive trends in Poland, particularly among the village youth.

FROM "SOCIAL IDEAS OF COOPERATIVISM"

(1907)

During every historical crisis, when great unnamed ideas, the property of all and of none, rise as harbingers of a new world, then, too, the criticism of personal life appears. This is the first sign of an inner struggle. The ideas loom huge and at the same time distant and foreign in contrast to the drab, daily life. In this world of ideas live the ageless dreams of humanity—the dreams of brotherhood, prosperity, freedom; there Isaiah's prophesies of plowshares forged out of armor and the evangelical predictions of a temple transplanted in the secret confines of human hearts are resurrected. But, before this vision of beauty crawls a soiled and shameful life—a life of profiteering, selfishness, and oppression of the weak; a life of offices, law-courts, exchanges and asylums; a turmoil of minor anxieties and petty ambitions; of limping thoughts and emotions.

Thus the problem of his own life, its edification and enhancement, faces whomever a breath of the new thought has touched; and the inalterable and self-evident postulate,

168

that a new social world requires new people, makes itself manifest.

Free institutions cannot rise from slave natures; democracy cannot spring from brigands and social parasites; social justice cannot be born of a people scurrying for gain and luxury. Even if, by reversing the order, we were to claim that political institutions of the new type would of themselves ennoble the human race and make life more wholesome, still unanswered would stand the question: "What powers will succeed in lifting these institutions out of chaos, in organizing, in preserving and in reviving them in the spirit of a renaissance? Whence will come the individuals capable of creating a social evolution? Whence those masses with their mature conscience of manhood and citizenship without whom a political democracy is only a fiction, a name without meaning—a whitened tombstone of the Pharisees?"

Democracy grows only where it has become a need of the masses. It appears as a reaction against absorption by the state; as a necessary defense of self-created institutions and of the people's organized economic and cultural interests against bureaucracy.

If the Swiss people defended their democratic order with such a logical stubbornness against the various demands of a central government, and if they succeeded in extending it to the farthest limits of political freedom, let us not forget that the defense of democracy in their case was the defense of their very existence. The political constitution which they created has for its broad and natural foundation thousands of unions, groups, organizations; thousands of self-created agricultural, trade, labor, and cultural organizations; democratic customs—the customs of equality and respect for man which are rooted in the whole civilization of this people; and, together with the habit and ability to attend to their own affairs and communal needs independently, a strongly developed civic sense and distrust of bureaucracy.

All this constitutes democratic culture—the first and indispensable principle of democracy and political independence.

The Polish people do not even now possess such a culture. They are not a modern society organized in multiform groups and free unions. Even until very recently they were no more than a loose collection of units always passively awaiting reforms and expecting to be shown new channels of government in which they might direct their lives. Without social institutions of their own which they could develop and perfect, they waited only for police reforms. So deeply did this apathy to self-initiated action pervade the character of the people, that not even the guiding minds of the parties or various fronts could think of any social slogans other than those included in the formula, "what to demand from the state."

We have long been accustomed to regard ourselves as the stuff out of which others mold various shapes: we offered ourselves constantly: make one thing or another of us, make of us a constitutional society, a democratic or a social-democratic society; build reform schools and hospitals for us, protect us from misery and exploitation. The sum of our political wisdom was contained in these petitions or demands for reform. All ideals bowed before the one State-Providence. It alone was to think and act for us. It was to feed, cure and protect us—and this we called "democracy".

In the course of such politics anything but democracy might develop. The first requisite of democracy is a strong feeling and instinct for social independence. Democracy requires a people that knows not only how to demand reforms from the state, but also how to effect such reforms by means of its own institutions; it requires the skill to organize social interests independently; it requires the development of societies controlling all fields of economy, culture, labor protection and health; and lastly it requires strong individualism and full consciousness of the need to regulate one's own life in accordance with one's own standards as well as respect for the independence of others. Democracy cannot evolve without these moral and social principles.

Were the most far-reaching reforms to be worked out in a ministerial committee or Duma; were we to acquire institutions of political self-government based on universal suffrage, all these would inevitably evolve into a government of officials and representatives, become centralized somewhere far beyond the people, and be comparable to the lowest level of political immaturity, if the task of creating a democracy from the very bottom—that free democracy of societies—were to be neglected by us.

Creation of democracy by society itself, the creation of its being, its inner strength, is both the salvation of life and the moral liberation of the people. Wherever institutions of self-sufficiency, cooperatives, agricultural cooperatives, and craft unions develop; wherever independent centers of education and culture arise, there also must occur and indeed do occur, serious changes in the customs and very souls of the people, in the rearing of children, in physical and moral hygiene, in the conceptions of life's problems and happiness. For it is the people themselves who create the conditions of their existence. On their capability, energy and sacrifice rests the communal well-being which the organization seeks. In the life of the individual appear goals which were non-existent before; appears the feeling of independent creativeness and communal solidarity. Then, not only do the petty sufferings of the slave soul disappear, but also those of the modern businessman who cannot conceive of a profit without pain. New categories of moral and social pleasures drive out the empty boredom of excesses, corruption and drunkenness. In short, a new culture, a new type of man evolves who is the differentiating principle of a democratic society.

A member of free organizations is one who regulates his life by the strength of his own mind, character and heart, and such a one is the citizen of a democracy. On the other hand the individual who wanders aimlessly among a herd is a gullible pawn in the hands of bureaucrats and party leaders. He is a slave of life conditions and is typical of a slave society.

These two basic sketches characterize the whole psychological and moral difference. They adjust to themselves conceptions, emotions and conscience, needs and the course of life, desires and ideals. The democratic type will demand above all the freedom to create; the slave type will demand "bread and games." The first seeks himself to improve and perfect his life; the latter demands this of the state.

In the democratic type the need for empty complaints and noisome grumbling vanishes, the struggle between individuality and conditions, between a nursed ideal and reality, disappears; because the member of a free society is able to create his own life and to adjust conditions to his own personality. Out of this there develops a perfect coordination of thought, emotion and action, a condition of salubrious unity.

In the slave type a great gap exists between the ideal and reality, between personality and environment. Man enters upon a life created for him under coercion. He tortures himself by seeking in vain to adjust himself to it, he castrates his individuality in the most varied ways, he suffers different disciplines—moral and conceptional—he loses the link between his hidden desires and the actual deed, and out of all of this he develops into a sickly, incomplete and perverted individual.

In this moral transformation of man from slave to free creator which is the profound personification of democratic culture, cooperativism finds its most important task.

FROM "COOPERATIVISM AS A MEANS OF FREEING THE WORKING PEOPLE"

(1911)

Creative freedom constitutes the essence of true democracy. Where citizens demand everything from the state or from the philanthropist, where they base all their hopes on reforms of one type or another instituted from above and by coercion, there is no democracy or free citizenship. There are merely subjects of a more or less progressive, and a more or less enlightened government. Democracy and freedom begin when citizens of a country, instead of demanding reforms from the state in the fields of economy and cultural conditions, bring them about independently, by the power of free unanimity; when a man is not merely an "electoral vote" to parliament, a pawn in the hands of bureaucrats or party leaders, but a free agent who is quite capable of working with others uncoerced and who knows very well how to improve life.

This democratic spirit, engendered in separate small cooperatives, must necessarily grow into one national economic organization and create what we call a "cooperative republic." Such a republic solves the problems which have most seriously troubled humanity for centuries. It reconciles the freedom of the individual with communal possession. By socializing production, business, and agriculture it forms a lasting basis for the self-government of the people and for the independence of man. It protects him from exploitation and slavery.

The advent of a cooperative republic is as quiet and calm as the advent of everything powerful and strong. It does not rise out of upheavals and rebellions or demagogic deception of the people. It takes the country slowly—one section after another, one city after another, trade after trade, village after village, home after home. It reaches into the newer branches of industry and commerce; not only internally, into the stores, workshops and unions, but externally as well, grooming the people mentally and morally for citizenship, for membership in democracy, for their function as workers in a cooperative national economy.

TRIBUTE TO FIGHTERS FOR FREEDOM*

* These excerpts translated by Edith and Sidney Sulkin

STEFAN ŻEROMSKI

(1864-1925)

*Żeromski was the leading Polish novelist of the period called
"Young Poland" (the end of the XIX century and the beginning
of the XX.) He established a new style and a new form for
the Polish novel. Besides being of the first order artistically, his
works were pregnant with socio-educational implications. He,
more than anyone else, deeply absorbed and portrayed the abysmal
misery and social deficiencies of the new proletariat.*

*Żeromski was Poland's candidate for the Nobel Prize. Among
his greatest works are "The Travail of Sisyphus," "The Home-
less People", "The Ashes", and numerous other novels.*

FROM "DREAM OF A LANCE"

Behind you, soldier of Poland,* when you hang by the
gallows noose, when, with a heart riddled with bullets, you
plunge into the bloody ditch of condemned, when you perish
in slow agony on the Siberian desert, behind you there wave
no mighty banners. There is nothing beside you and behind
you there is only a trench dug to the measurements of your
corpse. Before you there are armies. When you die no one
will feed your children in kindness, your fellow citizens will
disown you, fellow inhabitants will forget you; "Emotion
does not live long in their hearts, and in their heads a
thought has no more than an hour's life."†

The gutter will rear your offspring, latrines will shelter
them, and when they grow cut-throats will be their guardians. The world about you will not mark your death, neither
will the world afar, for you have not yet won your cause.
Beyond the rows of soldiers all is against you, reluctance,
fear, hatred, the shouts of the lords, the tolling of factory
bells, the intrigues of cowards, and the dark ignorance of
misery. The frightened eyes of national self-bondage peer

---

* Polish socialist workers who fought against the Czarist régime.
† Words of the Polish romantic poet, Juljusz Słowacki.

at you through cracks and holes, from behind buildings and corners. The hatred of all who have no need for greatness of soul, who have no need for strength, nor for the boldness of a raised fist which crushes ermine-clad tyranny at the risk of death,—such hatred conspires against you with its well tried doctrines of crooked philistinism and shrewdness and the eloquence of its newspaper filth. In the tracks of your martyred steps, taken as shrewdly as a fox, as quietly as a ghost, a murderer follows, imitating your gestures and your name . . . .

Your destiny is death for holy ideals, death without consolation, without fame. But your ambition was not fame, you set yourself the task of tearing the world—against its will—from the dark sovereignty of night. Your task was to destroy the power of man over man, to raise the human spirit from the ignominy of the body, and to plant love and the knowledge of their right to happiness among humans. And so you threw down the gauntlet to the ruling forces of the world. And next to your martyr's stake they raised the gibbet of a thief.* You crept out in the darkness of the autumn night with the wild wind moaning and the rain beating, while we, the twenty million of us, slept in our bedrooms, in our nooks, and attics, and underground holes, sunk in the deep slumber of slaves. You crept out like a thief, naked to the waist, on your back the dismantled parts of a printing press. You were stuffed with leaflets proclaiming the freedom of body and spirit. In your left fist you clasped a torch with which you sought the guard in the darkness, and in your right you gripped a revolver cocked to fire. Thus you crossed the border rivers, thus you entered the country, barefooted, bleeding. That very night Independence was brought to this land of miserable souls harassed by foreign soldiers. That very night the Declaration of Rights of the holy Proletariat, long trampled by the power of riches, was brought to the land. You brought with you the last remnants of the Polish creed out of the crumbling tombs of the exiles . . . .

---

* Polish rebels were treated as bandits by the Czairst régime and were hanged together with them.

Your sign posts were the groans of working people. Those of whom the Fatherland knew nothing, those by whose labor the world was fed, those you found and raised and called to fight for freedom.

Who could count the glittering foreheads numbed by the frosts of Siberia? Who could relate the harrowing agonies borne by Polish socialism in its manacles? Who could measure the road they trudged through snows and forests and marshes in their exile?

Today your stainless Polish honor is blotched by the newspaperman who profits from trampling the fires of idealism. Cleverly he confuses the noble spirit of the rebel with the image of a thief who has seized the spoils of another. But soldier, your steps resound with a lonely echo in the secret hearts of the people. You are the people yourself and your blood impregnates them. Out of the hardened puddles of blood as out of the secret thoughts of a maiden legends will rise, legends the like of which Poland has not yet heard. Dreams of the sweet taste of fame will rise . . . . For the poetry of Poland will not forsake you, will not betray or insult you. She alone will be unterrified by your dreams and exploits. However lost your case, she will be faithful. She will commemorate your days and nights, your efforts and fortunes, your labor and death. That broken head of yours, crushed by a soldier's club, she will place in the heart of her most beautiful poems, which, for you alone, she will mold out of the dust of the ancient tongue.

When the people exhume you from the mass grave to give you a pine coffin, that will be the most that people can do. But poetry will cover your corpse as it lies there, bare of golden belt or purple cloak, will cover it with a mantle of nobleness woven of the fairest colors known. Into your death-stiffened hands she will place her golden dream, the dream of so many youths, the dream of a knight errant's lance!

ANDRZEJ STRUG

(1873-1935)

Andrzej Strug's earliest literary efforts were dedicated to "the underground people" who were fighting for independence and social justice. Poland was under Russian occupation and Strug's mind was a ferment of revolutionary ideas. Artistic maturity came however, with "The Yellow Cross", a novel which pondered and dissected a vast array of political, social and international problems. It set Strug among the important writers of the day.

Besides writing, he engaged actively in the fight against fascism. When Pilsudski, whose legionnaire Strug had been, veered toward dictatorship, the writer did not hesitate to abjure allegiance. He held a profound grip on Polish minds with his writings and activities.

FROM "THE UNDERGROUND PEOPLE"

"The Obituary"

Everything took place as had been arranged. There were wreaths, there were crimson ribbons and a crowd of a thousand people. They sang *The Red Banner* over the grave, and there were encomiums to which the people listened. But the tributes went unfinished. The Cossacks burst into the cemetery and the horses trampled the graves with their hooves . . . . A skirmish flared briefly and died and a score or two were arrested . . . .

The people are stirred, they have felt the wild wind sweeping through the foul air of their basements. Even after death you are useful.

My task is to chronicle your deeds and bring your unsung name into daylight. They'll stand at the type-form composing the words letter by letter . . . . for the wide mourning box beneath the thin little lines of a cross. You must be honored . . . . but how?

Let them, the people, know that you existed; and those who knew you, let them understand at last that it was you, you that they knew. No need for secrecy now. You shall have fame. Not a few will be roused, fired by your tale; not a few sustained in suffering. You shall have fame.

* * *

You took your leave at the worst moment. Was it fair? The task is still great; whom shall we put in your place? Unfair . . . . Orphans were left behind. On Wola* they ask whither you disappeared: "Did Walter get himself into trouble, or what? Why doesn't he come?"

He got himself into trouble, you folk of Wola, he won't be coming any more . . . .

You could have waited for today—not much, just a brief while of living.

I've a deep sadness for your sorrow, a deep sadness . . . . Why did you hurry so? It was wrong of you . . . .

* * *

Listen, brother, listen well, the revolution's on its way, on its way and setting the earth atremble.

They're waking—even there below—waking powerfully, for they've been sleeping powerfully. Won't you believe it?

Listen! It's the truth, it's begun! New days are coming, day's we've not seen before. The people look up differently, breathe differently, the enemy has a different fear.

We shall rise out of the earth now, rise with our treasures and reserves, begin to boast with our work. Tomorrow is not far, we'll live to see it.

Listen, brother, listen well. We'll rise from our underground and do a little fighting. Eye him to his eye, measure him, size him up.

Only you will not rise from the earth depths to see that shining day. Wouldn't it have been better to see it? Fill your eyes with the brightness? Swallow the free air?

One sultry evening in the underground you said: "To have to keep your eyes about you all your life, to have to hide, never let a sound escape you—a terrible thing, a shame . . . ."

* The workers' district of Warsaw.

We swam a long, hard way, lost strength, were sucked under; now we've made it, here's the bank, here, you can touch it . . . . but you're at the bottom . . . . how will it be on the bright bank without you?

* * *

Remember?

Student discussions, long papers, quarrels, taking sides, relations broken, renewed, groups, circles, plans, plans, plans . . . .

This fame of ours dragged through the streets of Warsaw, this pride of ours . . . .

Where, when was there ever a Napoleon more certain of ruling the world than we two, then?

The university threw us out, we said: We are destined for higher goals!

Locked up, behind bars, we said: Be brave, the eyes of the world are on us!

They set us free a few months later and we were ashamed to be free, it was a crime.

Into the world, the far world, we followed the rest of them.

Parisian years, the work, the fights, do you recall that noble pride of ours? *Rue des Courcelles.* Behind the barricades, two miserable starved dogs. The last of the borrowed sous had gone for the printing of polemical pamphlets.

London, merciless, terrifying, miserable, unendurable. Remember the misty autumn night we lay lifeless with hunger in the dark, unheated suburban room?

And that star-studded summer night thick with the odor of pine sap and pasture flowers, when we crept over the border and returned to the fatherland . . . .

The unuttered, unconfessed thought lay in each of us, to swear that never would we leave our land again . . . .

* * *

Now, after the years, it is hard to believe. How did we endure thoes days? The Testament is right: Faith lifts mountains and moves them from their place.

Days of hunger, cold and wandering . . . . distrust, fear, envy . . . .

We did the work of ten, each of us did, and two of us ate for one. Our schemes tore like cobwebs in the wind and we patched them asking each of the other: Will anything come of it? Darkness, intrigue, betrayals, constant remorse engulfed us. It might have been worse. We were accustomed to fear.

We were lucky somehow. When inevitable disaster faced us we were saved by a miracle. We were astounded. You said: It's clear that God is on our side.

Do you recall how we fled into that little shop to escape? In the Old City?* No time to lose, and like that, instinctively . . . . The shopkeeper said nothing, we said nothing, not a word, there was no time; the police were there, hot on the scent . . . . Tell me, who told her, who taught her? . . . . "Two of them ran by here toward Bugaj,† I think . . . . " She slipped us out the back way through the gate, again without a word . . . . Is she still alive?

And that Jew at the gate. Remember him? "You gentlemen had better not go upstairs, the police are in the apartment." Who was he? How did he know us? Where did he come from?

We suffered it for the third, tenth, hundredth, thousandth time. Now our tribe has increased and even without us would endure.

Then why couldn't we have left together?

* * *

You died in a strange bed, they dressed you in a strange coat, strange boots for the coffin.

Listen, what did we ever possess of our own? Not a nook of our own, a moment, a secret of our own. Hardly a thought of such things . . . . Forever dragging ourselves about . . . . but always . . . . it was a dog's life.

You should have listened, you should have gone somewhere once in your life for a rest. You wouldn't listen to that.

You would have dragged on for another year or two. You would have seen something more, lived to see something—

---

* District of Warsaw.
† A street in "The Old City."

even if only a cleaner sun. And then it would have been easier for you . . . .

We prattled about it always: we would rest when they took us; in prison, in exile we would rest.

But there were moments of loneliness when a word tore out of us: "Let the devil send them for us already!"

To spite us they didn't come . . . . And so you fell, exhausted, like the end horse stumbling in the harness. Rest . . . . rest . . . .

*   *   *

I'll write your tale with vibrant, palpable words. Something to be long remembered. Great, eternal fame for you, man of the underground, man without a name!

Let your name, unfurled, be the pride of thousands, a living signal, a goad, a call to battle.

Let them know you!

I have to work now. The copy is ready, waiting only for you. We'll print it up tomorrow. I'll spend the night at the type-form setting up your deeds. A single column was all they allotted you. Your life must fit into that, and your soul. It'll be bright for you in the mourning-box and my tale will be short. I'll prepare it in the night, in the calm and safe night. This long night I'll spend with you alone, dead brother . . . . Setting type to type and reading the words off one by one.

Who knows? Perhaps out of the pain of memory, out of the sorrow of thought, perhaps out of the stillness of the night your shadow will rise and stand before me, quiet and sad, stand for a moment and nod and then drift away . . . .

*   *   *

Tomorrow the press will beat the pages off, one by one. The smithy will simmer with work. The quiet, skillful beating of the press, the rustle of papers and the heaps of newsprint rising hour by hour.

Your edition will go into the world by the usual routes. Throughout the Polish land the people will seize it and read it and shed a tear for you, a man's tear in which there is strength and an oath. It will spread through the world, passed from hand to hand, farther and farther until one day a crumpled, wrinkled scrap of it will fall somewhere sometime, borne by chance, blown by the wind, on an unknown road where an unknown man will find it and pick it up . . . .

POLAND LIBERATED

HISTORICAL BACKGROUND

(1918-1939)

The Russian revolution and the military collapse of Germany and Austria-Hungary prepared the way for the independence of Poland. While uprisings of the people removed German and Austrian authorities, Piłsudski's legions cleared away the last remnants of Russian domination.

On November 11, 1918, Piłsudski was proclaimed chief of the Polish state. Piłsudski's first cabinet of democrats, socialists and peasants was opposed by rightist groups which soon overthrew it. As a result a moderate government was established.

In 1921 a peace agreement between Poland and Soviet Russia determined the boundary between the two countries. A constitutional assembly injected a clearly democratic strain into Poland's constitution.

Among nationalistic groups semi-fascist tendencies began to grow and Poland's first president, Narutowicz, was assassinated by a member of one of these groups. Piłsudski consistently opposed the rightist government and in May, 1926, he seized control. Under his dictatorship Poland, however, turned toward reaction and semi-fascism. After Piłsudski's death in 1935 the situation became critical under the new dictator, Smigły Rydz. There were several unsuccessful attempts to create a governmental "monoparty". But the democratic opposition continued to strengthen itself and to fight the government's pro-fascist tendencies. These were the main problems of Poland's political life in the last years before the present war.

A DEMOCRATIC BEGINNING

FROM "MANIFESTO OF THE PROVISIONAL PEOPLE'S GOVERNMENT OF THE POLISH REPUBLIC"

(November 7, 1918)

The military defeat of the Central Powers and the revolutionary movements resulting therefrom opened the road to liberation for Poland. Disintegration among the Austro-Hungarian occupational authorities enabled the Polish progressive and independence groups to create a provisional government in Lublin. This government which included representatives of all democratic factions in Poland, though temporarily limited territorially to the former Austrian-occupied zone, nevertheless regarded itself as the legitimate representation of the whole of Poland. Headed by Ignacy Daszyński, it issued a Manifesto on November 7, 1918, containing the program on which the Polish state was to base itself.

* * *

To the Polish People! Polish workers, peasants and soldiers! Over blood-drenched, tortured humanity rises the dawn of peace and freedom . . . .

By order of the people's and socialist parties of the former Congress Kingdom and of Galicia we proclaim ourselves the Provisional People's Government of Poland and until the convening of the Constitutional Sejm we take over complete and full authority, pledging ourselves to exercise it justly for the good and benefit of the Polish people and state, not shrinking, however, from severe and absolute punishment of those who will not recognize in Poland the authority of Polish democracy. As the Provisional Polish People's Government we decree and proclaim the following laws binding the whole Polish nation from the moment of the issuance of the present decree:

The Polish state, embracing all lands inhabited by the Polish people, with a sea coast of its own, is to constitute for all times a Polish People's Republic whose first President will be elected by the Constitutional Sejm.

The Constitutional Sejm shall be convoked by us during the current year on the basis of general, equal, direct, secret, and proportional suffrage for both sexes. Electoral regulations will be announced within the next few days. Every citizen who has reached twenty-one years of age will have the right to vote or to be elected.

From this day we proclaim in Poland full equality of political and civic rights for all citizens irrespective of origin, faith and nationality, freedom of conscience, press, speech, assembly, procession, association, trade-unionization and freedom to strike.

All donations and majorats in Poland are hereby declared state property. Special prescriptions will be issued to counteract land speculation.

All private as well as former government forests are declared state property; the sale and cutting of forests without special permission is prohibited from the time of the publication of the present decree.

In industry, handicrafts and commerce we hereby introduce an eight-hour working day.

After we shall have finally constitutionalized ourselves we shall at once proceed to the reorganization of community councils, county assemblies and municipal local governments, as well as to the organization in towns and villages of a people's militia which will insure to the population order and safety, obedience to and execution of the orders of our legislative organs, and the proper settling of the problems of food supply for the population.

At the Constitutional Sejm we shall propose the following social reforms:

Forceful expropriation and abolition of big and medium landed property and its transference to the working people under state supervision;

Nationalization of mines, salt-mines, the oil industry, roads of communication and other branches of industry where this can be done at once;

Participation of workers in the administration of those industrial plants which will not be nationalized at once;

Protection of labor, unemployment, sickness and old age insurance;

Confiscation of capital accumulated during the war through criminal speculation with articles of primary necessity and supplies for the army;

Introduction of universal, obligatory and free lay school education.

We call upon the Poles living in the lands of the former Grand Duchy of Lithuania to strive in brotherly harmony with the Lithuanian and White Ruthenian nations for the reconstruction of the Lithuanian state on its old historical boundaries, and upon the Poles in Eastern Galicia and in the Ukraine to settle peacefully all controversial questions with the Ukrainian nation until they are ultimately regulated by competent agents of both nations . . . .

We consider it to be one of our most important and most urgent tasks to organize a regular people's army. We trust that the peasant and working youth will gladly join the ranks of the revolutionary Polish army, emanating from the people, defending the political and social rights of the working people, faithfully and completely devoted to the People's Government, subject only to its orders.

Polish People! The hour of your action has struck. Take into your worn, powerful hands the great task of liberating your land which is soaked with the sweat and blood of your fathers and forefathers and bequeath to subsequent generations a great and free and united homeland. Rise united to action, do not spare wealth or sacrifice or life for the great task of Poland's and the Polish workers' liberation.

We call upon you brotherly Lithuanian, White Ruthenian, Ukrainian, Czech and Slovak nations to live in harmony with us and to support each other mutually in the great work of creating an association of free and equal nations.

The Provisional People's Government
of the Polish Republic
Lublin-Cracow, November 7, 1918

FROM "THE CONSTITUTION OF MARCH 17TH, 1921"

(1921)

Having freed itself in the year 1918 the Polish Nation was faced with the problem of forming a constitution for its national life. This became the main task of the first parliament of the young republic, or the so-called Legislative Parliament. This parliament assembled in February, 1919, and worked under unusually difficult conditions. Poland was only then consolidating her borders and carrying on a war with the Soviet which burdened her further. Parliament became the scene of friction between the conservative and progressive elements represented by the labor and peasant parties. These clashes were most vividly accentuated by a background of constitutional debates. The left wing wanted to impose the most modern character upon the structure or Poland, particularly stressing the social factors. The right wing wanted to form the constitution in a traditional spirit and looked for inspiration to the Third French Republic. The final proof sheet represented a compromise between these two trends. Fundamentally it was based on the French pattern, though it greatly modernized it and introduced social motives. The constitution was truly democratic and belonged to the more progressive codes of contemporary Europe.

Following the coup d'état by Józef Piłsudski in 1926, the Constitution was partly revised to increase the powers of the Administrative Authorities. In 1935 the Government Party introduced a new, decidedly undemocratic constitution.

* * *

In the name of Almighty God,

We, the people of Poland, thanking Providence for freeing us from one and a half centuries of servitude, remembering with gratitude the bravery and endurance of the self-sacrificing struggles of generations, which unceasingly gave all their best efforts for the cause of independence, adhering to the glorious tradition of the immortal Constitution of May 3rd—striving for the welfare of the whole, united and independent mother-country and desiring her independent existence, might, security and social order, desiring also to insure the development of all moral and material powers for the good of the whole of regenerated mankind, to insure equality to all citizens of the Republic, respect for labor, due rights and particularly the security of State protection, we proclaim and vote this Constitutional Statute in the Legislative Parliament of the Republic of Poland.

The Polish State is a Republic.

The supreme authority in the Republic of Poland lies with the people. The Nation's Legislative powers are represented by the Sejm and Senate, the executive authorities by the President of the Republic together with responsible ministers, and the administration of justice by independent tribunals.

The Republic of Poland assures within its boundaries absolute protection of life, liberty and possession to all, regardless of descent, nationality, language, race or religion.

All citizens are equal in the face of the law. Public offices are available to all equally according to the conditions established by law.

The Republic of Poland does not recognize family or class privileges or escutcheons, family or other titles, except scientific, official and professional titles.

No one may be deprived of trial by court, to which he is entitled by law . . . . No statute may deprive a citizen of the right to claim damages and loss in court.

The Republic of Poland recognizes all property whether private or collective as one of the most important principles of the social structure and lawful order.

The land, as one of the most important national and state factors, may not be subject to unlimited turnover. Statutes will determine the law entitling the state to compulsory purchase of land and to regulate the turnover of the land, while considering the fact that the agrarian system of the Republic of Poland is to be based on farming units capable of adequate productiveness and constituting personal property . . . .

Labor, the principal foundation of the wealth of the

197

Republic, is to remain under the special protection of the State.

Every citizen has the right to State protection over his work and in case of unemployment, sickness, accident or incapacity the right to Social Security, which will be determined by separate statute.

Children with inadequate parental protection, whose upbringing is neglected, are entitled to State protection and help within the bounds determined by law.

Parents may be deprived of the authority over their children only by order of the court.

Separate statutes determine the guardianship over motherhood.

Gainful labor of children under 15 years of age, night work of women and adolescent workers in industrial branches, harmful to health, is prohibited.

Permanent employment in gainful work of children and adolescents of school age is prohibited.

Every citizen has the right to free expression of thought and conviction if he does not by such interfere with the order of the law.

Freedom of the press is granted.

Citizens have the right to coalition, gathering and forming societies and unions . . . .

Every citizen has the right to retain his own nationality and his own language and national character.

Separate State laws will grant the Minorities in the Polish State full and free development of their national character, with the assistance of autonomous societies of Minorities, having the public-law character, within the limits of common self-government organizations.

All citizens are granted freedom of conscience and faith. No citizen by reason of his faith and religious convictions may be limited in rights granted other citizens . . . .

Education in public schools is compulsory for every citizen.

Tuition in public schools is gratis. The State will grant to exceptionally talented pupils of moderate means scholarships in colleges and universities . . . .

198

ALEKSANDER SKRZYŃSKI

(1882-1931)

*For many years Polish foreign minister and delegate to the
League of Nations after 1919, Skrzyński was a "European" who
realized the necessity of Poland's close collaboration with the
Western and American democracies.*

*The following excerpts were selected from an address, deliv-
ered at the Institute of Politics, Williamstown, Mass., in July,
1925.*

FROM "AMERICAN AND POLISH DEMOCRACY"

(1925)

. . . . With your permission, Gentlemen, I propose to
consider the true and full significance of the words "The
Americanization of Europe" . . . .

By "American" I do not wish to imply a mere geographi-
cal expression, nor yet any ethnological, cultural, or economic
group. I have in mind a conception which expresses an
abstraction of the highest order. It is the comprehension
of America as a new historic, constructive force, which,
although it appeared in the arena of world events but a
relatively short time ago, reacts upon it with an ever-growing
effectiveness.

Analyzing this force, we find that it is, above all, a moral
force; that it emanates from a certain fundamental relation
to the world, from certain fundamental notions and certain
complexes of feeling, which are most characteristic of the
collective mind and sensibility of the Federated Nations of
North America. The material factors, such as the geographi-
cal position, the natural wealth of America, its energy and
its productiveness, these are but coefficients of this force.
They increase it enormously. They render possible its rapid
and intensive development, and its application to various
purposes, but they do not represent its essential nature.

This force may, I think, without violation of its essential character or of historical tradition, be described by the familiar but frequently misapplied term—democracy. Democracy, not as a name signifying a certain political system, nor as a definition of a body of customs, but as a comprehension of the collective life in all its aspects and with the entire mechanism of its directing impulses.

The American democratic type is the product of intricate historical processes and, like all products of an organized nature, possesses a complex structure. The elements comprising it are, however, not numerous. The peculiar properties of all living men, namely, the desire to live fully, the exercise of reason in the choice of means, idealism in the fixing of aims, constitute its few component parts. And yet how ingenious and intricate, how difficult to imitate is the formula of this compound! It embraces all that governs human life, all that adorns it and makes it worth living. And it creates a new structure of enormous activity which adapts itself to every situation, to every aim and to every means which it can use at any given time.

The eternal metaphysical yearning of the human soul which seeks consolation in productiveness and religious experience; adaptation to the strong and tenacious nature of a great and hard-won virgin country; the sense of solidarity of the group; the acknowledgment of the unlimited value of individual endeavor; all these were accommodated by this singular formula in such a way that the result is the strongest, most durable and most fertile product that humanity has so far invented.

American democracy is not an outline of theories, no matter how profound or how deeply pondered they may be. It is no Procrustean bed which man has built and continues to build with the aid of his formal logic upon one or another kind of foundation. It is rather a constantly varying, yet always biologically active, balance of the rational and irrational forces that govern human life. It violates none of these forces, nor does it attempt to deprive them of their existence. Furthermore it does not give to any one of these forces a preponderance over any other which it does not naturally possess.

American democracy unites in the most perfect way known the element of necessity with the element of freedom. It is thanks to this that nowhere else is the sublime idea of human solidarity so fruitful. At the same time, nowhere does the vital energy of the individual find a wider field of activity and production. And, even if the century old problem of the relation between the individual and the community has not been completely solved, it can nevertheless be emphatically asserted that in no other place does the attempted solution appear so bold and, in its practical results, so happy.

It is not without reason that we Europeans call America the "New World." We might also add "The Lucky World." This world is lucky because, conceived according to modern standards to meet modern requirements, and from the outset on a large scale, it does not know the difficulties connected with modernizing, hampered by the anxiety to preserve. It does not realize the discomfort of exiguity. When the United States adopted its political structure, the population amounted to something less than five million. The masses, flowing in at a rate which almost doubled itself with each succeeding generation, found their world ready to hand. It remained for them only to live and work in it, to love it and be justly proud of it. In a word, while in America democracy is much older than democrats, in Europe the reverse obtains. There democrats are, generally speaking, older than democracy—a distinction the significance of which you will appreciate, gentlemen, without elaboration on my part.

There is an ancient legend that even after the Catalonian battlefields had been covered with bodies of the slain and not a single warrior survived, the din of battle did not cease; for the spirits still warred with one another in the air. To such a legendary field post-war Europe may not inaptly be compared.

In this connection the international political conditions that prevail in Europe inevitably suggest themselves. To speak of these conditions, and in this place, is outside the legitimate province of an active European Minister for Foreign Affairs. I shall, however, devote myself to the consideration of a subject of even greater importance, from which, among many other things, international relations themselves arise. I shall speak of the post-war mentality of the nations of Europe.

This mentality is in a state of active ferment and chaos. The war and the series of revolutions in which it terminated have deprived the European mentality of the equilibrium afforded by a long, respectable, and now suddenly ruptured tradition. War and revolution have strengthened the emotional life of nations. Intensified in their power, collective emotions have destroyed the balance of mentality. All has become fluid. A modern social Archimedes would call his *dos moi pou sto* (give me a pivot), even more hopelessly than his predecessor of Syracuse. All the points that were stable until yesterday are agitated and vibrant. *Panta rhei.* (Everything flows). Individuals, groups, social classes, nations and states, all have lost their feeling of security. One has something to defend, another something to acquire. All anxiously await some kind of lottery, some sort of decision. This waiting exasperates. It falsifies perspective and distorts the vision of reality.

Before the war, the European mentality was distinguished by its tranquil faith in evolution and progress. The strength of this faith compensated for its lack of philosophical foundation. Its establishment was favored by the splendid technical developments, the dazzling scientific advances, the generally efficient machinery of government and particularly the varying yet continous march of universal prosperity. Technical art produced, each year, greater amenities of life. Earnings increased. States proved that their legislative and executive machinery was equal to every task imposed upon it. In England the Parliament Bill was carried through in the course of one election. A few decades ago, it would have required a bloody revolution. Under pressure from its aged emperor, monarchist and conservative Austria accepted the principle of a general election to Parliament, a thing which, a few years back, would have been considered inconceivable. The European looked upon all this and strengthened himself in the belief that the era of evolution had at last commenced; that this all powerful and beneficient goddess would successfully deal with growing armaments; that she would be able peacefully to dispose of the energy accumulated in European militarism at some fifth or tenth successive conference at the Hague; that this same beneficient goddess would point out to the different classes of society the road to a successful settlement of their conflicting interests; and that, in the deepening and spreading atmosphere of culture, the sharp edges of national, social, and political opposition would gradually disappear.

In the midst of this tranquil dream burst the most terrible of wars. After the war came revolutions. After the revolutions came a wave of inflation with its economic bankruptcies unexampled in history. It inundated many nations and shook the foundations of what appeared to be the strongest social and economic structures.

. . . . The problem of contemporary Europe reduces itself to clear and simple alternatives: either it must, by the development of democratic principles, recover its psychological balance and rebuild its faith in the efficacy of evolution, or it is destined to a destructive welter of nationalist conflicts or social revolutions.

Shortly after the Treaty of Versailles, there appeared a German book entitled "Pax Americana." In this book the author dwelt upon the analogy between his theme and the ancient *Pax Romana.* He endeavored to show that in relation to Europe, America, in the course of the war and the succeeding peace, occupied a position similar to that held by ancient Rome in relation to the Hellenic world after the battle of Cynoscephalae. He was concerned primarily to record the pain and disillusionment of a nation rudely awakened from its dream of world dominion by the reality of military defeat. He nevertheless gave expression to an incontestable truth in stating that, by reason of what happened since the great war, the establishment of *Pax Americana* in Europe, however distant its realization may be, has become the only positive ideal to which the harassed and shattered people can and should direct their course.

In its final practical consequences it is the suppression of traditional antagonism. It is the mutual economic, political, cultural and psychological intercourse which leads to real brotherhood and to the obliteration of the physical barriers of fear, suspicion and hatred.

Upon the remote horizon of human vision has appeared the image of a United States of Europe . . . .

The realization of this idea of the United States of Europe, what is it but the corollary of the great *Pax Americana?* What else but the Americanization of Europe in the fullest and noblest sense? And yet it is far from having become the watchword of the masses.

. . . . Old Poland was not a democracy in the modern sense of the word. No such democracy existed in Europe before the nineteenth century. She was, however, a democracy *sui generis,* a democracy based upon the social and political principles which had marked her unbroken historical evolution. Poland was both a democracy and a republic. Political rights were, it is true, the privilege of the nobility, but this class was so numerous and was so freely and copiously renewed, that Poland possessed, without question, the most liberal political system that Europe up to that time had produced.

When the State found itself in mortal danger, the better elements among the democratic nobility, under the leadership of the last king of Poland, framed and passed a new constitution, on May the third, 1791.* Considered in the light of the ideas and conditions prevailing in Europe at the time, the brightness of the thought that inspired it and the liberal nature of its covenants are truly astonishing. It aimed on the one hand at strengthening the authority of the monarch, on the other at broadening the basis of state by the extension of political rights to the entire middle class.

* See page 52

This great national impulse, unfortunately, came too late . . . . The first to draw his sword against the invading hosts was Tadeusz Kościuszko,* who while fighting at the side of Washington for American independence, had imbibed the spirit of modern democracy.

It was no more caprice of chance that brought Kościuszko, the defender of a perishing old democracy and the hero of its re-birth, to this free land and to the side of your illustrious forbears to fight a disinterested battle for the ideal of liberty and progress. The Kościuszko statue in Washington is a great deal more than the commemoration of a curious or even touching historical anecdote. It symbolized in Kościuszko's act the existence and the disclosure of a certain deep spiritual and idealistic union between Poland and the United States, which existed before any mind was able to detect, describe or explain it. It is a union of the same yearnings, the same affections, and of the same ideals in which these yearnings and affections became incarnated. And when on the most prominent spot in Warsaw there stands a statue of President Wilson, then will the symbolic feature of this union become fulfilled, and then will it be distinctly indicated that this union was and is reciprocated.

. . . . Democracy in Poland is objectively driven to model itself upon the democracy of the United States; to adopt its patterns; to pursue its aims. It not only desires, but is compelled to be its most faithful ally.

---

* See page 61

MIECZYSŁAW NIEDZIAŁKOWSKI

(1894-1940)

During the Polish war with Germany, Niedziałkowski acted as assistant to Stefan Starzyński, civilian chief of the defense of Warsaw. When the act of the city's capitulation was set before him, Niedziałkowski refused to sign. "Polish workers never capitulate," he said.

He had been editor-in-chief of "Robotnik", the central organ of the Polish Socialist Party, and for many terms a deputy to the Polish Parliament. After the fall of Warsaw he was arrested and imprisoned contrary to the conditions of the capitulation.

When Himmler, who was then in Warsaw, entered his cell to ask whether he wished anything, Niedziałkowski retorted: "From you—nothing!" On June 26th, 1940, he was secretly shot at Palmiry near Warsaw.

FROM "THEORY AND PRACTICE OF SOCIALISM IN THE FACE OF NEW PROBLEMS"

(1926)

Parliamentary democracy did not spring from the heads of theorists of the radical wing of liberalism. It arose where and when people reached such a level of interest for public affairs and desire of participating in them that "ruling the subjects as if children" became impossible. On the other hand political liberties overcame in a violent or peaceful manner the obstacles put in their way by routine, tradition and the written law, and the restriction of civic laws by legal privilege was forced to yield before a new sense of law, new tendencies and . . . . demands. The main advantage of the system lies in the following circumstances.

It is the most elastic, the subtlest form in which the play of class forces is manifested. Capitalistic society, especially after the war, may be likened to a kettle filled with boiling water. If the cover is hermetically sealed to the sides the kettle will burst, or at least the cover itself will fly into the air. If—on the contrary—the cover is loosely laid on top it reacts to each pressure of steam, to each gush of water by jumping and the kettle is in no danger. Parliamentary democracy conditions state policy in matters great and small upon fluctuations in public opinion, the balance of parties, the numerical influence of organizations, etc. The extremely accelerated, nervous, intense pulse of contemporary life requires such a construction of the system; the more subtly the government and parliamentary machine responds each time to the tone of the people, its various social classes and political groups, the greater are the chances of a *peaceful* development of the state and nation both internally and externally.

But is the above statement not contradictory to what I have written about the oligarchic tendencies in democracy?* For oligarchy, when it has marks of durability, appears not to take into account the sentiments of the people.

There is nothing more untrue.

Every oligarchy that completely and for long isolates itself from social reality is eventually broken and destroyed. In a democratic society, an oligarchy maintains itself by elastically and subtly reacting to the needs, changes, ebbs and tides of sentiment, interests, tendencies, and desires of the crowds. It has a hundred times greater difficulties in that direction than its predecessors of centuries ago. It has adapted its methods of action, the facility with which it modifies them, the vigilance with which it listens to the "voices from below", to the spirit of the epoch. Very often a kind of refinement replaces brutal ruthlessness which nevertheless continues to be the attribute of extremely strong individuals outgrowing their surroundings . . . .

FROM "ROADS TO SOCIALISM"

The reconstruction of Independent Poland was achieved amid the clang of arms, amid a growing wave of powerful

---

* The author refers to one of his earlier writings.

revolutionary movement. The fall of three empires, Russia, Germany and Austria-Hungary, which for decades were the mainstay of European reaction, was necessary—as foreseen by Polish democracy—before independence could be reestablished.

The young Polish state was at once faced with colossal social, political, economic, and cultural problems. Our generation does not yet realize the difficulties which Poland had to overcome after 1918. It does not sufficiently appreciate its own effort. Polish socialism constantly endeavored to convince Poles of the historic principle that Poland can sustain herself in post-war European life only as a democracy, that the struggle for Socialism in the young state can be won only if that state develops in democratic forms.

Hence our bitter conflicts with "pre-May" reactionary trends;* hence the necessity of absolute struggle with the "post-May" system of government† . . . .

---

* Nationalist trends embodied in the National Democratic party. Reference is made to the period preceding Marshal Piłsudski's coup d'état in May, 1926.
† The rule of Marshal Piłsudski and his group.

WINCENTY WITOS

(1875*)

Wincenty Witos was among those imprisoned by Marshall Pilsudski in 1930 at the ill-famed fortress of Brest. He had been for many years the leader of the Polish peasant movement. In 1920, during the war with Soviet Russia, he headed the Cabinet of National Defense; and later, in independent Poland, he was deputy to the Lower Chamber and minister in several cabinets.

On his release from Brest, he emigrated to Czechoslovakia, whence he exercised a strong influence on the peasant movement in Poland.

In the days before the German occupation of Czechoslovakia, Gestapo agents attempted to lure Witos to Germany, presumably to bring about an agreement between the Nazi government and the Polish peasants. Needless to say, Witos was not drawn into the trap.

After the occupation of Czechoslovakia, Witos returned to Poland.

FROM "THE SPEECH ON AGRARIAN REFORM."

(1919)

. . . . If today we take the stand that the soil should belong to those who work it, those who have nursed it for Poland, it is above all because we believe that the more such soil there is the greater will the fatherland be.

If the soil is torn from under our feet, if it passes to our enemies, we shall be no more than helots with no alternative left but to act the part of slaves. It was not the Potockis or the Branickis* or even those whom Moscow presented with whole Bialobrzesk districts for their services, it was not they who tilled the soil. If we look to Silesia, or the District of Posen, or to any other province perhaps less affected in this case we will see that those who clung to the soil, who refused to let themselves be dispossessed, who, however unprepared

---

* Representatives of Polish aristocracy.

they were, weathered all storms, were the peasants, the common people, and no one else. And for that reason, whether one likes it or not, justice must be rendered.

Whoever first gave the opportunity of acquiring land to the (German) Colonization Commission or to the various Russian Banks, whatever his name was, Radziwiłł* or otherwise, whoever it was that first introduced these foreign, enemy elements into Poland must surely have been heir to a great family and proud name. Such are the men who claimed and still claim to be the fathers of the nation,—for my part I should be ashamed to have them as stepfathers!

If these peasants, these workmen, these common people in general could keep their soil, and preserve their Polish character, certainly they are beholden to no one but themselves. What they did was without outside help, indeed they did it in spite of the obstacles raised by those who should have come to their aid, and today they can face them and say: "In spite of all you have done, here we are and here we will be! . . . ."

If we wish to carry out an agrarian reform at this time, two aims must be kept in mind: the national aim and the social-economic aim. Let us consider the national aim. I have mentioned earlier in my speech that the soil is safest in the hands of the peasant, of the people, that only the people can preserve and defend it, as has been shown by many instances. When the first news arrived that Cossack troops were approaching we watched all the thick-skulled landowners who lived in manors do nothing more effective than pack their belongings and flee to Vienna.

Is the soil to be used only when we feel safe on it? Does a true lover of the soil leave her at the first tremor of fear and seek refuge under foreign protection? I do not think so. But there was another man who remained on that land, who plowed and sowed it under flying shells, who did not flee when his neighbor was killed by a bullet, because he loved

---

* Representative of Polish aristocracy

that Mother-Earth, because he knew well that it was his right and duty to love her to the last drop of his blood. And he did not retreat though often it cost him not only his health, but his life.

Not without emotion and not without some pride did one behold even women, those Polish womenfolk, peasant women, harness themselves to the plow and the harrow and alone perform the heaviest task—not once, not twice, but for years to keep this soil which was meant to produce and nourish from lying fallow and falling into enemy hands . . . .

I firmly maintain that the Polish state can be founded in the future on the common people alone . . . . I admit that other classes have the same rights . . . . But we know that the hub of the state must be and is the Polish people: the Polish peasant and the Polish workman . . . .

Those gentlemen who believed that our future could be built on the aristocracy and the nobility were writing off Poland . . . . Those gentlemen who believed that our future could be based exclusively on towns . . . . were greatly mistaken. And even those who thought that our future could be founded on bureaucracy . . . . were also mistaken. There must, therefore, be something else that could serve as a foundation. If this class or these classes to which we must look for our future and on whose shoulders we place the burden of work are to carry that burden we must do everything possible to give them a firm base upon which to stand.

In Poland, if anywhere, the soil is the basis of our national existence. Those who have led the fight to keep every inch of this soil in Polish hands have long understood that. It was the wasters of the soil who did not understand it . . . .

The peasant element has proven itself to be impregnable even to the enemy. That is why we wish to plant it all over the Polish soil and in that way preserve this soil for Poland . . . .

Gentlemen, inasmuch as we have come here to the Sejm (Lower Chamber) and are permitted to speak and make decisions, we have not the slightest desire to pass judgment upon by-gone centuries. We leave such judgments to history and throw a veil over the past. We do, however, wish to establish a new life, a life in which all Polish citizens are treated as equals. We do not wish to create new privileges for anyone, but neither will we leave old privileges to anyone. Those gentlemen must reckon with this and be prepared for it. One of the princes of high-sounding name, whose record in Polish history is good though slightly tarnished since the partitions, protests against the agrarian program and argues that . . . . it will satisfy neither the interests of the representatives of large estates nor the objective criterions which will be accepted here . . . .

We know that he is not an exception, that there are many more of his kind and that we shall meet them more frequently as we go along. But they will not deflect us from our course.

If we accept the axiom that the greatest wealth of a nation is man then we must also admit the next axiom—that the state should make the greatest effort to protect and support that man . . . . Homes have been ruined, all the possessions of men destroyed by the hurricane of war; it has struck the great and small, the peasant, the townsman and the workman, but it has hardly touched the great landowner who fled to Vienna, Berlin or St. Petersburg to avoid the storm and to engage in new political intrigues and spin new schemes. The peasant did not escape, he felt that he himself was the master of his soil . . . .

. . . . In conclusion I should like to say that I consider agrarian reform to be separate from other matters of national importance. It is a problem which must be solved by the Sejm as soon as possible. If the Sejm does not rise to the occasion then I shall have to place a question mark upon our whole future. Gentlemen, we all have that future at heart. Because we are aware who is with us and who against us we look into that future undaunted and we trust that not even those gentlemen who believe it to their own interests to do so will dare to rise against the Polish people. The future belongs to us!

*   *   *

FROM AN ADDRESS AT STAROGARD* ABOUT THE GERMAN
MINORITY IN POLAND
(1920)

. . . . Once Germans lived here with you as today they
also do; but once it was they who ruled, today it is we.
Poland, however, will not enact special laws against anyone
—laws are the same for all. We cannot follow the example
of a state which acted otherwise. We shall follow in the
footsteps of civilized nations. We shall proceed in that direction only and, I hope, give Poland a firm foundation . . . .

---

* A town in western Poland

STRUGGLE AGAINST REACTION

RESOLUTION OF THE CONVENTION OF THE PEOPLE'S RIGHTS AND FREEDOMS

(1930)

In Poland the year 1930 introduced a period of intensification of the struggle against the dictatorial system of government. In view of the open violation of the law by the government and the fact that the government evaded public control of state expenditures, the opposition parties prepared a large scale mass action of the population in the defense of democracy. The resolution reproduced below was adopted by the Convention of the Defense of the People's Rights and Freedom, and subsequently by a meeting of 30,000 workers and peasants who came to Cracow on June 29, 1930, summoned by the Polish Socialist Party, the Polish Populist Party "Liberation", the Polish Populist Party "Piast", the Peasant Party, the National Workers' Party and the Christian-Democratic Party. The resolution was confiscated in Poland by the censorship.

The above action induced the government to arrest the leaders of the opposition parties and imprison them in the military fortress of Brześć. At the trial, at which a delegate of the League of Nations was present, all defendants were pronounced guilty in compliance with the will of the government. The Convention of the People's Rights and Freedom was an important step in the struggle for freedom and democracy in Poland.

* * *

The representatives of Polish democracy, assembled on June 29th, 1930 at Cracow, declare the following:

WHEREAS:

Poland has been living for more than four years under the power of the actual dictatorship of Joseph Piłsudski; the will of the dictator is carried out by changing governments; the President of the Republic is subject to the will of the dictator; the nation's confidence in law in its own state has been undermined; the public life of the country is constantly fed by rumors and indications of new coups d'état; the people have been deprived of any influence whatsoever on the Republic's domestic and foreign policy.

217

Since now, in consequence of the decree of the President of the Republic the constitutional voice of the Sejm has been silenced, as the President has neglected his duty and has neither carried out the demands of the National Representation nor referred to the country by way of new honest elections—we, the representatives of Polish democracy assembled at Cracow,

Be It Resolved:

1. The struggle for the rights and freedom of the people is not only the struggle of the Sejm and Senate, but the struggle of the nation;

2. Without abolishing dictatorship it is impossible to get the economic depression under control or to solve the great domestic problems which Poland must solve on behalf of her future;

3. The abolition of dictatorship is the indispensable condition of preserving the independence and assuming the integrity of the Republic; democracy means peace.

We Declare:

1. That the struggle for the abolition of Joseph Pilsudski's dictatorship has been undertaken jointly by all of us and will be continued jointly until victory; 2. that only a government possessing the confidence of the Sejm and of the nation will meet with our determined support and the assistance of all our forces; 3. that any attempt at a coup d'état will be met with most determined resistance; 4. that in relation to the government in power by the coup the nation will be free from any duties, and the obligations of the illegal government towards foreign countries will not be recognized by the Republic; 5. that every attempt at terrorism will be met by physical force. We further declare that since the President of the Republic, unmindful of his oath, has openly taken his stand with the dictatorship that rules Poland against the will of the country and allows the government of Mr. Sławek to abuse the constitutional rights

of the Head of the State for the government's current political aims—Ignacy Mościcki should resign from the office of President of the Republic.

The Convention states that it is the will of the broad masses of the Polish people to maintain peaceful relations with all neighbors and to cooperate actively in the preservation of the peace of the World. The Convention states that any action aiming to change the boundaries of the Republic will meet with the determined resistance of Polish democracy which warns world democracy against any new attempts on the part of imperialists who provoke international conflicts.

Long live the Independent Polish People's Republic! Down with Dictatorship! Long live the Government of the Workers' and Peasants' Confidence.

IGNACY DASZYŃSKI

(1867-1936)*

THE SPEAKER OF THE POLISH SEJM APPEALS TO THE
PRESIDENT OF THE REPUBLIC FOR HONEST
AND DEMOCRATIC ELECTIONS

(1930)

MR. PRESIDENT:

The events of the last days compel me to address you once more. Many phenomena of our public life indicate that Poland is on the verge of a precipice. It may fall into that precipice of disorder and anarchy . . . .

For several years such methods have been used in ruling Poland that the culmination was bloodshed on September 14.† These methods may sooner or later cause dangerous shake-ups and a complete disorganization. These methods have fostered the growth of destructive forces in the most important branches of public life, without allowing for the emergence of any creative elements. This state of affairs is seen and understood by every honest, thinking man but the most fanatic. Not everyone, however, dares to speak of it.

Contempt and scorn for the Constitution—the nation's fundamental law in the name of which every oath of office is taken,

The breaking of laws recently sanctioned,

Insults and the defamation of ministers and deputies who were called to help in 1920,

Calling the people, who saved the country in 1920, a "nation of idiots",

Governing with the help of the police and censorship, so sharply fought against only a quarter of a century ago,

---

* Biographical note, see page 159.

† This is a reference to the attack of the police on members of the oppositional parties parading in the streets of Warsaw after holding meetings directed against Piłsudski's dictatorship.

—all this is destroying the citizens' confidence in the state and his love for the state's institutions.

Do the people not know that the authority and dignity of your Presidential Office is based only on the Constitution? Does the road to freedom and power ever lead through the humiliation of human dignity, trampling on legality, freedom and honor, through the rearing of cowardly menials, through terror and insults?

With such methods one cannot long rule over a modern state which is based on labor, diligence and the attachment of millions as well as on citizens' rights and dignity. . . .

There is even today a way out, a normal and pacific way out. It is honest, legal elections without fraud or terror, and immediate return to legality. If we do not take this opportunity, the elections will become terrorism by the governing rather than the expression of the will of the governed— and then, I fear, we shall be called to account by future generations.

That is why I cannot remain silent. I appeal to the President, as the Constitutional head of our Republic, and petition him to use his moral and legal influence to secure honest and free elections in Poland on November 16 and 23, 1930.

Ignacy Daszyński,
Speaker of the Sejm (House of Deputies.)

Warsaw, September 24, 1930

HERMAN LIEBERMAN

(1869-1941)

A lawyer by profession, Herman Lieberman was for a long time one of Poland's most prominent labor leaders. His efforts during the struggle for universal suffrage won him election to the Austrian parliament. During the World War he joined the Piłsudski Legion and attained the rank of colonel.

When Poland regained independence, Lieberman soon achieved prominence in the young Polish parliament; at the same time he made a name for himself as a brilliant defense counsellor in political trials. He denounced the abuses of dictatorship and defended the principles of democracy. In September, 1930, along with a group of other opposition leaders he was thrown into the military prison of Brest, mistreated and tortured. After the trial he sought refuge abroad.

When Poland fell he was called upon to become vice-chairman of the Polish National Council. A few months before his death in 1941 he was appointed Minister of Justice in the Polish Government in London.

FROM A SPEECH IN DEFENSE OF LAW AND CONSTITUTION*

(1929)

. . . . This match between the legislative body and a minister is no common quarrel between the Parliament and the Government. No, this is a historic event, and each of you, gentlemen, assumes a historic responsibility for the way it will be solved . . . .

Your Honors! Whoever demands the acquittal of Minister Czechowicz demands that you, Your Honors, admit that all that was done is right, that the so-called law binds only the small and weak, and not those at the top who hold supreme power. To demand the acquittal of Minister Czechowicz means to demand the approval of the fact, that the Government can take money, as much as it pleases, and

---

* The speech of a representative of the Polish Sejm, delivered at a session of the Supreme Court in the case of Minister Czechowicz, Minister of Finance, accused of spending public funds without parliamentary control. This case became an accusation of the whole system of dictatorial rule.

without accounting, for the political party which it supports, that Poland is ripe for the willfulness of the strong. It sincerely believes, however, that the sentence will be given in accordance with conscience and law. I believe that the law will win. To kill the law means the beginning of slavery. This would be contrary to the very soul of the Polish nation which is not a nation of slaves. *De profundis*, from the depth of centuries of Polish history rises the cry of masses clamoring for freedom, and all enlightened minds have always linked that cry for freedom with the watchword of victorious law. Freedom and law, those are the ideals towards which Poland was steadily progressing. At the beginning of the sixteenth century an immortal monument of law and freedom was founded at the Sejm of Radom. The Constitution of May Third was inspired by the flame and breath of the French Revolution, which in turn was caused by the uncontrolled fiscal policy of French kings and the longing for equality before law. When Poland fell and her sons fought in the ranks of the French Revolutionary Army, then, as Karl Marx said, they went to help wipe out Feudal Europe. Adam Mickiewicz flung into the soul of the nation these flaming words: "The heroism of slavery is a virtue in a dog, in a man it is sin."

No! the Polish nation is a nation of democrats, not of slaves. We all lived through those memorable moments, when from across the ocean came the words of President Wilson: the aim of the war is to determine whether all people will be ruled even in the realm of internal politics by factors of slavery, or according to principles based on freedom and the will of citizens. Hundreds of thousands of Poles died on various fronts of the World War with just that dream, and the thought never entered anyone's mind that Poland might become a paradise where one man could be a sovereign ruler, and all others would have to obey in slavish submissiveness.

. . . . We beg you, Your Honors, to help society to rise from the abyss of lawlessness, to help our state, so that with the support of law it may acquire strength enough to hold its own in international competition. Help us! We do not

demand political decisions, we ask you only to declare yourselves on the side of the law. Our country has turned into
a spiritual casemate; a great number of noble and non-
partisan men are suffocating in this casemate, they cry and
suffer and beg that the days of their lives may be shortened
that they may no longer have to look upon what is happening. These are not empty words, not exaggerations.
Everyone serves the country according to his strength and
heart. In spite of insult I can state—and forgive me, gentlemen, this personal allusion—that I have served the country
according to my means in certain situations which were
discussed with me by the present Marshal Piłsudski, but
no matter what sacrifice I may have to make in the service
of the ideal of the Law which I represent here, I will be
happy if even in the slightest degree I succeed in persuading
you, Your Honors, that your sentence must be a great civil
deed. Life flies away, but let not the future generations say
that we were too weak to set Poland on the road of lawfulness, that we were unable to oppose forces, which sought
to push Poland down to the level of spiritual slavery, that
we were indifferent when right trembled before might.
Poland stands on the crossroads: East or West, the willfulness of an individual or the will of the whole, the rule of the
law or the whim of the great and strong. Remember, gentlemen, that an error committed in the passing of sentence may
fall upon society in the form of many complications, dangers,
and sufferings. Gentlemen, in trying this case you stand on
a mountain-pass of time, you must look to the deep and
distant future. Does that might which already holds sway
over right need the additional aid of your verdict? Who in
Poland today is more miserable than the law, distorted and
ridiculed as it is by those who hold the supreme authority?
To whom but you should the nation turn for protection of
its right, to whom but you, gentlemen, should the legislative
authority, deprived of its right, appeal? Speak, Your Honors! Give an answer to that burning question: shall the
right of the people continue to be trampled upon, and shall
the will of the strong be respected? We stand at the turning
point of history and for that reason, free of all personal

hatred and resentments, mindful of nothing but the welfare of the state and the people, and supported by the sense of justice of millions of citizens who stand behind us, we ask you: give your verdict, a verdict of guilt, and impose adequate sentence upon a Minister, who after concentrating in his hands a tremendous amount of authority, deliberately broke the law.

*　　*　　*

FROM "A NEW PAGE IN POLAND'S HISTORY . . . ."

(April 1939)

. . . . The solemn guarantee of Poland's independence and Great Britain's offer of unlimited help in case of actual or threatening attack has stirred public opinion all over the world, but naturally enough nowhere more than in Poland. The solemn pledge made by Chamberlain in the House of Commons is a great historical event; it marks a turning point in the life of a torn and tortured post-war world. Under the pressure of its own public opinion, and in spite of all the obstacles raised so far by its Minister of Foreign Affairs, Poland has at last joined the bloc of nations which defend freedom and the principles of international ethics against the ruthless dictatorships that blackmail big and small nations alike. This is a tremendous moral triumph for Polish opposition parties, which, ever since 1934, have fought with great courage, devotion, perseverance and foresight for a reversal of our official pro-German policy. Once the London conferences are brought to a favorable conclusion, Poland can breathe freely and hopefully look to the future. The bond of alliance with the British Empire, added to our own strength, will be from now on the rock-bottom foundation of our importance in the family of free nations. In England—as you know—psalms are held in high esteem. The English call Psalm XV "the gentleman's psalm" for it blesses the man "who gives a promise to his neighbor and keeps that promise". Let us therefore trust that the pact signed in London will be kept in a gentlemanly fashion and that it will assure durable safety to our country. The healthy instinct of the Polish nation has won out at last. After many years of aimless wandering in the shadow of Hitler's politics our diplomacy has at last brought our state's vessel to the right harbor.

Our internal policy, however, does not look so sound. The whole nation clamors for a government of national defense and urges that large masses of people deprived of parliamentary representation be allowed to participate in shaping the country's destinies. But the leaders of OZON* have nothing but disregard and contempt for the clamor of the masses even though they constantly demand that they sacrifice life and property in the defense of a Fatherland in danger. "You ask for a Government which would command the confidence of wide masses of population? Nothing doing," they answer. "We the privileged ruling party have full confidence in our President and Commander in Chief—that is quite enough. The majority of the nation can keep their mouth shut, obey, pay, and when required die on the battlefields. All the rights of the nation will be replaced by an order from Ozon!"

That arrogance of the ruling group may cost us a lot some day. No matter how great a genius the President and the Commander in Chief may be, they will not replace those millions of peasants and workmen, whose strong will and deep love of the ideal of freedom constitute the greatest warrant of victory.

One of the most brilliant military experts, in a monograph devoted to the great battle, which took place on March 9, 1814, near the French city of Laon, analyses the reasons why that battle was lost by Napoleon and thus became the cause of his later abdication and downfall. "His genius did not leave him in this battle," the author says, "but the French people were not favorable to Napoleon's army and without them neither preparations, no matter how careful, nor genius, no matter how great, can achieve victory."

Who is this author so enlightened and astute? Marshal Foch, the greatest of victors known to human history . . . .

---

* The Camp of National Unity in favor of tendencies represented by Pilsudski's clique.

WINCENTY WITOS*

THE PEASANT PROBLEM

(1936)

The peasant problem has for some time now been one of utmost urgency. The peasant, his numerical strength and his fate, the value and importance of the common people, has suddenly come to the fore in Poland as in the rest of the world. Some countries have attacked the problem in all earnestness either solving it completely or creating conditions favorable to a positive solution. In others, however, interest has been aroused rather for tactical reasons, out of temporary needs.

For that matter, the peasant problem is not the same everywhere. There are countries where peasants are in the majority, there are others where they constitute a minority. But everywhere one thing is certain. Regardless of their number, universally and invariably, they represent a valuable and most reliable element in any state, as providers of its sustenance and its defense.

. . . . In politics you need not take sentiment into account, you may ignore the peasant, ask him no questions, forget justice. You may outlaw him, make a pauper out of him, you may use him as a blind tool. All this you may do but only if you have no regard for the future and only to those who have little or no self-respect. Fortunately there are few such in Poland, as was painfully discovered by those who attempted to establish outrageous systems in the villages.

Will their blindness not allow them to see the truth or let them, once and for all, put the welfare of the state above the interests of their clique? I might say that, were Poland to be exposed to a crucial test in the near future it would be not hirelings or slaves but free and conscious citizens who would be able to stand. And I point out that peasants constitute three-fourths of the nation.

---

* Biographical note, see page 209

The importance of the problem is so great that it must be stated with brutal frankness without the fantastic yarns and tricks employed by the Sanacja.†

. . . . Whoever thinks of the future of Poland without ulterior or hidden motives must accept the truth that the future cannot be built by scoundrels or individuals who are devoid of beliefs, conscience, or will. It can be built only by the entire nation, and mainly by those who not only constitute the majority but also possess such qualities as nothing and no one can replace.

---

† Piłsudski's party

RYSZARD GANSZYNIEC

In his book, "Poland, Key to Europe", Raymond Leslie Buell writes:* "A considerable amount of literature opposing anti-Semitism has developed in Poland in recent years. University professors, writers, social workers and others have opposed anti-Jewish excesses and the methods of the nationalists. A large section of the press has refused to follow the anti-Semitic trend."

Ganszyniec is an outstanding scholar in classical philology and a professor at the University of Lwow. In the article reprinted below he opposes the restriction of the number of Jewish students in the Polish Universities.

FROM "THE QUESTION OF THE 'NUMERUS CLAUSUS' "

(1925)

"FOR THE JEWISH POPULATION'S RIGHTS TO EDUCATION"

What is the *numerus clausus?* It is a euphemistic designation of a problem which the authors of that designation lacked courage to name accurately, numerus clausus Iudaeorum, the restriction of the number of Jewish students. For only the Jews are involved, this regulation has been devised only for them, applied only to them. Since this is, therefore, a manifestation of anti-Semitism in the universities it should be examined from that very angle, and not only from the purely academic standpoint. For the scholar the question of *numerus clausus* is a problem, and he must acquaint himself with all its aspects. I present my thoughts here in the form of an objective examination of the recriminations levelled at the Jews. Of these recriminations, besides simple deliberate lies and calumnies, there are so many and the Jewish problem is so complicated that all particulars, sometimes very interesting, cannot be discussed. I limit myself neces-

---

* "Poland, Key to Europe". New York, 1939, 3rd edition, p. 307.

sarily to certain fundamental points, namely to those on which the theory of anti-Semitism is based.

As the main causes of anti-Semitism are enumerated: race, religion, ethics, nationality and character.

Let us start with race which is regarded by anthropologists as the ultimate cause of all differences, not only physical but intellectual and psychological as well. All anti-Semitism, if it at all seeks a rational and scientific cover for its statements, is based on the fundamental assumption of the difference between the Aryan and Semitic races. The ideally pure form of the Aryan race is supposedly represented by the Hindus of India and above all by the Germanic peoples of Europe; the ideally pure form of the Semites is supposedly represented by the Jews. Obviously such a statement is sometimes inconvenient. Since scientific anti-Semitism is an export article of the intelligentsia for the broad masses that are still Christian, out of consideration for them also the question must be solved, Who was Jesus, and what is Christianity? If the Semitic race is really so underprivileged mentally and of such low moral standing, then obviously also Jesus, as a Jew, and Christianity as originally a Jewish sect, cannot be better. A slap levelled against a Jew, falls on a Christian face. However, the anti-Semites find various subterfuges to counteract this. They proclaim the Aryan origin of Jesus, and give the lie to the Gospel: thus some make Jesus descend from non-Jewish parents, others identify Jesus with the Celtic God Hesus. The aim of these arguments is one and the same, namely to harmonize anti-Semitism with the foundation of the anti-Semite's religion, to create a distant and deep division between Christianity and Judaism. However, these are either open deceptions, or dilettante, non-scientific inventions laughed at by the educated anti-Semite. Consequently it is true that Jesus was a Jew and that Christianity was originally only a Jewish sect. If it is therefore true that race leaves its spiritual imprint on its product, Christianity, insofar as it still preserves its views and strength is Jewish, and Christians combating the Jewish race, by that very action condemn

230

their own religion. For this very reason German anti-Semitism went a step further and, rejecting Christianity as a Jewish product, wants to introduce an Aryan, namely the old-Germanic, religion—a perfectly logical step.

However, there is no need for so much speculation in a question that can be experimentally examined by the anthropologist. It is a truism of scientific anthropology that the Jews inhabiting Europe do not represent any homogenous race, but rather a racial mixture, linked in a certain whole rather by negative bonds than by positive ones of language and religion. We find the explanation of this mixture in Jewish history. It seems to me that the admixture of Jewish blood is to be traced to the beginning of the Jews' political life when, after the conquest of Canaan, the Jews refrained —out of greediness though, and not pity—from carrying out Moses' cruel order when he demanded a radical extermination of the Canaanites who belonged, together with the Philistines, to a non-Semitic race. The newcomers preferred to keep them as slaves and taxpayers. The Canaanites were much more civilized than the Jews who, in spite of the priests' orders, concluded marriages with them. This fact explains the Jews' similarity to Greeks and Italians descended from nations of the same race as the Canaanites. A further admixture of foreign blood occurred during the dispersion in foreign countries. This dispersion began for the Jewish people in the 8th century B.C. and since that time has continued almost uninterruptedly for twenty-five hundred years in spite of temporary concentrations of Jewish factions in Judaea. In the course of history a mass of proselytes was added as whole tribes accepted Judaism. As far as the Polish Jews in particular are concerned, we must reckon with the probability of a considerable admixture of Slavonic and Tartar blood, because, among others, a great portion of the Khasars together with their Khan accepted the Jewish religion, a fact that, in my opinion, was not without effect on Jewish sectarianism.

The conclusion from such a state of affairs is simple. Though racial differences should not cause racial struggles, for this would lead to the extermination of mankind, in our case the reference to the allegedly eternal antagonism between the Semitic and Aryan races is entirely out of place since the Jews do not represent the Semitic race. One may therefore speak about the Jewish race in Poland in a negative sense as of a non-Polish or not purely Polish people. Is it, however, a just principle to regard every Polish citizen of non-Polish or not purely Polish origin as an intruder? If somebody advocated this principle and wanted to purify Poland in accordance with it, he would have to start with the expulsion of the Armenians* and above all with the expulsion of the gentry which is of German, Lithuanian, Ruthenian, etc. and consequently of non-Polish origin: he would also have to expel the major part of the townspeople of Cracow and of other trade centers in general, for they are of German origin. Following an exact scrutiny of family records there would remain in Poland, after such a purification, only peasants and workers, and even they in great part only because they have no family records for which one cared in the past. Yet it is not the peasant and worker but the bourgeoisie and the gentry, who, incidentally, resemble the Jews, that demand the ejection of the Jews.

The anti-Semites say that it is not the religion established by Moses, nor the Old Testament, but the Talmud that is the source of evil in Judaism. Indeed, the influence of the Talmud, especially among the uneducated masses is tremendous for it has almost completely obscured the Bible which is understood in a Talmudistic spirit. But how many anti-Semites know what the Talmud is? How many have read it? The Talmud is a legal book which, using a scholastic dialectics, discusses and explains the ritual prescriptions and illustrates them by casuistic application to the various cases of life. Moreover, there is not to be found in it a plan such as appears in legal commentaries. The absence of a leading idea, the fragmentariness of the presentation, for these texts are designed to be supplemented orally by the teacher, make the comprehension of both Talmuds difficult. It is easy for

---

* In Southwestern Poland, there exist settlements of Armenians who came there in the XVIII century. Today they are completely Polonized, having preserved only the consciousness of their origin and religion.

some one looking for evidence of the Talmud's immorality
to find individual phrases and take them out irrespective of
the context. Whoever reads books knows that in this way
one can present the opponent's and not the author's thoughts.
I have read both Talmuds—very dull and tiresome reading,
for the contents is uninteresting to a non-jurist—but I have
not found any immoral statements in them beyond the level
of the culture of the time, which in ethics differed little
from ours . . . .

I conclude. We have seen that the *numerus clausus* forms
only a fragment of the general Jewish problem, as a manifestation of the anti-Semitism of the university caste. In
general anti-Semitism is only a safety valve through which
the various classes release in different forms their grievances
and complaints caused by disappointments and failures
whose source is their own ineptitude, their own dishonesty;
numerus clausus is also partially such a safety valve. As an
exceptional law applied to a certain class of Polish citizens,
the *numerus clausus* is contradictory to the Polish constitution, it gives occasion for the introduction of more politics
and unrest to the Polish universities: the *numerus clausus*
has a demoralizing effect on Polish scholarship and the
education of youth by maintaining protectionism and developing among Polish youth the sense of a privileged class: it
has a demoralizing effect also because it creates a precedent
for other spheres of life, for other classes of the population.
Therefore I oppose the present *numerus clausus Iudaeorum*
as a man and educator, as a scholar and a Pole.

STANISŁAW KULCZYŃSKI

The introduction of the "ghetto benches" in Polish universities was opposed by a number of prominent professors. A collective protest of Polish professors was also published at the time in the American press. The rector (president) of the John Casimir University in Lwów, the outstanding Polish scientist, Prof. Stanisław Kulczyński, opposed the "ghetto benches" determinedly and in protest resigned his position. He published an open letter in the press from which the following excerpts are quoted:

FROM AN OPEN LETTER IN DEFENSE OF THE FREEDOM OF LEARNING

(1938)

. . . . I have resigned from the office of rector because I did not want to put my signature to an act which in name is called "decree of the rector's authority", but which in essence is a check exacted under terrorist pressure to be cashed by a political party and paid for by the University at the expense of its prestige and its vital interests.

The political party which is responsible for the terror practiced in the University proclaims the motto of absolute struggle against the economic and cultural preponderance of the Jews in our life, while it simultaneously proclaims the principle that this struggle should be waged not only from below, by organizing boycott and competitive struggle, but also from above by creating special legislation restricting the rights of the Jews in the state and in the nation.

. . . . There are . . . . in the Polish state legal authorities, very high authorities at that, who are powerless in the face of terror. They are the rectors and academic senates. These authorities are entitled to issue certain decrees of a general character. These authorities are at the head of independent and respected institutions which exercise a very important influence based on the authority of learning on the nation.

There is no obstacle in the way of terrorizing these very authorities and these institutions and thus creating a precedent and an example, which will have a strong effect on the nation, on how the system and legislation of the state should look. This example based on the prestige of learning is to open the way for the introduction of analogous arrangements in the state. Hence the "official ghetto "catchword . . . .

Everyone may have his own opinion about the purposefulness of the special laws in relation to the Jews, and about the question of the wholesomeness of the political régime prescribed by the groups advocating the monopolistic totalitarianism of a political party. Only the political party that is the author of these prescriptions is responsible for their effects. Neither the rector, the University, nor Polish learning has, can have, or desires, any responsibility for the effects of these prescriptions.

Forcing the university authorities to introduce a political party's conception of law is blackmail—it is abuse of the prestige of the universities and of learning for the benefit of the party.

For this blackmail of the universities, these venerable institutions pay not only with their prestige, but also with their ability to work and with the disintegration of their organization. It can easily be seen that under cover of the beautiful mottoes of national solidarity and the defense of the Polish spirit of our culture, autonomous university authorities are brutally stripped of their dignity, and Polish learning is deprived of the rights of freedom which alone can insure its development.

Learning cannot develop under conditions of compulsion, not because such is the whim of professors, but because learning is free thought, and thought that is not free is not scientific thought. Without learning life will be difficult not only for scholars but also for those by whose hands the destruction of Polish learning is effected.

Dr. Stanisław Kulczyński
Professor of the John Casimir University

Lwów, January 11, 1938

THE MEMORANDUM OF THE POLISH LABOR MOVEMENT TO THE PRESIDENT OF THE REPUBLIC OF POLAND

(1937)

For many years the Polish Workers' and Peasants' Movement led the fight for democracy in Poland. Strikes were organized under the political banner of the reestablishment of democracy: strikes of workmen, farmers (who refused to supply the cities with their products), and even of white collar workers (teachers). In the face of an increasingly precarious international situation the Polish Labor Movement found it advisable to address a memorandum to the President of the Polish Republic, Ignacy Mościcki. On November 13, 1937 a joint delegation of the Central Executive Committee of the Polish Socialist Party, the Central Committee of the Trade Union Congress and the Board of the Workmen University Society handed to President Mościcki the following Memorandum:

On behalf of the Polish Socialist Party and of the professional labor and educational organizations bound to it by fraternal collaboration in the great common cause of the social liberation of the Polish people, and with the deep conviction that Poland, whose rebirth and independence was primarily due to the heroic struggles of the working masses, is faced today with an extremely grave situation, we, with a full sense of responsibility raise our voice to express the opinion of labor.

We wish, first of all, to point to the very grave international situation, so much graver, in fact, when one realize that confidence in the effectiveness of the League of Nations and in the binding force of treaties has almost completely broken down. In the light of war-torn Spain, of the embattled Far East, of the ever-growing international conflicts inspired and staged by Fascist states all illusions of security and peace are shattered. The threat of an immediate outbreak of war faces us, and war-mongers who lie in wait for other people's territory and freedom will certainly not be deterred by its horrors. Poland is already confronted with immediate danger, for the attempts to incorporate Danzig into the Third Reich and to detach Upper Silesia from Poland show the true, war-like intentions of the Hitler régime.

At such a time the foreign policy of our state can no longer bind us to nations whose vengeful aggression will soon, no doubt, be directed against Poland, as it has been against others. Upon this decision depends not only Poland's security but her independence and integrity as well.

The social and economic situation, too, requires careful attention. Temporary improvements in the economic life do not dispose of problems which can be solved only by a reconstruction of the entire system. The already proverbial poverty of the village has assumed in some parts of the country the proportions of a disaster affecting thousands of people, thousands of families. Adjustment of the domestic market cannot be even begun without a considerable improvement in the standard of living of the masses of workmen and laborers. The influence of foreign capital on many branches of industry and agriculture makes itself frequently and painfully felt. Poland must adopt a planned economy; it must remodel its whole agricultural structure, it must take over those branches of industry which are essential to its defense and which are indispensable to a planned economy conceived on a nation-wide scale, an economy which would liquidate unemployment.

As for internal conditions, the nation has been forced into a political system long condemned and rejected by the majority of the people—the system of voting privileges for the ruling groups and police repressions of anyone outside these groups. Consequently, open and constructive conflicts between ideologies and policies have given place to disgraceful squabbles for power among various cliques and factions. This was demonstrated clearly when the "Camp of National Unity" under the leadership of Colonel Koc attempted to "consolidate" the nation with the sole result—a result which, incidentally, could easily have been foreseen—that at the price of its tradition of independence a small fraction of the "National-Radical Camp" merged with a part of the *Sanacja** camp; the old *Sanacja* camp as a whole disintegrated even further and internal fights gained in intensity.

This tension finds an outlet, particularly (though not exclusively) with regard to the Jewish problem, in incidents which deprave the streets of Polish cities and towns.

Manifestations of violence, punctuated by bomb explosions and assassinations, which undermine the very foundation of state life have become rampant. This monstrous degradation has reached the point where advocates of a "bloody purge" find refuge in an organization protected by certain privileged circles.

In such an atmosphere there can be no solving of national problems. The great task of economic advancement, the struggle with the dreadful calamity of unemployment among both city and country dwellers necessarily—and obviously— is neglected. Neither can the capital problem of armed forces and national defense, which by its very nature must be kept aloof from internal political struggles, be completely solved under the circumstances.

The authority of the government has been seriously shaken. This constitutes a grave danger, not simply to an ephemeral system, but to the actual existence of Poland. This is a fact generally known and admitted by the consensus of independent opinion. In this light we hold it our duty to point out that the authority of the government cannot be restored by purely external means, by raising the ranks and insignia of authority.

No administrative and economic policy can function creatively unless it is based on actual trends and forces latent within society. Only by actually linking the state with the large masses of its citizens, by basing its very existence on an active participation of the people in causes of common

---

* The popular name given to the régime which came to power by Piłsudski's coup d'état in 1926.

238

interest, and by a strong-minded repudiation of cliques known for their hooliganism and their dirty, cheap demagogy, can the true authority of the state be restored and launched on the road of progress.

We can see but one path of wisdom for the government out of the present impasse:

(a) THE ELECTORIAL LAW AS APPLIED TO THE LOWER CHAMBER (SEJM), FORMALLY IN FORCE SINCE 1936, SHOULD BE QUICKLY AND IMMEDIATELY AMENDED.

(b) As soon as the said Law is amended in accordance with the principles of universal, secret, direct and equal suffrage and the principle of the proportional count of ballots, THERE SHOULD BE NEW ELECTIONS—FREE AND HONEST.

(c) The people must be certain that the government which has charge of the election *will not have recourse to the methods* used in 1928-1930: since those methods have demoralized the administration and introduced anarchism into the country.

Poland can wait no longer!

Laborers, peasants, white-collar workers, in mass demonstrations, at public meetings, in the peasant strike, in general strikes in many cities, in all the public utterances of the social organizations in which the working population of Poland is united, have taken a firm stand in their demand that THE PRESENT SYSTEM OF GOVERNMENT BE CHANGED AND TRUE DEMOCRACY ADOPTED. The essential steps in that direction are: THE AMENDMENT OF THE ELECTORIAL LAWS AND THE ORDERING OF ELECTIONS AS SOON AS POSSIBLE FOR LEGISLATIVE BODIES AND LOCAL GOVERNMENTS BASED ON FIVE-POINT SUFFRAGE.

The adoption of these measures has become the most pressing need of the state. For this reason the organized forces of democracy are determined *to use every available means* to shatter the selfish complacency of privileged groups, to shake

239

the conscience of those who by their obstinacy obstruct national recovery, and to paralyze the attempts of all who corrupt the collective and political life.

THE WORKING MASSES OF ALL POLAND CLAIM THE RIGHT TO DECIDE THE FATE OF THEIR COUNTRY; THEY CLAIM THIS RIGHT WITH DETERMINATION AND WITH A FIRM WILL TO ATTAIN THEIR GOAL!

IGNACY JAN PADEREWSKI

(1860-1941)

*World famous pianist and composer, Paderewski began to take
an active part in political life at the outbreak of the first World
War. In 1919 he became head of the Polish Government, but soon
(1920) withdrew from public life. From time to time, however,
he made public utterances in the defense of democratic ideals.
After the outbreak of the second World War he returned to active
political life assuming the presidency of the Polish National Council (i.e., Parliament in exile) in France. After the French collapse
he came to the United States where he died on June 29th, 1941.*

*In March, 1939, the German armies occupied Czechoslovakia.
On that occasion I. J. Paderewski wrote a letter, subsequently
published in the press, to Edvard Benes, who was at that time
in Chicago.*

FROM A LETTER TO EDVARD BENEŠ

(1939)

.... A crime has been perpetrated. The most sacred rights
of a nation to independent life have been trampled by
marching troops.

The ruthless invader of your national soil, in spite of all
his solemn assertions, has broken once more his freely given
word and daringly challenges the right of self-determination
and democracy which have been looked upon as cornerstones
of our civilization.

The differences that separated our countries for many
long years have been settled by mutual agreement. Those
differences could not have had a lasting effect upon the sentiment of blood that unites both our nations . . . .

From the bottom of my heart, with the fullest indignation
I protest against the enslavement of your nation!

It brings humanity back to the epoch of dark barbarism:
it is a triumph of evil forces over the right, a triumph over

that divine spark implanted by the Almighty in our immortal souls, the conscience.

If the world's conscience is not yet dead, if that divine spark is not yet extinguished in the human race, all our efforts should go to assisting your nation in her ordeal, to strengthening her will of resistance, to helping her legitimate struggle for the recovery of her full independence . . . .

I. J. PADEREWSKI

ADAM PRÓCHNIK

(1894-1942)

Adam Próchnik's researches on the social movements in Poland have won a place for him among the ranking historians of the day. In his youth he was active in the struggle for Polish independence; and when independence was won he represented Polish labor in Parliament. Until his death he took an active part in Poland's fight for freedom and democracy.

FROM "YEARNING FOR DEMOCRACY"

(1937)

The desire for the introduction of a truly democratic system, which is felt today by the greater majority of Polish society, is by no means the result of some momentary political mood, nor is it only a reaction to the disappointments experienced under the influence of experiments by the authoritative régimes. It is merely a stage in the process of democratizing contemporary society . . . .

The process of democratizing must, in the first place, embrace all societies, all peoples and nations, must include in its scope the whole world. In the second place it must reach the depth, must plough through every field of life. Political democracy is only the introductory phase, a road to real democracy which must penetrate the whole of life. There must follow the democratizing of culture, the democratizing of social foundations above all . . . .

It is possible to persuade a person temporarily to relinquish his freedom, for one reason or another, persuade him that there is someone who will make the best decisions in his interests. But deep down in his soul everyone considers this to be an abnormal state, a temporary evil. With an unabated force there awakens the longing for freedom and the will to decide one's own destiny oneself. And this is the real

243

yearning for democracy. For democracy is the only system permanently suitable for the man of today. He will tolerate a fascist or dictator system for a longer or shorter time, but he can live only in an atmosphere of democracy. The man of today is a democratic being, a being desirous of freedom and conscious of his active part in the making of history . . . .

FROM "IN THE HOURS OF GREAT TRANSFORMATION"

(1938)

We have come to a period of upheavals. We cannot yet perhaps evaluate the far-reaching effects of the events now taking place in Europe, we cannot yet define the point to which they will go and especially we do not realize exactly the part which will fall to Poland, but we see very clearly that events of great historical import are taking place and we have no doubt that owing to the geo-political situation in which Poland is placed, she cannot be indifferent. There can be no doubt that the vital interests of Poland must come into play. Our situation is such that every serious upheaval in Europe brings to the fore, in full intensity, the problem of our existence and, in general, our whole future . . . .

Let no one think that the greatness and importance of events and the international situation can overshadow the vital question of our internal structure, the great problem of democratizing our political life. On the contrary. This problem becomes, in the present political situation, still more vital; it comes more aggressively to the fore of the political life in Poland.

There certainly can be no doubt that democratizing our political life and bringing the masses into the orb of national existence is at present a necessity. This is unerringly voiced by public opinion. It is pure and simple. Society wants to decide its own destiny and has every right to do so. The great movements which today represent the vital force in Poland, put forth this demand most emphatically. The social classes that portray the nation as a whole, laborers, peasants, white collar men, in other words the whole working world, both physical and mental, this nation has expressed itself decisively. And in crucial historical moments the voice of Polish society must be expressed strongly and emphatically.

FROM "THE NATIONAL WAR"

(May, 1939)

The Polish Nation finds itself in a state of Moral Preparedness. This is no less important than military preparedness. We do not want to forestall the further currents of events, but there is one thing we must state. If Poland becomes involved in a war it will be a national war.

What is national war? It is a war fought by the whole nation, without exceptions, for its existence. This is something more than a war waged by even the greatest army comprised of millions . . . . It is fought by the nation as a whole, the young and the old, men and women and even children. It is fought with arms and without arms, with rifles or with bare fists. It is a tremendous collective gesture of the whole society. A national war is one in which everyone must give his share, everyone must make his greatest effort. During a national war there are only two things to be done: fight, or work for those who are fighting. A national war is a spiritual crisis, which we all undergo, a crisis in which nothing has any meaning outside of freedom. Human life loses its value even in one's own consciousness. Everyone feels as a reality, not just as an empty phrase, that it is better to die fighting than live as a captive. In national warfare it is not sufficient to state that everyone shall do his utmost. Everyone must do more than his utmost, a superhuman effort is necessary . . . .

Propaganda, agitation, appeals of the press and appeals to sentiment do not have much meaning in this case. This force which should be possessed by all, must be brought out from within. National warfare is no miracle, it has to exist potentially in our hearts. Undoubtedly this is a certain emotional quality, but the emotional factors do not exist independently. These are plants that spring from the most real relations . . . . Poland is so situated that national warfare for her is essential. It is necessary to realize this and draw all conclusions consequent to it.

FROM "THE STRUGGLE OF IDEAS"

(August, 1939)

If anyone who faces a threatening conflict between nations tries to eliminate all ideological meaning, he purposely minimizes the very cause which motivates the struggle, he reduces the color of the flag under which the battle is to be waged. This is a harmful act since it diminishes our strength. When one demands great sacrifice of a man, even the sacrifice of life, one must give him a worthy symbol . . . .

Why should we add to the enemy's strength by concealing his faults? Why should we not openly and frankly admit that he is not only an enemy of our nation, but the enemy of all humanity? . . . . We cannot consider our controversy with Hitler's Germany as an ordinary feud between two neighboring nations. If this were so, we would, in all probability, have to fight alone . . . . If we omit all ideological meaning, what would our fate matter to an Englishman or a Frenchman, why should he decide to give his life for Danzig? . . . . We have once lost our freedom because of the world's indifference. If such indifference does not exist any longer, if the world has begun to understand what Danzig stands for (which formerly was beyond its comprehension) this is because our cause has become part of the cause of freedom for the whole world, because we are fighting not only for our national freedom, but also against a hegemony of one or two nations over other countries, and against a general rule of tyranny . . . .

We have therefore become united with other democratic countries by clearly ideological ties and we, of all countries, certainly have the least reason for denying this. In these ties lies our strength. . . . What aim have we in constanly stressing that our controversy with Germany is not a fight with Hitlerism, but a struggle between two nations! It would be understandable if this were done by the German internal propaganda to unite against us the whole nation, including all those whom the Hitler régime oppresses. But surely it is in the interest of strengthening our defensive power that all our sentiments, national, political and social, should be uniformly directed against the enemy. In truth every one of these emotions represents a certain total of powers, which must be pooled for the fight and for the assurance of its victory. If the Germans say that this is only a struggle between two nations, then they unite themselves and divide us; if we, though, stress strongly that this is not only a struggle with the Germans, but a struggle with Hitler's Germany we divide them and unite ourselves. Why should we put ourselves and domineering Germany on a basis of equality where such does not exist? Why should we renounce that important moral factor namely, that every Pole feels justly endangered by a German invasion, whereas no German can feel threatened by a Polish invasion?

Let us not belittle the justice and greatness of the cause we are defending. Let us not disturb the harmony which exists between the cause of external and internal freedom. In this harmony lies our strength.

FLORIAN ZNANIECKI

(1882*)

Florian Znaniecki, whose "Polish Peasants in Europe and America" (written in collaboration with W. Thomas) made a deep impression on modern sociological research, is an important link between Polish and American culture. While he was a professor at the University of Poznań, he introduced into Poland many valuable elements of American thought. His educational ideas, for example, were eagerly received in Poland and he became the leader of a whole school of sociology and pedagogy. His works have also left their mark on the culture of America, where he is now teaching at the University of Illinois.

FROM "PRESENT DAY MEN AND FUTURE CIVILIZATION"

(1934)

We live in a historical period of greater potentialities than humanity has ever before faced. There is the possibility of a new civilization, differing from all those that have existed or exist now, not only in its unprecedented wealth but in its very nature. Cultural developments are taking place in the world which may bring about a complete transformation of the structure and vital functions of all fields of culture. No utopia can give a picture of that future civilization. All that can be foreseen with a certain amount of probability are some of its fundamental characteristics, provided, of course, the rudiments perceptible now will attain full growth.

But this great future is uncertain. And, as an alternative possibility, we are confronted not with a further gradual evolution of the present world, be it hesitant and devious, but with the decay and destruction of a large portion of the cultural gain accumulated in the last few thousand years, with an impoverishment both in the quantity and quality of civilization for many centuries to come . . . .

Yet, there exist in the modern world indubitable signs of a new civilization—not "international" but human, containing not elements common to all national civilizations, but the most valuable elements of various national civilizations combined in an unprecedented synthesis, based on forms of social intercourse unknown in the past, and developing along a course that, so far, cannot be foreseen. On the other hand there exist indubitable but more apparent symptoms of the collapse of national civilizations through external struggles, internal crises, through creations that elude their creators' control. We are faced with an alternative. Either there will emerge an all-human civilization which will not only save everything that is worth saving in national civilizations but will raise humanity to a height far exceeding the boldest dreams of utopians, or national civilizations will crumble to pieces; which means that although the world of culture will not be destroyed, its greatest systems, its most precious patterns will lose all meaning in the life of human communities for many generations to come . . . .

An all-human civilization, if it comes into existence, will differ from national civilization not only in that all humanity will participate in it. It will also be a humanistic civilization with a preponderance of spiritual culture, whereas all the civilizations up to now have been naturalistic ones with a preponderance of material culture. It will be a socially harmonious civilization, free of conflicts and antagonisms that fill the history of today's civilization. And finally, it will be a fluid civilization, with a dynamic equilibrium, in which free creative activity will be the normal cultural function of all individuals and social groups; creative activity will not have to overcome any resistance nor will it produce crises as it has done so far in all existing civilizations, fixed or static. Only such a humanistic, harmonious and fluid civilization can be an all-human one.

249

FROM "THE CULT OF THE STATE"

(1936)

To this day for the majority of theorists or men engaged in state activities the problem of the relationships between the state and social groups is a fairly simple one. The state, they believe, is a self-contained unit which has to deal with two kinds of problems: those of internal policy and those of external policy. The sphere of internal policy includes all problems of relationship between groups formed by the population living on state territory. The state tries to solve all these problems in accordance with the principle of "right of state" (*raison d'état*), which expresses the precedence that "general" state interest, conceived as a whole, takes over the "particular" interests of these various groups, treated as parts of the whole. Since the interests of these groups are widely divergent and often conflicting it is in the general interest of the state to unite and harmonize them in such a way that their divergence shall not weaken the state and impair its unity. This can be achieved, more or less successfully, in either of the two following ways: by a durable, strong and wise government which is completely independent of its people, and which, from the heights of its absolute sovereignty, carefully notes the aspirations of individual groups and tries to satisfy them as far as possible, mitigating their conflicts and forcing them to mutual concessions; or by a government which emanates from the people itself and which represents at any one time the common denominator of group powers, with public opinion acting as a regulating factor in the free interplay of these powers,— but, that is to say, a public opinion guided, in principle, by state interest which is more or less understood depending on the general level of education.

The external policy, on the other hand, is a matter of competition between states, in which every state tries to secure the greatest advantages at the expense of other states, while representing the common interests of its own entire population. "The right of state" coincides in this case with common interest; and it is particularly apparent in war-time when the divergent interests of various groups of the population are completely overshadowed by the obvious fact that defeat of the state would be a loss to them all and victory a common benefit.

This whole conception always has expressed rather an ideal than a reality, but an ideal that some states in antiquity as well as in more recent times were able to approximate. It is increasingly difficult, however, to reconcile this conception with facts; any approach by an isolated country to the ideal of the "right of state" as the final criterion of state activities not only must surmount ever greater impediments but is possible only at the cost of increasingly serious cataclysms visited upon civilization.

While considering the problems of various social groups to which the population belongs we have observed the existence of certain groups which include parts of the populations of several states. The interplay of social forces in which the solidarities and antagonisms of these groups find their expression cannot be controlled and regulated within the framework of one state. What is more, we witness in the civilized world of today a constant growth of common aims and conflicts among powerful interests, independent of territorial boundaries, and these common aims and conflicts lead to the formation of new super-state or inter-state groups, combating each other. Confronted with these conflicting social forces an isolated state saves itself from disintegrating only by becoming the tool of destruction.

The facts are well known, only the ideologists of the state fail to draw conclusions from them. It started in the West with religious wars in the sixteenth and seventeenth centuries, wars which set back for at least a hundred years the growth of European culture. The state determined to preserve its internal unity could find no other solution but to ally itself in the name of "right of state" to one of the combatant sides, destroy the dissenters within the country and try to conquer, destroy or weaken the rival state which had allied itself with the opposite side. The problem was effectively solved in accordance with the principle of religious tolerance only in countries with protestant majorities owing to the fact that protestantism broke up into separate sects and lost its belligerency. Besides, other conflicts overshadowed the religious one; the struggle of bourgeois democracy against a monarchy based on nobility was not an internal problem of individual states; the inter-state forces which participated in that struggle did not allow any state to recover its internal equilibrium until monarchic powers were overthrown. But while that struggle lasted there arose the national problem, and again states were unable to solve it in any other way except by becoming instruments in the hands of their major national groups, by "denationalizing" national minorities and struggling with other states for territories which either were already inhabited by a population belonging to their "national majority" or could become a sphere of expansion for those majorities. And no sooner did the short-sighted ideology create the ideal of "national state", which sees in the union of the nation with the state a means to preserve the sovereign "right of state" of each country, independent of the rest of the world, than new inter-state forces arose dragging individual states into the whirlpool of new solidarities and antagonisms, both internal and external.

The traditional isolation of a state leaves it confronted with an inevitable dilemma: whether it will become the passive battlefield of those forces which have already organized or are organizing competitive groups, or it will in each struggle ally itself with one of the sides. In the first case, if it does not disintegrate it will become the prey of its combatant neighbor; in the second case, by putting its material resources and military organization at the service of a nation, a class, a race, or an economic organization, it makes possible the conversion of the struggle carried on in other forms into a war, and everyone knows where repeated wars would lead today.

The only solution outside this dilemma is the creation of a new "right of state", not of an individual state but of a union of states (if not a sort of world super-state) which would put the common and general interest of all states above the one-sided interests of religious and anti-religious groups, nations, classes, races and economic organizations. Such a union would have to be an ultimate peace preserver, harmonizing the conflicts of social forces throughout the world in the same way that a wisely administered state harmonized the less important conflicts which have their causes and effects within its own boundaries. It would be necessary that in a union of that sort (unlike the League of Nations today) each state should represent only its own interests, as a territorial group, regardless of the aggressive interests of super-state groups, but at the same time in conformity with the interests of other states. Such mutual state conformity would probably be impossible for states which want to expand at the cost of other states, because they identify their general state interests with the interests of an aggressive ruling group. Yet the state, as a complete territorial group, in which all citizens participate actively and which endeavors to maintain and improve social order and to nurture the material and spiritual culture of the entire population, has, as a matter of fact, no interests contrary to those of other states which, as territorial groups, are working towards similar aims. The reverse is true: as modern culture grows, so does the field of interests common to many, if not all states. Medicine, hygiene, eugenics, technical progress in exploiting the wealth of nature and the growth of general prosperity; the release of economic conditions from the pressure of class differences, the intellectual and moral education of youth, as well as science, literature and art, all these are fields in which it is to the advantage of the state not only to avoid any conflict with other states but to seek ever-widening, more harmonious cooperation and mutual assistance. The superior rationalism of the state as compared with other groups enables it to put this cooperation into practice, thus breaking away from the conflicting, irrational social traditions. The first step in this direction would be to get rid of the traditional conception of the state as an isolated organism in which men are integrally enclosed, like cells, and all groups formed by these men constitute the organs. This conception is outmoded and harmful to civilization at large but particularly harmful to the state itself.

It is in cooperation with other states, and not by drawing away from them, and still less by fighting them, that each modern state can find the necessary inner strength to end its role as a passive tool in the hands of social groups. Only thus can it rise above them, gain control over their conflicts and induce them to subordinate their aims to the cause of "the common good". That "common good", set up as the goal of joint, inter-state cooperation, would, of course, mean the good of all humanity. Serving such an ideal the state would achieve a moral superiority over all other social groups; it lacks such superiority today when it borrows ideals from the nation, the church, a class or a race.

A sociologist, observing the activity of the foremost ideologists (of the state) in different western and eastern countries, sees clearly not only that they fail even to approach realization of their ideology, but that they actually move in the opposite direction by arousing and nourishing social forces, which, if not checked will sooner or later bring about the ruin of all states either through disintegration from within or destruction from without or through the combination of both. The impartial, objective observer is amazed. How to explain this phenomenon? The ancients had a simple explanation: *Quos deus vult perdere, dementat* (Whom God would destroy He first deprives of reason). But an explanation of that sort could not satisfy us. The unreasonable actions of statesmen and party leaders is not a matter of individual or even mass insanity. Their primordial sources lie deeply hidden in the life of society; to discover them is one of the hardest but most interesting of sociological problems.

POLAND DURING WORLD WAR II

HISTORICAL BACKGROUND
(1939–1945)

The German invasion of September 1, 1939, terminated Poland's brief period of independence. On September 17, 1939, while the Polish army fought the Germans, Soviet troops attacked from the east. The Nazis' plan to subjugate the Polish nation was to be accomplished by liquidating its political and intellectual elite and by enslaving the working class. Their methods included arrests and deportations, forced labor, starvation, executions, concentration camps, and other forms of terror. Although the Soviets' plans for Poland were different from those of the Germans, the Communists used every means of compulsion to secure their domination of Polish territories.

Many political leaders and thousands of soldiers and civilians went into exile. The Polish government established itself in London, organized on foreign soil a new army, navy, and air force, and directed its own foreign policy. As a result, Polish soldiers took part in major combat during World War II, shedding their blood during the Battle of Britain and at Tobruk, Narvik, Monte Cassino, and elsewhere.

Eventually, other political centers were established, both within Poland and in the Soviet Union. Although political views differed on what the future of Poland was to be after the war, the various groups were united in their determination to liberate Poland. Following the outbreak of war between Germany and the Soviet Union, a Polish army was also organized in the U.S.S.R.

While Polish soldiers were involved in the war on both the western and eastern fronts, most of those on the home front were fighting a day-to-day battle with the Nazis. Of the many underground military organizations, the best known were the Home Army, the Gray Ranks of Polish Scouts, the Jewish Fighting Organization, the Camp of

257

Fighting Poland, the National Armed Forces, the Peasant Battalions, and the People's Army. They committed acts of sabotage, derailing trains and destroying arms supplies; they published underground newsletters, organized clandestine schools and universities, aided their persecuted countrymen by smuggling arms and food to the ghettos, and, above all, prepared for a nationwide uprising. Countless deeds of heroism and sacrifice demonstrated their fighting spirit and culminated in two armed uprisings: that of the Warsaw Ghetto in April 1943 and that of the entire capital in August-September 1944. Both were brutally crushed by the Nazis, who finally razed Warsaw. The immensity of the tragedy that befell the country can be measured by six million deaths, irreparable cultural losses, and a completely devastated economy.

By the end of the war Poland's fate was sealed. The Yalta Agreement between the Big Three powers, represented by Roosevelt, Churchill, and Stalin, decreed that the Soviet-Polish border should follow the so-called Curzon line. This arrangement gave almost fifty percent of Poland's prewar eastern territory to the Soviet Union. The Agreement recognized the Polish Committee of National Liberation, which was created by Polish Communists in the Soviet Union, as the nucleus of the future Polish government. This decision also marked the beginning of Communist rule in Poland. Later, at the Potsdam Conference, Poland's western border, at the expense of Germany, was extended to the Oder-Neisse line. East Prussia went to Poland.

The documents on the following pages manifest the struggle of the Polish nation for liberation, justice, and human dignity throughout World War II.

IN EXILE

IGNACY JAN PADEREWSKI
(1860-1941)*

FOR YOUR FREEDOM AND OURS!

Appeal to the Polish Soldiers

(1941)

For what do you set forth to fight, Polish soldier? For a hundred years these words have appeared on the glorious banners which led you to battle: "For your freedom and ours." What is the meaning of these words?

For our freedom means:

That the monster of evil, paganism, and slavery shall be expelled from Polish soil,

That your father and mother, your brothers and sisters, subjected today to the most cruel persecution, shall throw off the yoke of slavery,

That to each Polish home, to each farmstead, and to each workshop there shall again return the smile of victory, the happiness of freedom, and the sun of peace,

That the Poland of tomorrow shall become not only great and strong, but also a solicitous, good and noble mother of free and equal citizens.

For your freedom means:

That, after this most frightful war in the history of the world, after the eradication of evil and paganism, no nation shall be able to oppress and exploit other nations,

That the sun of freedom may shine equally on all, and that all may realize that there is no happiness at home when wrong is done to one's neighbor,

---

* For editorial note on I. J. Paderewski, see page 241

That the future order which shall prevail in the world shall not be based on violence and force but on the principles of the teachings of Christ, justice, and the consonant thriving of the great family of free peoples.

Your ancestors fought for such freedom and, in such struggles, won immortal glory. For such freedom, for the most sacred cause of Poland and of all nations, you today set forth to fight, Polish soldier.

March onward to glory and triumph! March to victory! The sacred cause of your homeland calls you!

WŁADYSŁAW SIKORSKI
(1881*)

General Władysław Sikorski is Premier of the Polish Government-in-Exile and Commander-in-Chief of the Polish armed forces. During the first World War he was a Colonel of the Polish Legions and later commanded one of the armies in the Soviet-Polish war. He was minister of war and premier of the Polish Government in 1923. In his political activity he was an adversary of the policy of Marshal Pilsudski. As a leading representative of the policy of rapproachment with the Western democracies Gen. Sikorski also combatted the policy of Colonel Beck. He was a prominent military writer and authored a series of important works in that field. During the war in Poland in September, 1939, Marshal Śmigły-Rydz did not allow Sikorski to assume a separate command. After the defeat of Poland he went to France, where he immediately began to organize a Polish army and assumed the premiership of the government.

FROM THE ADDRESS AT THE OPENING OF THE POLISH
NATIONAL COUNCIL
(January, 1940)

Every government draws its vital juices from the masses supporting its activity. In Poland it was otherwise. The prevention of the nation's collaboration in, and responsibility for, the existence of the state had severe consequences for us the moment the war was imposed on us.

Poland bravely resisted the united destructive forces that sought to annihilate the world. She accepted a struggle too uneven to be won. But that she lost it so quickly was the fault of the system which was in disharmony with the nation and used its energy in a useless and injurious spirit.

The government over which I preside has broken radically with these methods. It avoids exercising uncontrolled authority. And though the war requires quick and energetic action we wish to be controlled, with the natural reservation that this control will not restrict us in our creative work . . . .

Rejecting totalitarian models so absolutely foreign to the Polish spirit, following the beautiful examples of our allies, Great Britain and France, we prepare the foundations for a truly democratic, and consequently just and orderly Poland. One of the most important problems which the tragic historical moment poses before us is the rebuilding of the Polish Army . . . .

I can . . . . state that after the catastrophe that destroyed our armed forces their rehabilitation on a new basis proceeds successfully . . . . I personally as well as my immediate assistants and higher commanders strive assiduously to introduce a new spirit into the officers' and non-commissioned officers' corps, and to bring about a unification of the commanders with the generally excellent soldiers of the emigration in a spirit of cordial fraternity, mutual respect and modern discipline.

The Polish soldiers stand aloof from politics. They do not regard the army as a springboard for careers in other state services. Educated in the spirit of sacrifice and complete devotion to the homeland, they dream of the moment when they will be able to follow the example of the heroes of Warsaw, Hel, Westerplatte, Lwów, Modlin and countless other places and avenge the wrongs of their brothers.

The Poland that we shall rebuild will be based on new foundations of international order. The ideals for which we fight at the side of our allies, France and Great Britain, are universally human ideals . . . .

DECLARATION OF PRINCIPLES OF THE POLISH GOVERNMENT IN LONDON

(July, 1941)

The Polish Government in Exile has given frequent expression to its democratic attitude. By a series of government acts issued during the war some of the pre-war undemocratic decrees, enactments, and institutions, introduced by the pre-September, 1939, Polish Government, were abolished. In July, 1941, the principles on which the Polish Government bases its activity and which it intends to present at the peace conference were ultimately defined.

* * *

An independent Poland, with a completely democratic political system, is the chief aim of the Polish Government of National Unity.

The Government is an instrument in the service of all Polish citizens and of the Republic. There can be no return to any system of personal, clique, or oligarchic rule. There can be no return to irresponsible government, evading democratic popular control by National Representation.

The chief immediate task of the Government is fully and actively to participate in the war and in the subsequent Peace Conferences, to ensure for Poland a direct and adequate outlet to the sea, and frontiers which will guarantee the future security of the Republic.

Without infringing upon the unquestioned right of the nation to decide what political and economic system Poland shall have after the war, the Government pledges that:

1. The Polish State will be based on Christian principles and culture.

2. Poland will be a democratic State. All her citizens will enjoy equal rights and equal treatment by the Administration and the Courts, regardless of race, creed or nationality. Personal liberty, the democratic rights of individual citizens,

and the national rights of the minority groups (Slavs, Lithuanians, and Jews) will be fully respected.

3. Poland's administrative apparatus will be responsible to and controlled by the National Representatives, elected by the secret, equal, universal, and direct vote of all her citizens.

4. Economically and socially Poland will strive to realize the principles of social justice. Every citizen's right to work will be assured and safeguarded, every peasant will own the land he tills. A just re-distribution of the land will be effected by the Government. Manual and clerical workers will have a voice in the control of industrial production, and a share in its fruits. The productive system will be reorganized according to just and rational principles, and workers will be protected from exploitation and assured a decent standard of living and health.

THE STATUS OF JEWS IN FREE POLAND

(Declaration presented on behalf of the Polish Government by Minister of Labor and Social Welfare, Jan Stańczyk)

(December, 1941)

The Polish Government in Exile has twice defined its position regarding the Jewish question in the future Poland. It did so for the first time at a great public meeting in London on November 3, 1940, when the Polish Minister of Labor and Social Welfare, Jan Stańczyk, leader of the Polish Socialist Party, read a declaration concerning the complete equality of rights and obligations of Jews in free Poland. In December, 1941, in New York at a meeting of the Council of the Jewish Labor Committee, Minister Jan Stańczyk made a second declaration which was an elaboration and crystallization of the first.

* * *

A new world order, based on the principles of Liberty and Social Justice, will emerge from the present war. Already the war is bringing great changes into social relations. In the face of common disaster, in the course of the common struggle against the common foe, old prejudices and conflicts must rapidly disappear. In the future Poland—as I stated on behalf of the Polish Government on November 3, 1940, in London—there will be no place for racial discrimination, and none for the social wrongs of pre-war Polish life. The war has wiped out the institutions and destroyed the power of groups which formerly strove to foment hatred among the people of Poland. Their common fate has created a strong bond between Gentile and Jew. In the ranks of the Polish Army they fought and still fight side by side. The Jewish underground movement is part of the great Polish underground army waging the struggle for the common cause of Liberation.

Future relations between Gentiles and Jews in Liberated Poland will be built on entirely new foundations. Poland will guarantee all her citizens, including the Jews, full legal equality. Poland will be a true democracy and every one of her citizens will enjoy equal rights irrespective of race, creed or origin.

The psychological and social changes taking place in Poland today are the best guarantee that this pledge will become a valid fact. The democratic forces of Poland have always fought against the policy of national discrimination and racial persecution. In the new Poland these forces will decide the future of the country.

Jewish cultural life in Poland was rich and manifold. Poland has always been one of the centers of Jewish culture, and the Polish Jews have created a literature, an educational system, and a press of their own. The right of the Jews to possess and to develop a culture of their own will be fully recognized. The system of cultural autonomy seems to be the best method for the realization of full and unhindered development of the Jewish cultural life.

The question is often raised whether the Polish Jews who are not at present in Poland will be permitted to return to a liberated Poland. There must be no doubt whatever that every Polish citizen, irrespective of creed, race or nationality will be free to return to his country. The Polish Government has clearly stated its position with regard to the political rights of the citizens of future Poland. The constitutional guarantee of legal equality and equal responsibility excludes any possibility of exceptions. The Polish Jew, like any other Polish citizen, will be able to return to Poland.

All this, of course, concerns the future solution of the Jewish problem in Poland. Today, with all of Poland under the Nazi yoke, the Polish Government has little opportunity to put its principles into practice. However, even now it does all in its power to redress all old wrongs against any group of citizens. A decree of the pre-war Polish Government depriving of their Polish nationality persons who had resided abroad for many years without maintaining contact with the home country, was one such wrong. This vicious decree has been revoked by the present Polish Government.

Democratic Poland, freed of the Nazi yoke, will give the Polish Jews, as well as all other national minorities, a home and an opportunity for constructive activity for their own good, for the sake of Poland and of mankind.

BRONISŁAW MALINOWSKI

(1884-1942)

Born and educated in Poland, Bronisław Malinowski's anthropological researches carried him to remote corners of the earth. He conducted field studies in New Guinea, on the Triobrand Archipelago, in Africa, Australia, Mexico, and on several islands of the Pacific. The school of functionalism in anthropology and sociology was founded by Malinowski. For several years before he came to Yale University in the United States, he held a professorship at the London School of Economics.

In America, Malinowski was elected chairman of the Board of the Polish Institute of Arts and Sciences. The last work completed by him before his recent death was "Human Nature, Culture and Freedom", which is the crowning synthesis of all his previous research. It was his wish, expressed the day before his death, that a fragment of that work be included in the present anthology.

FROM "HUMAN NATURE, CULTURE AND FREEDOM"

(1942)

An inquiry into the nature of freedom and its relation to human nature and to culture is not out of place in a fighting democracy. We are now engaged in a war against the greatest threat to freedom which humanity has ever known. We fight for freedom. Do we really understand what it is, appreciate its value, and realize that it is in fact the very foundation of our civilized life? We are surrounded by many magnificent slogans, some of them true and significant. We know that this is "a battle of free peoples against slavery"; we hear that this is "the fight for freedom"; we have been officially told that this war will establish "the four freedoms" firmly and permanently . . . .

The principles upon which the Nazis have transformed Poland, Czechoslovakia, Serbia, Greece, and other parts of conquered Europe into actual slave communities are neither temporary nor metaphorical. The German nation, partly through the cunning trickery of the Nazis, partly through brutal coertion, partly willingly, partly through the indoctrination of the young, have accepted their historic mission of masterhood . . . .

The new German system would mean a slavery numerically so strong that it could never be really quelled, and let us remember the nations which the Germans want to enslave are sufficiently strong, numerous, and developed to continue their culture, their education and their public opinion, and to fight even as now the Poles, the Norwegians, the Hollanders and the Serbians, the Greeks, and some of the French are fighting. The German nation, turned into a large Gestapo force, would have to continue the battle against its slaves. The picture is so fantastic that it baffles imagination, but if Hitler wins this will be the reality even as all the unthinkable horrors of this war are reality. Hitler, however, will not win. It was necessary to draw the outline of the Nazi daydreams primarily to show that what we are fighting for now is nothing short of the survival of culture and humanity. Any of our slogans which appear somewhat ambitious are really understatements as regards the evils which the democracies now are opposing by force of arms. It was also necessary to draw the outline of this nightmare which we have allowed to creep upon us so near that only a supreme effort can prevent it, because another such disaster must be prevented . . . .

THE FREEDOM OF ORDER AND ACHIEVEMENT

Freedom is the most dynamic, essential, and general factor in the problem of planning and reconstruction. Democracy is freedom in action. Freedom of conscience is the essence of religion, and religion is the core of civilization. Cast off Christianity, and religion enters as the Nordic myth of Aryan superiority, the ritual of Hitler worship, and the Nazi ethics of domination. Proscribe God through the anti-God campaign in Russia, and you will worship the spirit of Marx and his gospel at the shrine of Lenin's embalmed body.

"Fascism is the new religion of the Italian people," is being proclaimed by Mussolini.

The principle of self-determination of nations, groups, and persons can be defined only by making clear how far the freedom of collective decisions has to be related to rights of minorities and to legitimate claims of individuals. Justice again, which is the spirit of laws, is the balancing and the portioning out of freedoms. Security is freedom from fear; and prosperity, freedom from want. We shall even be able to come near to the definition of that most elusive concept, the pursuit of happiness, and relate it to our description of freedom in terms of human needs and their satisfactions.

Freedom as the driving force of the cultural process challenges us also theoretically because it is the most difficult to define. Philosophers and political thinkers, theologians and psychologists, students of history and moralists have used this word with an excessively wide range of meanings. This was due very largely to the fact that the word "freedom" for very definite reasons has an emotional force and a rhetorical weight which make its use very handy in harangue, moral sermon, poetic appeal, and metaphysical argument. Since it is also used in scientific or near-scientific reasoning, the word "freedom" leads a hybrid existence. It is used in propaganda and in the appeal to what is best and what is worst in human nature under the false pretense that the appeal is founded on profound wisdom and even on scientific cogency. The duty, therefore, of making clear scientifically to what realities the word "freedom" can be legitimately applied, and where it appears out of bounds insofar as any semantic legitimacy is concerned, is not to be shirked.

The essential nature of the concept of freedom can only be understood with reference to culture and in relation to the processes of culture. In other words, freedom is an attribute of organized and instrumentally implemented phases of human action. Its great emotional potency is due to the fact that human life and indeed the pursuit of happiness depend upon the nature and the efficiency of those means which culture gives man in his struggle with environment, in his cooperation and conflicts with other human beings, and indeed in coming to grips with Destiny herself. Hence, unless we refer freedom to the techniques and technicalities of culture, that is, unless we understand it in terms of anthropological analysis, we shall never be able to establish real semantic criteria for the distinction between legitimate and illegitimate uses of this word. Freedom is a symbol which stands for a sublime and powerful ideal; the same symbol, however, may become a dangerous weapon in the hands of the enemies of freedom.

All this already implies the definition of the term. Freedom means the smooth and effective, as well as successful, run of an activity undertaken by a group of men, with a clear aim in view, who combine for the task, fit themselves out for action, and achieve the desired end. Each member of such a group enjoys his own differential freedom in the measure to which he has a part in the planning, a full access to the means of execution, and a share in the rewards. Even in its smallest and most insignificant manifestations, freedom gives any and every member of a society the sense of achievement and through this the sense of personal value. In a free culture people can form their purpose, undertake activities and enterprises, and enjoy the gains from work thus undertaken. The essential nature of freedom thus conceived is pragmatic. Freedom comes into being when activities of organized behavior follow human choice and planning. Freedom is determined by the results of action as well as by its prerequisites. The individual's freedom consists in his ability to choose the goal, to find the road, and to reap all the rewards of his efforts and endeavors. Those men are free who are able to decide what to do, where to go, and what to build. All claims for freedom remain idle and irrelevant unless planning and aiming can be translated into an efficient execution through well-implemented and well-organized behavior. The determining conditions of freedom are therefore to be found in the manner in which a society is organized; in the way in which the instrumentalities for action are made accessible; and in the guarantees which safeguard all the rewards of planned purposeful action and insure their equitable distribution.

These considerations indicate why little attention will be given to those approaches to the problem of freedom which treat it as a negative attribute. To define freedom, as is usually done, as the "absence of restraint" amounts to a statement that freedom is not no-freedom. This is mere verbal substitution of two negatives and two words for the bare tautology that freedom is freedom. Equally irrelevant are those conceptions of freedom in which it is defined as a mere movement of the mind, as a goal which can be reached by the untrammeled spirit of man alone. Only when freedom of thought or of inspiration becomes embodied into an active performance does it become relevant to the student of organized behavior, that is culture. The freedom which we need to understand is that powerful force which moves men to deeds, which inspires martyrdom and heroism, which precipitates revolutions and mobilizes nations into wars. Such freedom cannot be born or bred by any abstruse and recondite metaphysical speculations, nor yet by processes of idle daydreaming, or of free association of ideas. True freedom—the freedom of order, of action, and of achievement—enters into the very texture of human life and of ordered, organized human societies. It is a reality to be found in the conduct of domestic life, in processes of learning, in the acquisition of values, in the administration of justice, the protection of life and property, and in the cultivation of science, art, recreation, and religion. In all this we find that freedom is a gift of culture. It might as well be said that culture is a gift of freedom. For from the very beginnings of humanity freedom is a prerequisite of the exercise, maintenance and the advancement of cultural achievements.

Yet, as we shall see, culture also supplies all the means for the curtailment and denial of its most precious gift to humanity.

FREEDOM AS A GIFT OF CULTURE

Culture consists from the outset in the organized exploitation by human intelligence of environmental opportunities, and in the disciplining of drives, skills, and nervous reactions in the service of collective and implemented action. The earliest human groups and the individuals who form them achieve a much greater integral freedom of mobility and environmental adaptation, freedom of security and prosperity, by the use of tools, by following the principles of knowledge, and by loyalty to a system of activities started with a purpose and carried out concertedly.

Culture in its initial stage grants the freedom to live in order and safety and with a margin of surplus, while at the same time it implies obedience and submission to certain restraints. These restraints consist in the rules of technique, and of knowledge how to exploit the environment and avoid its dangers. Bound up with these are the laws of custom and of social give and take. Ethical principles, partly implicit in submission to the supernatural, partly arising out of organized emotional reactions, impose also certain restraints from the very beginning of culture.

The integral freedom, given to a man as an animal species through the development of his cultural instrumentality, is thus objective, tangible, and specific. It consists in the indefinite extension in the range of human mobility. It is a new type of environmental adaptation. It is brought about by the use of tools, artifacts, machines, and weapons; by the organization of human beings in relation to the apparatus, and co-ordination of their actions through rules of concerted behavior; and by the development of symbolic means of communication, more especially of language, which allows man to accumulate his tradition and to transmit it from generation to generation. In all this man establishes a new self-made environment, to which in turn he re-adapts his own organism.

This new artificial environment obeys a determinism of its own. There exist laws of cultural process, of the constitution of culture, and of the efficiency of concerted activities. Hence culture inevitably becomes a source of new constraints imposed upon man. The *leitmotif* of all our arguments will be that all those constraints which are dictated by cultural determinism are as indispensable to successful behavior as are the laws of nature and of the organism. Freedom, indeed, consists in the lead and guidance which the rules and laws of culture give man. At the same time we shall see that most of those rules of cultural determinism imply the element of power, placed in the hands of one or of a few. This power can be abused in the form of wealth, of physical violence, and of spiritual intimidation. When the work, the effort, and the risks, as well as the punishments of an enterprise, are imposed on one section of the organized group, and the advantages are enjoyed by only a few, we have a differential distribution of advantage and effort respectively. This constitutes a denial of freedom. The denial may refer to initiative and planning, or to the distribution of the benefits, or else to the control of cultural instrumentalities. In every case the distinction between freedom and bondage turns around the question whether the constraint is necessary for the successful execution of the activity, or whether it is exercised to the advantage of a few and at the expense of others.

In its earliest beginnings, as well as in its fundamental function throughout evolution, culture satisfies first and foremost man's basic needs. Culture thus means primarily the freedom of survival to the species under a variety of environmental conditions for which man is not equipped by nature. This freedom of survival, as was already stated, can be analyzed into freedom of security and freedom of prosperity. By freedom of security we mean the protective mechanisms which culture gives through artifacts and cooperation and which endow the species with a much wider margin of safety. Freedom of prosperity refers to the increased, widened, and diversified power of exploiting environmental resources, allowing man to prepare for periods of scarcity, accumulate wealth, and thus obtain leisure for many types of activities which man as an animal could never have undertaken. Indeed, in a scientific analysis of culture we have to state that as humanity advances, there open up new vistas for human desire, interest, knowledge, and belief.

All those ever-widening, ever-unfolding gifts of culture to humanity remain contingent upon the basic freedom of survival. The archeologist can show from magnificent remnants of extinct communities that in the course of evolution there has been a disruption and annihilation of whole cultures. This means that at many periods in evolution the foundations of security and prosperity were destroyed. The student of history knows that wars and epidemics, droughts and natural disasters, as well as mismanagement of national resources have led to the disappearance of specific cultures, to the death of empires, and to the depopulation of once thriving regions.

These facts contain an important lesson for the present. The world is now once more threatened with a denial of the two fundamental freedoms of security and of prosperity. Thousands of human beings are perishing daily by sword, disease, and starvation. This is the denial of the biological freedom in the satisfaction of primary organic needs. This abrogation of the freedom of survival and existence does not affect man merely in his animal interest and needs. It also automatically disorganizes human groups, destroys loyalties, and lowers the standard of life in its finer intellectual, artistic, and religious values.

Culture, now as always, is one and indivisible. Today it also embraces humanity as a whole. Its deterioration is as total as war itself. It must now affect the basic functions of culture, that is the maintenance of our commissariat, of our social and legal order, and of our educational systems. This deterioration affects also all the fundamental values of loyalty, decency, ethical principle, as well as of invention, scientific work, and technical skill. Culture in its higher spiritual achievements, and in its fundamental functions cannot survive the shattering lessons of total war. If might is right, if brutality pays, if ruthlessness, perfidy, and the argument of violence become the fundamental doctrine of civilization, then humanity is doomed.

ALEKSANDER HERTZ
(1895*)

Formerly Professor of Sociology at the School of Political Science in Wilno, Aleksander Hertz is the author of a number of sociological works. His dissertations, "Mission of the Leader", and "The Leader and His Group", bold analyses of the characteristics of dictatorship, attracted wide attention when they first appeared in Poland during the period of reaction. Before the first World War, Hertz was an active liberationist. He took part in Polish military organizations during the war, and later devoted most of his energies to the Polish Labor movement. He has been in the United States since the autumn of 1940, when he came here from France.

FROM "THE RISE OF PEASANT DEMOCRACY"

(1940)

Among three neighboring peoples, the Poles, Rumanians, and Hungarians, there are certain common developments, which have played and still play a notable part in their culture. In these three countries the basic factors in the picture of rural life are the relations between the gentry and the peasants. And since the structure of these countries is distinctly agrarian, the relations of which we speak are reflected in the whole system of community life, whether it be in the country or city.

The essence of democracy is often said to be the realization of equality of opportunities. It is not enough to have this equality set forth formally in written laws. These have little significance if there is actual inequality resulting from unwritten social, economic, and cultural mores. True equality, as the basis of real democracy, exists only when the individual himself as well as other individuals recognize his personal worth and his right to attain a place in the sun. But this in turn cannot exist if the individual himself has no feeling of his own worth, of the power, and social role of the group to which he belongs. This is particularly important when it concerns groups spread over extensive territory and whose impress upon society as a whole is deep. If democracy is to arise, the members of such groups must become conscious of the great part they have to play, they must be proud of membership in such a group. A condition for the practicability of democracy is the emancipation of the masses, the development in them of the conception of their significance, their worth as individuals and as groups, of the will to play as great a part as that played by the classes heretofore recognized as leading or superior.

Thus, the feudal order is broken up from within. For it exists only so long as the masses of the people look upon the apparent social superiority of the gentry and their own inferiority as a part of the natural order of things. In independent Poland we were witnesses of the breakup from within of what remained of the feudal conception of life, which disappeared with the coming to maturity of the most numerous element of the population—the peasant masses. Conditions became favorable for the development of a people's democracy which was making its appearance as a result of the great changes in community life. Similar processes made themselves felt in Rumania and Hungary, where a consciousness of their historic role and its incompatibility with the present order has arisen in the minds of the peasants . . . .

In our analysis we shall limit ourselves to Poland, never losing sight of the fact that phenomena similar to those of which we shall speak may be found in Hungary and Rumania.

The gentry and nobility tradition is the outcome of a definite social and cultural structure. Essential for that structure is the glaring division of the whole of reality into two separate spheres, into two separate worlds—that of the gentleman and that of the peasant, and the patronizing attitude of the former toward the latter. This structural characteristic was an inheritance from the old gentry of Poland. It was carried over through the period of subjection into independent Poland. But there it reached a stage of decadence and disintegration. This process of the gentry's internal disintegration in independent Poland may be considered one of the most important phenomena of her history. It was at the same time an extremely dramatic phenomenon. For in independent Poland the gentry endeavored to wage a last desperate struggle for existence. In that struggle which was doomed to failure, the gentry sacrificed the state itself, as well as its defense . . . .

The group which ruled Poland for thirteen years embodied in itself and its rule the spirit of the nobility tradition. Its nucleus was formed of men who in their youth showed élan, fighting spirit, romantic enthusiasm. It was a romanticism of the nobility pattern, though displayed in its most beautiful aspect. The men referred to represented, at any rate in their youth, the best characteristics of the nobility climate. However, even these characteristics were part of the distorted nobility tradition and eventually it won the upper hand.

It found expression in the élitarianism of the ruling group. The élite theory is a pseudo-rational attempt to prove that a given ruling group has the right to rule and that this right belongs to it alone. This theory is used by every monopolistic clique, irrespective of whether it is called Nazism, Bolshevism, Fascism, or what not. In Poland it was cut to the measure of the requirements of the nobility tradition. It was an élitarianism which fed on lordly patronage—a farm and overseer philosophy transferred to the whole nation as its object.

In all spheres the country was treated as a big farm. And as a matter of fact, the totalitarian tendencies of the ruling camp were closer to the overseer mentality of the squire than to German, Russian, or Italian models. It was a sort of semi-totalitarianism, inconsistent, vacillating in its undertakings, weak in contour . . . .

Thus, behind the facade of modern totalitarian ideologies, were to be found anachronistic contents. The system of government and the whole mentality of the ruling group became the more anachronistic as fundamental socio-cultural changes occurred more and more behind them in the whole of Poland. Life itself liquidated the gentry tradition for which the ruling camp became a last stronghold. The history of recent years is the history of the desperate struggle of the political gentry tradition against those forces which were completely changing the face of Poland. In that struggle the camp of the gentry tradition could lean only on physical force . . . .

The transformations taking place in the country were undoubtedly the most significant event in the social history of independent Poland. Their meaning lay in the fact that the peasants were changing from a passive mass weighed down by traditions of serfdom into a social class conscious of its historical role and its political and cultural tasks, that they were acquiring a sense of their power, their dignity, their class distinctiveness. This evolution of the peasant became apparent in all possible fields: political movement, cultural and trade economic organizations, in the tendency to develop a peasant intelligentsia closely linked with the countryside, in the extremely interesting young peasant movement. In all these fields the will to independence was the dominant factor. The emancipation of the Polish peasant rejected the patronizing protection of the nobleman, did away with the traditional division into a gentleman's and peasant's world. It was a profoundly democratic process creating foundations for Poland's real democratization . . . .

The Polish village experienced such an emancipatory process in recent years. The ideal of a people's democracy ceased to be an abstraction and became a concrete goal of endeavor, became a part of the experiences of great human collectivity. This was most profoundly displayed in the young peasant movement, reflecting the tendencies of the young people reared in independent Poland. No doubt the programs of these young people were not free from internal contradictions and ambiguities. But these were natural sins. What is important is that the whole movement was a complete rejection by the young peasants of the old serfdom traditions, the old definitions of the peasant's social role.

281

It was directed against the gentry tradition and its anachronistic survivals.

Thus the gentry tradition was breaking down where it had had its main foundation of existence. Its vitality depended on whether the peasants preserved the traditional picture of reality, whether they acquiesced in the social role which grew on the basis of serfdom, and in the obligations resulting from them. Irrespective of any political movements, the ruling group was becoming socially and culturally isolated. In her internal processes Poland began to be modernized. The most important obstacle to this was the ruling system— the main stronghold of the old gentry tradition.

The war swept away the political gentry tradition. The Polish people found themselves under the terrible yoke of the invaders. But the great historical process cannot be turned back. The gentry tradition cannot be revived. The pages of its history are filled to the end.

ANTONI SŁONIMSKI

(1895*)

Słonimski's weekly articles in the Warsaw paper "The Literary News," were widely read for their biting wit and boldness. His comedies were stamped with a fine European sense of humor. But by far his most profound and natural medium is poetry. He is generally accepted as one of the leading Polish poets writing today. Though he writes rarely now in England, he does occasionally address an article to his compatriots—especially when he feels that the truth requires restatement. He recently started the publication of a literary monthly "New Poland".

FROM "THE PEOPLE'S WAR"

(July 13, 1941)

. . . . We have already seen the results of that "political realism" which is based on rapacity and the disregard of ethics. We have already seen those politicians reducing the world to the level of the jungle, where nations swallow one another by the dozens, where the stronger tusks and the greater cruelty decide the right of the individual and the nation to live. Disregarded moral criteria are the most obvious cause of the development of Hitlerism and Fascism. That does not mean that only the totalitarian states have rejected morality as a superfluous ballast; it means that the opposing side also has been guided neither by ethics nor morals. Whatever we think of the Soviets, the fact that the democracies armed and urged the Hitler gangster to fight against the Bolsheviks does not speak too well for the morality of pre-war politics. Concerning the subsidizing of Hitler by big international capitalists, we may find new and quite revealing details in the recently published memoirs of the American ambassador to Berlin, Dodd. The attitude of the democracies toward Abyssinia and their acceptance of this criminal attack was the first and decisive cause of the bold-

283

ness of the leaders of Hitlerism. We, ourselves, have seen
how the rejection of moral criteria has repaid us! And today
again Polish political thought is being formed in the same
direction. And once more those who would like to see morality in politics and ethical criteria in world government are
being told: "enough of those dreams", "enough pacifism",
"enough of your idealistic illusions". Again, they say that
the future Europe should be divided into strong armed
states, or perhaps federations, to watch the Germans and the
"European balance of power". But what next? If the future
of Europe is to be built on old governing systems, on the
old immorality and hate, it is easy to imagine that the armed
nations or federations will find new causes for war among
themselves. I am not a believer in a post-war understanding
with Germany, even with a most democratic Germany.
Criminals and madmen should be placed in strait-jackets.
I should warn against freeing them too soon. I must say,
however, that he who imagines that madmen are cured by
strait-jackets alone only deceives himself. Germany must
pay the price—and a painful one—it must be deprived of
its bite and its poison, it must be severely controlled for a
long period of time, but I believe firmly that even Germans
can be educated. The maintenance of the principle of hatred
and chauvinism is a plan for the reconstruction of the world
on the principle "My uncle changed his hatchet for a stick",
but, in the last analysis, it is all the same to us whether our
heads are going to be struck off with a small hatchet or a
large stick.

. . . . Only a clear and definite war aim may give . . . .
strength. Only the belief that the world is indeed fighting
for a great cause, for a true universal democracy, will conse-
crate the new sacrifices and give us the unbreakable strength
and will to persevere.

Before us there arises a great family of nations fighting
for a new world. The word "democracy" takes on new
significance. Democracy does not today mean only the right
of the people to live, to work, to create, the right to safety
and liberty. The definition of these rights the reader may
find in many publications. Their finest formulation is the

"Declaration of the Rights of Man" given by Wells in his "The Common Sense of War and Peace".

True democracy will treat not the symptoms but the causes of evil. True democracy means the rejection of racial and class hatreds, the union of continents into a common United States of the World. Those who are afraid of bold ideas, those who react with cowardly habit, and not with mind and heart—will turn away discouraged at the clarity of this picture. But nevertheless, the time has come for our thoughts to become bold and our hearts truly noble. The world has undergone tremendous shocks. History lies in ruins and geography is overturned by the victorious airplane.

Today it is necessary to work toward a Poland to which one may return, where moral laws will become the *raison d'état*, toward a Poland where for every wronged prisoner there will be the enthusiasm of an eager defense, toward a Poland where morality will not be a gala banner, but will serve our everyday life, will stand behind the desk of the official, will guide the pen of the writer.

We wander as if in a dark room, where a body lies in its casket and beyond whose curtained windows glows the dawn. Let us close the casket and open the windows. Those who, like blind men, wander about the room arguing about the arrangement of the furniture, see neither death nor the newly awakening life. We must open the windows as wide as possible. Close the casket with nails. Let us look carefully into the future, freed from the superstitions of the past. *The aim of this war must be the introduction of moral criteria into the life of the individual and of nations. The aim of this war must be concern for the individual.* Only then can this war become the people's war, for which Mickiewicz prayed,* and only then can it be truly victorious.

---

* See page 82

UNDERGROUND POLAND

"We do not know when these materials will reach you. We do not even know whether we shall succeed at all in sending them to countries remote enough from us so that a free book may appear in the broad light of day. But if we should succeed, we want you to know how these materials originated and why we hand them over to you . . . ." These are words taken from one of the secret reports that reached this country from Poland.

Poland's political and social life continues to develop despite the frightful terrorism of the occupying powers. It has been forced into the underground of conspiracy, but it is nevertheless extremely exuberant and creative. The wave of the democratic and socially progressive underground movement is powerful and increasingly strong. It leans on the masses of the peasants and workers and on considerable portions of the professional intelligentsia. Poland is one vast concentration camp; in that camp every spark of "free life" must be carefully hidden from the eyes of the new masters. Nevertheless these sparks are numerous. The whole population is one great mass of conspirators. The sparks of real life are hidden deeply underground, but they have a very high temperature. Its testimony is the uncommon readiness of sacrifice, unusual courage, heroism and boldness of thought of the thousands of nameless fighters on the underground front.

From the texts which we reproduce there emanates a new force, a force which, when the hour of victory strikes, will build a new world of freedom, democracy and social justice.

The texts are translated from originals printed secretly in Poland by underground democratic and liberationist organizations. The materials have been smuggled out of the country through the channels of those organizations.

The names of the authors of the articles and of the co-authors of the manifestoes who live in the occupied territories cannot, of course, be made public.

(1943)

FROM "MANIFESTO OF FREEDOM"

(November, 1939)

The first document of great political importance published by the underground democratic movement of Poland was the "Manifesto of Freedom" first published "somewhere in Poland" on November 7th, 1939. This document, reprinted many times, circulated from hand to hand, spread in thousands of copies over the whole of Poland. It formulates a positive program for the future in the name of which the Poles fight and die.

* * *

After the years of independent political existence, Poland has fallen victim to the imperialism and unprecedented aggression of Nazi Germany.

At the moment of greatest strain, the fate of Poland was disastrously burdened with errors in foreign policy, infiltrations of reactionary ideologies, with the existing government itself, with its negligence in the economic and social fields and its policy of oppression of national minorities. During the first twenty years of her independence, Poland failed to fulfill her obligations to the masses of working people, who were not permitted to exercise any influence on the fate of the country.

The chief aim of the régime in power had been to perpetuate itself and to oppose any expression of the independent political aspirations of the masses of the people. The régime had betrayed the tradition of the struggle for independence and had accepted a reactionary fascist ideology. The standard slogan of Hitlerism—anti-Semitism—became the bridge between the régime in power and the nationalist fascist groups .... The territory of the Republic has been occupied by foreign armies bringing violence and injustice. As long as the struggle continues, however, Poland has not lost her independence.

Europe has been thrown into the abyss of war, the first act of which was the sacrifice of Poland's blood. Nazi Germany has imposed this war upon the world in the name of her imperialistic aspirations, which conflict with the imperial interests of England and France. Besides its imperialist character, this war has, however, still another aspect: it is a war between Hitlerism and democracy, between totalitarianism, barbarism, cultural and moral savagery and the ideas of Freedom and Justice. Such is the meaning of the present war, as understood by the masses of the working people of oppressed Poland as well as those of England and France.

Hitlerism must be defeated in this war; however, the victory of the allies should not induct the hegemony of one group of nations over others. From the chaos, there must rise a new Europe organized on the principles of political freedom and social justice. Such a Europe is the desire of millions of workers, peasants, and intellectuals, as well as of the soldiers who fight on all fronts.

Poland, in spite of military defeat, continues to fight. On Polish soil the people carry on a daily heroic struggle against the occupation, preparing themselves for the moment when the final battle will take place. In the West the Polish army fights in cooperation with the armies of France and England . . . .

In order that the sacrifice of blood so freely given through so many years shall not again be in vain, we formulate our aims as follows:

1. The chief aim of the struggle of the Polish working masses is the reconstruction of the full political freedom and independence of Poland, and the establishment of her existence on the principles of democracy and social justice.

2. In the New Poland the decisive influence of the masses of the people on the future of the country, the influence of the peasants, the workers, and the intellectuals must be secured. The political constitution and the social and economic structure of Poland must once and for all preclude the possibility of the existence of privileged social groups which strive to seize power and economic supremacy.

3. The political constitution of Poland must be based on the principles of political democracy guaranteed by: a

democratic representation of the people elected on the basis of equal, secret, universal, direct and proportional suffrage; responsibility of the government before Parliament; independence of the Courts of Justice; extensive democratic self-government; freedom of speech, of the press, of assembly, and of association; and personal immunity of the citizens. Under these conditions the political and social aspirations of the working masses will find their expression in the emergence of a workers' and peasants' government, endowed with the confidence of the people and representing the interest of all working men.

4. The influence of big capitalist and landlord groups on the fate of Poland must be removed through the abolition of large landed estates by means of a thorough and immediate agrarian reform, through socialization or through the subjection to strict social control of the credit system and of large scale industrial establishments, and through the abolition of monopolistic organizations such as cartels, syndicates, etc.; and through support of small-scale agriculture, of the cooperative movement, and the protection of small business men.

5. The military forces of Poland must be based on democratic organization which precludes any caste systems.

6. All nationalities living in Poland must be guaranteed full political, economic and cultural equality. Race doctrines and anti-Semitism must be eliminated from public life in Poland.

7. Universal and free education must be provided for all citizens, particularly for the children of peasants and workers.

8. The freedom of science and of religion must be guaranteed.

9. All citizens of the New Poland must be guaranteed the right to work, the protection of labor and health. It is necessary to expand social insurance on the basis of democratic self-government.

10. The foreign policy of Poland must be based on full cooperation and mutual understanding with all free peoples

of the world, and particularly with the nations with which Poland must live in good neighborly relations.

The struggle for such a Poland is a struggle for Freedom, Justice, and Peace. The struggle for such a Poland is a struggle for Socialism. In this struggle the masses of the working people are not isolated. It coincides with the struggle of the masses of the working people in the whole world against totalitarianism which brings slavery and destruction to the people of Europe. Fighting for the Freedom of Poland, we fight for the fate of all oppressed nations. We fight under the noble slogan: "For Your Freedom and Ours!" . . . .

"FREEDOM"
Executive Committee

November 7, 1939

FROM "MANIFESTO TO THE PEOPLES OF THE WORLD"

(February, 1941)

This Manifesto comes from "somewhere in Poland" .... There is no one, however busy, however pre-occupied with other things, who cannot afford the minutes needed to receive its message .... Let no one shirk his duty by saying that the Manifesto is a forgery. I give him the fullest personal guarantee that it is not. From the beginning of the struggle I have been in contact with the delegates whom these Polish organizations have sent abroad. I have seen the "underground" newspapers which they have circulated in every region of Poland; I have seen the reprints of broadcasts from London which they pass secretly from hand to hand; I have seen the earlier manifestoes which they issued to their compatriots at home.

The Manifesto is not a forgery; the picture which it paints is all too true. As its authors say, Poland shows the world what Hitler's New Order would be like, if he should win. But the Manifesto gives us the assurance that he cannot win. For close on two years he has tried everything which even Himmler could invent to break their spirit .... Yet, after two years of that rule, the spirit of those Poles is still unbroken. "Every day," they say, "we feel stronger". It is their unbroken spirit which is the ultimate guarantee of Hitler's failure.

Written under the lash of the Gestapo, these are noble words, and they are noble people who wrote them. In our duty to them, both now and when the war is over, we must not and we shall not fail.

(From the Foreword to the first issue of the Manifesto, by P. J. Noel-Baker, prominent member of the British Labor Party and Member of the House of Commons.)

*   *   *

The organized workers, peasants, and intellectuals of occupied Poland, through the secret convention of their delegates, representing over two thousand groups, proclaim their solidarity with the social and political aspirations of the working people of the world. In the name of the Polish people, we call to the peoples of Europe and of the world to join with us in the struggle against totalitarian tyranny.

We were the first to oppose the barbarian onslaught against free peoples. The first victims of the superiority of the brute force and its military machine, we were also the first to begin underground resistance against the invader whose iron heel tramples Poland and the other countries of Europe. All who fight against the tyranny and crimes of Nazi-totalitarianism are our natural allies. To them we address this message . . . .

We have been driven underground. Every day a blood-thirsty terrorism takes its toll of victims from among us. The slightest association with the struggle for freedom, even the reading or possession of an illegal newspaper, may mean death at the hands of a firing squad or imprisonment and martyrdom in a concentration camp. Yet free life has been born and is developing in the darkness of conspiracy, swelling into a powerful, unconquerable tide, which will sweep over the occupying Powers, who are surrounded by the implacable hatred of all Poles, and will prevent the enemy from striking root and strengthening his hold on our country . . . .

We are still a nation of thirty millions free in spirit, united in the common effort to overthrow the brutal tyranny of the invaders. No force will break us, and we shall defeat the ruses, tricks, and stratagems of the enemy by our own methods of revolutionary work, evolved in a hundred years of struggle against oppressors. Our movement grows daily in scope and strength, negating all attempts of propaganda to undermine our faith in the ultimate restoration of Poland.

A triple wall of occupation frontiers cuts us off from the outside world. The radio forbidden—but carefully concealed from the enemy's eyes—is our only link with other nations. But we know that the spirit of resistance is already awake in the peoples enslaved by Hitlerism and fascism. Every manifestation of revolutionary activity, every news of secret preparation for the overthrow of the oppressor, awakens echoes of solidarity in Poland. Warm comradeship links us with all subjected nations which fight against the intolerable tyranny of the occupation. Our common fate must lead to common action. Cooperation today in the underground struggle to hasten the moment of liberation, to weaken the enemy and thus render the final blow more decisive, will build a firm bond of understanding between the peoples of Europe. This cooperation will enable all the peoples fighting for their deliverance to create a new life on the basis of mutual understanding, a life that will spring up in a free Europe after this war, based on the principle of freedom and equality . . . .

We are fighting, as is every other conquered nation, for freedom and social justice in the several countries and for a new and better life in a Europe organized as a Commonwealth of Free Peoples.

We are firmly convinced that the enemy will be overthrown in the end. At the first opportunity the conquered peoples will rise to strike the death blow to the invader. Therefore, in the name of the Polish people, working and fighting in underground conspiracy, we call to the peoples of the world.

We call to all who have risen in arms to fight the powers of oppression, to all who wage an underground struggle against the dark terror.

We call, too, to the nations which are still outside the armed conflict in this historic tragedy.

We call to the people of Germany, of Italy.

We call to the people of Russia . . . .

We speak to you so that you may know that in even the worst conditions and under the worst persecutions we hold aloft and unfurl the flag of national and social freedom and we shall not lower it or let it fall.

We call to the peoples of the world to join with us.

Look at the bloody face of the "new order" which a victorious totalitarianism holds in promise. Look at our country which is transformed into a vast graveyard! This is the fate which awaits the conquered. . . . The brutal methods of wholesale extermination, the systematic moral and physical tortures which are inflicted today by the invaders upon millions of people outdo the darkest pages of human history.

The war of today, the war against the instigators of war, is above all a defense of the very foundations of civilization, a defense of the most elementary human rights. In this conflict no one can remain neutral. We call upon the working people of the world to unite with us in the struggle against the new tyranny. Let the century old slogan of Polish liberation—FOR YOUR FREEDOM AND OURS—lead us today in our fight for FREEDOM, EQUALITY AND INDEPENDENCE!

THE LEADERSHIP OF THE UNDERGROUND MOVE-
MENT OF THE WORKING MASSES OF POLAND

Somewhere in Poland
February, 1941

THE WARSAW GHETTO UPRISING
OF 1943

*The following excerpts from the clandestine press were printed
and circulated throughout the country at great risk.*
On April 29, 1943, the Information Bulletin *of the Home
Army (No. 17/172) published the following article:*

THE LAST ACT OF THE GREAT TRAGEDY

A week ago, the second act of the savage extermination of
Poland's Jews was initiated. As the Germans began deporting
the forty thousand Jews who still remained in Warsaw, the
ghetto responded with armed resistance and the Jewish
Fighting Organization enlisted in the uneven fight. . . .

Hitherto, the Jews' passive acceptance of death could not
evoke a fighting spirit in the people of Warsaw, but taking
up arms to meet death in this uneven fight ennobled their
martyrdom. The people of the capital listen with approval
and admiration to the sound of the defenders' salvos, as they
anxiously watch the blaze and smoke of the ever-spreading
conflagrations. . . .

It is our strict, Christian duty to help those who have
escaped from the ghetto's flames until the reborn Polish
Republic restores full security and freedom to this part of
Europe. . . .

On May 7, 1943, the Polish Socialist Party organ, Wolność,
Równość, Niepodległość *(Liberty, Equality, Independence), No.
9/115, appealed to the people of all nations to help the fighting
Warsaw Ghetto:*

Comrades and Citizens!

Since April 18 there has been strong resistance in the Warsaw Ghetto to the invaders' determination to massacre the
remaining Polish Jewry. Though condemned to death by

Hitler, the Jews have decided not to surrender themselves to their executioners, and by defending their honor as men and as citizens, they heroically resist the bloody henchmen. . . .
To those Jewish workers who, faced with inevitable death, preferred to perish fighting rather than passively surrender, we send our brotherly greetings and our assurance that their heroic deed will not pass unrecognized. As part of the legend of a fighting Poland, it will help form the foundation of a future, reborn Republic.

We appeal to the nations of the world. Confronted by the monstrous plans for extermination that the Nazis have realized in the past three years, and under the yoke of terrorism that rages over our land, the fiery protest of Poland's sons constantly bursts forth. It calls for the most urgent, immediate support, so that the enemy will be vanquished, before our strength is completely exhausted.

In appealing for the quickest possible attack from the outside, let us now increase our efforts to engender a general Polish uprising that, synchronized with the Allied offensives, will strike the deathblow to all shades of totalitarianism.

THE WARSAW UPRISING OF 1944

The Warsaw Uprising ended in the city's complete devastation, and two hundred thousand people lost their lives. By August 1, 1944, the Poles saw armed struggle as their only course of action. During five years of occupation the inhabitants of Warsaw lived under unspeakable terror and humiliation. They had initially clandestinely resisted the occupation; they now realized the time for taking up arms had come. Aware of the great risk their people would incur in an uprising, the Underground leadership had repeatedly postponed such action. In the spring and summer of 1944, however, the political situation had further deteriorated: the Soviet army had quickly moved into Polish territory; in July, in the eastern town of Chełm, the Communist Polish Committee of National Liberation was proclaimed as the official government, with complete disregard for the legitimate Polish government exiled in London. That the Soviet intention to establish dominion over all Poland would soon be a reality appeared certain.

Under these circumstances, the Home Army command could no longer ignore the mood of Warsaw's populace. While it was unthinkable to allow the Germans to go unpunished, it was equally unacceptable to be liberated by the Soviets, who were already approaching the right bank of the Vistula River. In the capital, forty thousand Home Army soldiers anxiously waited for action, and on August 1, 1944, they received the following order:

TO THE SOLDIERS OF WARSAW

Today I issued the long awaited order to begin open warfare with Poland's eternal enemy—the German invader.

After almost five years of unrelenting underground fighting you now openly take up arms to give freedom back to our Motherland and to mete out the deserved punishment for the atrocities the German criminals have committed on Polish lands.

> General Bór-Komorowski
> *Commander, the Home Army*

THE SURRENDER OF WARSAW: PROCLAMATION OF THE COUNCIL OF NATIONAL UNITY

The Council of National Unity functioned as a democratic parliament for Underground Poland from early 1944 to July 1945. In their founding declaration, representatives of the four major political parties of prewar Poland (Socialist, Peasant, National, and Labor) outlined a progressive program for political and social development in the future Polish Republic.

Excerpts from the proclamation issued by the Council of National Unity at the moment of the tragic Warsaw surrender on October 3, 1944, follow.

TO THE POLISH NATION

Throughout the centuries the Polish national spirit has been shaped by the idea of freedom. We fought for this freedom without help, without compromise; the bones of Polish soldiers have been scattered throughout the world. Such is our historical tradition.

Faithful to this tradition, we undertook, in September 1939, a lone struggle with an enemy superior to us in numbers and arms. We were the first barrier through which the entire German war machine rolled, thus starting World War II. Although defeated, we have not succumbed to the oppressor's yoke. We continue to fight openly in the West and covertly in our country to defend our freedom and that of others and to build a new Poland.

We began open warfare with the Germans in Warsaw on that first day in August 1944. At that time Russian troops were at the gates of Warsaw; our Western Allies were marching toward Berlin; and the Home Army had grown to a size that could not be concealed. We acted when the yearning for freedom that had gathered momentum during the long years of occupation could no longer be controlled, when, finally, the German army rounded up and deported our youth and threatened the capital's destruction.

In undertaking this warfare in Warsaw we could not hope to defeat the Germans alone. Ill equipped, both in numbers and in arms, we counted on aid from Russia and from our Western Allies. . . .

We were deceived in our expectations. . . .

For nine weeks, we fought alone. We fought in the ruins of Warsaw, in the ruins of all we loved. The blessed Polish soil has soaked up our blood.

But when our soldiers fired their last bullets, when mothers could no longer feed their children, when long lines of people could not find water in the empty wells, and when the bodies of those who had died of hunger were brought up from the cellars, we could not continue fighting. We now have to give up.

While the Polish army provides aid to France, Belgium, and Holland so that they may regain their freedom, the Warsaw Uprising fails from lack of assistance. We reserve judgment on this tragic turn of events.

Let a righteous God judge the great wrong that has befallen the Polish nation and mete out just punishment to its perpetrators.

Warsaw, the once glorious capital of Poland, has again passed a heroic test amid its smoldering ruins.

The heroes are the soldiers whose only arms against tanks, planes, and cannons were handguns and gasoline bottles. The heroes are those women who under fire cared for the wounded and delivered dispatches, who cooked for and fed both children and adults in shelled-out cellars, women who, in the midst of the dying, maintained their calm. The heroes are the people of Warsaw.

Immortal is the nation capable of such heroism. Those who died have already conquered; those who live will continue to fight and will conquer.

THE TESTAMENT OF FIGHTING POLAND

The new political circumstances, created by the Yalta Agreement, and especially the recognition of the Communist Provisional Government in Lublin by the Western powers, deprived the Council of National Unity of its right to exist. On July 1, 1945, the Council announced its bitter decision:

The end of the war against Germany left Poland in an extremely difficult, even tragic, situation. While nations in the West regained their freedom after throwing off the yoke of German occupation and could resume their independent existence, Poland, in the wake of a war in which it had suffered the most, found itself under new occupation, under the rule of a government imposed by a foreign power and with no prospect of help from its Western allies.

In these circumstances, the rejection of the Yalta Agreement by the government in London could be no more than a solemn protest. . . . The establishment of the new government and its recognition by the Western powers puts an end to the possibility of an underground resistance openly associated with the generally recognized government in London. The task now before us is that of a determined struggle of the democratic parties in Poland to achieve the national goals and the realization of their programs.

In this struggle Underground Poland does not wish to create difficulties for men of good will who are associated with the Communist Provisional Government of National Unity. Neither does it wish to restrict particular political parties in their choice of tactics that they may want to make or be forced to make.

At a session held on July 1, 1945, all the democratic parties of Underground Poland, represented by the Council of National Unity, unanimously decided to dissolve the Council and to proclaim its dissolution at home and abroad.

303

THE KATYŃ MASSACRE
NOT FORGOTTEN

On April 11, 1980, the Social Self-Defense Committee (KOR) published the following statement:

ON THE FORTIETH ANNIVERSARY OF THE KATYŃ MASSACRE

Forty years ago, the NKVD massacred thousands of Polish officers in the Katyń forest. The date remains merely symbolic, for the crime was not committed [only] on April 11, but the victims were taken gradually from the Kozielsk camp to the place where, only later, the mass graves were found. The date only designates the day when the last letters were sent by the soon-to-be-murdered prisoners of war from Kozielsk, Starobielsk, and Ostaszkowo. In April 1940, one of the prisoners of the Kozielsk camp, Professor Stanisław Świaniewicz, was taken to the NKVD prison in Moscow for questioning. He traveled on the same train that carried the prisoners to the place of the Katyń massacre. The number of people shot in the Katyń forest is still unknown, as is the location of the graves of the prisoners of Starobielsk and Ostaszkowo. Since it has long been known who is guilty of the crime, few believe the gross lies of Soviet propaganda, which has tried to blame the Nazis for it. The direct and indirect perpetrators of the crime were never punished or ever interrogated in the U.S.S.R. In the name of the Polish nation, we demand the disclosure and punishment of the guilty. We do not demand this in the name of revenge, but in the name of justice and truth. We also demand punishment for the crimes committed by the Soviets on Polish citizens after September 17, 1939, when the Red Army in cooperation with the Wehrmacht and the government of Nazi Germany occupied part of the territory of the Second Polish Republic. The government of the Polish People's Republic makes no attempt to disclose the truth about the Katyń crimes and other crimes of genocide committed by the U.S.S.R.; instead it persecutes those who demand such disclosure and who wish to pay tribute to the memory of the victims. Such repressions have an effect contrary to what the authorities intend, for they simultaneously expose the Polish authorities before the public and confirm the truth of the Katyń incident. We believe that the disclosure and punishment of the Stalinist crimes against Polish citizens is crucial to our friendship with the Soviet nation. Our belief is strengthened by the Russian dissidents who also demand that the truth about Katyń be disclosed. We are grateful to them for joining us in this demand. It allows us to hope and trust that true brotherhood between our peoples someday will prevail. We call on our people both here and in exile to observe the sad anniversary of Katyń, and we warn that government repression of our right to commemorate the Katyń crime would evoke our people's contempt.

THE STRUGGLE FOR
FREEDOM AND DEMOCRACY
UNDER COMMUNIST RULE

HISTORICAL BACKGROUND

(1944–1980)

MAREK TARNIEWSKI

The author of the following article is a Polish historian and political essayist.

POLAND'S STRUGGLE FOR DEMOCRACY UNDER COMMUNIST RULE

(1981)

The fate of postwar Poland was shaped by the military situation at the end of World War II. In the beginning of 1944 the Soviet army had already driven the Germans out of eastern Poland and started to exercise full jurisdiction over it. In July 1944, under the aegis of the Soviet government and the Polish Communists, the Polish Committee of National Liberation was established in Moscow. This committee was to govern the territories to which Poland had been restricted.

At the Yalta Conference, in February 1945, the Western powers granted the Soviet Union further concessions regarding Poland. Among other things, it was agreed that a provisional government, supported by the U.S.S.R., would be established. This government was to carry out, as soon as possible, free elections based on a universal and secret ballot. Elections were held two years later. Meanwhile the Communists continued to consolidate power. Aiding in this was the Soviet police apparatus and Soviet advisers, all under the protection of the Soviet army. The Soviet secret police arrested Polish citizens and deported them to the U.S.S.R. Such was also the fate of wartime resistance leaders who, arrested by the NKVD near Warsaw in March 1945, had to stand trial three months later in Moscow. This trial of Polish leaders (Trial 16) demonstrates the degree to which the new Polish state, ruled by Communists, was subjugated by a foreign power.

The new order imposed on Poland in the late 1940s often met with armed resistance. The various political parties still hoped there would be free elections, as stipulated in the Yalta Agreement. Instead, the Communists prepared for these elections over the two-year period in such a way as to ensure the defeat of the Polish Peasants' Party. This party, led by Stanisław Mikołajczyk, was the strongest and the one most opposed to Communist rule. The remaining parties were either not given legal status (the National Party), broken up (the Christian-Democratic Labor Party), or maneuvered into an alliance with the Communists (the Polish Socialist Party). The last, following a purge in the cadres, was thus absorbed in December of 1948 by the Communist Party, and renamed the Polish United Workers' Party (PUWP), while the other two parties were dissolved. Therefore, by the end of the 1940s a forced unification of political organizations had been brought about. The same thing happened in other countries under Soviet domination. For the sake of appearances two substitute political organizations were preserved, namely, the United Peasants' Party, embracing the countryside, and the Democratic Party, made up of the intelligentsia and artisans. These parties were actually subordinated to the PUWP.

Social changes instituted by the Communists in Poland were the nationalization of large industrial plants, commerce, trade, and banking. Large agricultural farms were also nationalized, while plots of land were distributed among the peasants. Nationalization of land occurred mainly in the western and northern territories after the eviction of former German landholders. After the elections, the government began to harass private businesses. Through economic sanctions and police action, private agriculture was suppressed in order to force peasants into collectivization. At the same time, rural self-governing organizations were wiped out, as were other village associations that had been independent of the State. Similarly, in the cities, not only political life, but life in general was brought in line. Independent organizations were liquidated and terror was applied not only against actual political adversaries but also against potential opponents. Primary targets were participants in the anti-German underground movement of World War II, former soldiers of the Home Army, and members of the Polish army who had returned from the West.

The government saw to it that it put its hands on the instruments of force: the police and the army and the means of economic control and of information and influence—censorship, education, and the mass media. Nevertheless, in the early 1950s the majority of peasants' farms still operated outside State control, as did the Catholic Church, which played a significant role in Poland; since the war the country had become almost exclusively Catholic. The government, in an attempt to dominate the Church, created nominal Catholic organizations that were infiltrated by the all-powerful secret police. In addition, many priests and bishops were arrested.

In 1953 this anti-Church campaign culminated in the arrest of the Primate of Poland, Cardinal Stefan Wyszyński. In the early 1950s, some members of the Communist Party were also terrorized, including those who had previously taken part in the organization and consolidation of this system. Władysław Gomułka, the former Secretary General of the Party, was imprisoned. In 1954 he was freed; Cardinal Wyszyński was released two years later, after the death of Stalin, when there was a thaw in the Eastern Bloc. Communist rulers reduced the use of terror, which had ultimately backfired. The trend toward liberalization carried broader social implications and encouraged political demands.

In June of 1956 the workers of Poznan took to the streets shouting "bread and freedom." The crowd, bearing Polish national banners, stormed the Party headquarters, the secret police office, the local prison, and the radio-jamming station. But military troops entered the city and the rebellion was quelled. The Polish United Workers' Party, supposedly representing the interests of the working class, proved to be an instrument of Communist suppression. Strikes and demonstrations of workers broke out in 1970, 1976, and 1980, each time bringing about a policy of "liberalization," or at least a temporary diminution of the Party's drive to monopolize power.

In the mid-1950s police terror was significantly reduced and steps taken to rehabilitate its former victims. Enforced collective farms were broken up and censorship was eased. In 1956 the State and the Church reached a settlement; the official Communist youth organization disbanded, and new organizations arose, which the Party later managed to suppress. In October of 1956 the government promoted "the Polish path to socialism," and the words "Polish sovereignty" were frequently used. In November many Soviet military advisers were withdrawn, and a Polish delegation headed by Władysław Gomułka was received in Moscow. The Soviet Union granted Poland some economic concessions, established regulations regarding the "temporary" stationing of Soviet troops on Polish territory, and also set down conditions for the return of Polish citizens who had found themselves in the Soviet Union after the country's frontiers had been moved westward.

In the Polish press there was a noticeable revitalization. Polish newspapers again carried interesting articles on political and economic topics, and several works of literature and history that would have been banned earlier were now published. Liberalization, however, did not last long. The Party had no intention of allowing freedom or democracy. The government made an appeal to the people to vote for Communist candidates, threatening that otherwise Poland would be erased from the map. Decentralization of industries and the creation of workers' councils were soon aborted, and they fell under the full control of the Party.

After 1956 some gains were maintained. Peasant farms remained independent despite antipeasant economic policies and the permanent threat of collectivization. Actions against the Church did not yield the intended results either. Religion was taken out of the schools, but influence of religion did not diminish, in spite of the 1966 propaganda campaign against the bishops, who were accused of meddling in politics when they wrote a reconciliatory letter to the bishops of Germany. Many Catholic discussion clubs are still extant. Some Catholic periodicals are still published, e.g., *Tygodnik Powszechny* (Universal Weekly), *Znak* (Sign), *Więź* (Tie), and within the limits set by censorship, they try to preserve as much independence as possible.

In the universities, limited independence existed until 1968, when several professors and students were expelled and the propagandistic character of teaching was intensified. The events of 1968 mark the culmination of an anti-intellectual policy, which had already manifested itself in the early 1960s in excessive censorship and in court trials of writers accused of maintaining contacts with émigré organizations.

In January of 1968 a production of the nineteenth-century drama *Forefathers' Eve* by Adam Mickiewicz was closed down in Warsaw. The banning of this work, which deals with Polish-Russian relations, caused protests among intellectuals and students. The authorities responded by initiating a brutal campaign against "revisionists" and "Zionists." In March 1968 a peaceful protest movement that included nearly all the universities in Poland led to the creation of student committees and to the formulation of social programs, which were also to provide assistance to those persecuted and arrested. The government's propaganda campaign virtually ignored this student movement.

After March 1968 one of the darkest periods in the suppression of cultural activities began. Unapproved writings had to take refuge in émigré publications, such as the Paris-based monthly periodical *Kultura,* while a few works that had escaped censorship still circulated in Poland in the form of typewritten sheets.

In December 1970 the announcement of a price increase for food provoked strikes and demonstrations, particularly in the cities of the Baltic coast—Gdańsk, Gdynia, and Szczecin. In Gdańsk, troops opened fire on workers leaving the shipyard—ten years later a monument was erected in honor of those who died there. In Gdynia workers were shot on their way to work. The workers' protest was suppressed and followed by changes in the ruling elite. Edward Gierek replaced Władysław Gomułka as First Secretary of the Party. Gierek announced a program for economic growth based on an increased number of Western credits. These credits were to enable imports of Western technology and patents, which were to raise the quality of Polish products, improving their competitiveness on world markets. The organization of the centrally planned economic system remained unchanged. By the mid-1970s, it became evident that the "economic miracle" was an illusion and that more investments were required, for which new credits were necessary.

The government sought to legitimize the specific role of the Communist Party and to solidify the special relationship that binds Poland to the Soviet Union. It was announced that necessary amendments to the constitution would be introduced. This announcement created a wave of protests. In February 1976 the final amendments were ratified, although formulated in a rather vague fashion. These amendments were, above all, an expression of the self-assured isolation of the rulers and their insensitivity to the mood of the people. This was again demonstrated after the price increases announced in June of 1976. Workers' protests, particularly in Radom and Ursus, both near Warsaw, compelled the government to rescind these increases in less than twenty-four hours. The government took action against the workers by using police force and propaganda. These measures, however, were counteracted. Following the workers' demonstrations, students and intellectuals announced their solidarity with the workers and offered legal and financial assistance to those who had been arrested or dismissed from their jobs. In August 1976 the Workers Defense Committee (KOR) was founded as the body to coordinate these actions. One year later, after personnel changes, the committee was renamed the Social Self-Defense Committee-KOR.

The changes in the constitution resulted in a proliferation of independent publications, circulating as typewritten and mimeographed copies. Distributed in this manner, among others, were texts published by the Polish League for Independence, a group of writers who remained anonymous.

In March 1977 the Movement for the Defense of Human and Civil Rights was formed. This group, like KOR, did not seek the permission of the government, which, however, chose not to interfere with these activities. Other groups of this kind were also formed: Farmers' Self-Defense Committees, Founding Committees of Independent Trade Unions, Student Solidarity Committees, and the Society of Scientific Courses. This type of independent organizations had previously not been tolerated. All these groups aimed at a common goal: the country's independence and the building of a democratic society.

Since the war the Communists have directed many campaigns against the Catholic Church. In general, they have mainly tried to reduce its influence. The building of churches was not permitted, seminary students were conscripted in the army, the Church was denied practically any access to the media, and persons professing their religious beliefs have been refused higher positions. Nevertheless, the influence of the Church in Polish society remains substantial. When in 1976 the archbishop of Cracow, Cardinal Karol Wojtyła, was elected Pope and a year later visited Poland, not only the intensity of the people's religious feeling was evident but also their ability to organize themselves.

The new price increases, introduced in July 1980, again triggered a wave of strikes, which eventually spread throughout Poland. Workers formulated their demands, which at the end of August became the basis for their negotiations with the government representatives. The consolidated and well-organized activity of the workers brought about the signing of agreements between representatives of the government and the Inter-factory Strike Committees in Gdańsk, Szczecin, and cities of Silesia. The principal victory won by the workers was the government's consent to the creation of self-governing trade unions operating outside the control of the Party, the State, and existing government unions.

The new unions adopted the name "Solidarity," and despite obstacles presented by the government they began to organize, consolidate, and defend workers' interests as well as the interests of society at large, such as freedom of expression and the observance of laws by the rulers.

In late 1980 the threat of armed Soviet intervention appeared not only in official propaganda but also in troop concentrations on the borders. Poland's struggle for democracy, for achieving conditions of greater national freedom, has again proven difficult. But in Gdańsk, on the monument that commemorates the tenth anniversary of the massacre of the shipyard workers, the anchors attached to three huge crosses symbolize hope.

VOICES OF THE OPPOSITION

EDWARD LIPIŃSKI

(Born 1888)

The economist and statesman Edward Lipiński was a member of the Polish Socialist Party prior to its liquidation. A university professor and member of the Polish Academy of Sciences, he is one of the most influential representatives of the Polish Human Rights Movement.
Excerpts from his article published in the Polish samizdat Krytyka, *No. 4, 1980 (reprinted by Aneks, London), follow.*

FOR POLAND'S FREEDOM

. . . The Polish struggles for independence resulted from the determination of those who chose to be the makers of history. Władysław Gomułka became the gravedigger of the limited freedom Poland did achieve in 1956.

We have begun our struggle for freedom of thought, our struggle against Russification, which has deprived Poland of its chances for full development. But we are confronted with brutal police repression, punitive sentences by servile courts, and dismissals from work. The entire government apparatus conspires to perpetuate our bondage—army, police, and courts, as well as the hundreds of thousands of individuals who engage in these outrages. Thirty years of Russian domination did not pass without affecting morality, and so it has not been difficult to find collaborationists.

Even in the period when Poland was partitioned, the vital core of the nation was not as seriously endangered as it is now. The censorship, which under tsarist rule destroyed all manifestations of a free spirit and undermined the aspirations of Polish culture, was not as brutal as it is today. Upon a nation of Christian and liberal roots that has placed freedom above all else, the Russians have imposed a political system derived from Asiatic despotism. The introduction of a new economic system and the proclamation of a new epoch of growth have caused severe deficiencies in all areas of life

319

while simultaneously destroying the possibility of self-government and individual initiative. The imposed dependence on
Russian expansionary imperialism has burdened the country
with obligations that are to the detriment of the people's
welfare.

. . . Although Poland's chances in the struggle for freedom
remain uncertain, the idea of freedom must be kept alive in
both thought and action. An omnipotent and ubiquitous
bureaucracy has caused untold damage to our nation. The
bureaucracy in our economy, in the life of our towns, settlements, and schools, has deprived citizens of any influence
on their daily life and their future. In this Asiatic political
system, a person is state property and, as such, must recognize the monolithic character of views set forth by the party
tsar of the day. Such a system impoverishes the life of the
entire nation and impedes its growth.

We must not waver in the belief that history will again
afford us our chance for independence. But have we done
all we could to take advantage of the possibilities that already
exist? It seems to me that we have not. Terror paralyzes the
will to fight of the intelligentsia, who bear the heaviest responsibility for our people's destiny. Although some opposition movement has grown in Poland, those who should take
a stand have still not engaged in the fight. Far too many
members of the intelligentsia have opted to collaborate with
the regime. Far too many of the nation's leaders refuse to take
a stand even when such action would result in no more than
the possible loss of minor privileges. If the intelligentsia,
particularly its prominent members, were to participate actively in the dissident movement, the political situation
would radically change for the better. . . .

ZYGMUNT ŻUŁAWSKI

(1880–1949)

Zygmunt Żuławski, a leader of the Polish Socialist Party, retained his ideals to the end of his life. Following World War II, during the period of the power struggle of the various political parties, he opposed both the Communists and the compromising Socialists in his own party. In Parliament, he protested censorship, the fixing of elections, and the lies of Communist propaganda.

The following excerpts from speeches he delivered to the Polish Congress in 1947 were first published in the Polish samizdat Krytyka, No. 4, 1980 (reprinted by Aneks, London).

PARLIAMENTARY SPEECH AT THE
FOURTH SESSION OF THE CONGRESS
(February 8, 1947)

... The July Manifesto, the program of the Polish Workers' Party and the Polish Socialist Party, as well as the Governing Coalition in their electoral proclamations, guaranteed freedom of expression.

I thought that if I joined you, the Polish Socialist Party, I would be able to elaborate on my views of freedom and social justice, especially since both were officially guaranteed. But these promises have not been kept. They have prohibited me from speaking and writing freely.

Thus, I was very surprised to hear a Polish writer on radio praising the present freedom of speech in our country. It was explained to me that censorship of the press was necessary in regard to foreign policy. However, the opposite seems to be the case. Restrictions on the press and on elections discredit us. We have nothing to hide from the world, and I do not know what the world could "spy out" of us. America is far away, and more importantly, whenever we received anything from her, it was goodness itself. During World War I, President Wilson first supported our struggle for independence, then Hoover's Committee helped us to survive, and now UNRRA [United Nations Relief and Rehabilitation Administration] does it. And we will never forget that, had it not been for England's resistance, the Nazis would have crushed us. Finally, regarding the Soviets, despite past and present differences, we want to live in friendship with them, not only because of our Slavic kinship, but because we realize that any Polish government that did not cooperate with the Soviets would not be viable.

Since it is not without risk for me to speak, I shall be very careful in whatever I say. At a banquet in Moscow, in the presence of Mr. Stalin, I expressed our sincere wish for friendship with the Soviet Union. But I now declare in bitterness that those who persist in calling us reactionaries do not promote this friendship.

Mikołajczyk and I are the Polish reactionaries!

One can tarnish the reputation of Chairman Mikołajczyk, one can even crush the Polish Peasants' Party, and yet Mikołajczyk's name remains today a symbol of the peasants' ideals. And even though Mr. Mikołajczyk may fall under the blows of his accusers, protest for the sake of freedom, supported by the Polish Peasants' Party, has at least saved our country's honor.

For my part, I want to defend socialism and its purity. I also want to be the conscience of those who despite their declarations and promises could not resist the lure of power. Prime Minister Osóbka can present me to foreign journalists as a feeble old man, and Doctor Drobner, long suffering from self-exaltation, can send me to an early grave, but I would rather be dead than live betraying my ideals.

PARLIAMENTARY SPEECH AT THE
SEVENTEENTH SESSION OF THE CONGRESS
(June 20, 1947)

The duty of government is not to create mammoth armies and security forces but to be just, to ensure the fair distribution of wealth and to guard against exploitation.

Before making further promises, what have you, gentlemen, achieved in living up to your duties? The people ask:

Is this truly the new social order? Is this freedom and social justice? Has exploitation really been eliminated? . . .

Before the war, I wrote in the workers' press that nationalization [of industries] alone will not obviate social wrongs, will not free one man from being exploited by another. Whether a capitalist or the government is the exploiter makes no difference to the worker. It also matters little to him whether he is paid by a nationalized or a private industry, whether he buys in a cooperative or a private store. What does matter is how much he has to work to earn enough to buy his necessities.

Law and order, so eloquently described by Prime Minister Cyrankiewicz just a moment ago, applies not only to the citizen but also to those who make the laws and those who execute them.

Finally, since I disagree with the policies of this government, I will vote against the proposed budget, which guarantees neither general freedom nor social justice.

MIECZYSŁAW JASTRUN

(Born 1903)

In both his literary works and his political views, the poet and essayist Mieczysław Jastrun expresses moral and philosophical concerns. Following the events of the "Polish October" of 1956 and Władysław Gomułka's return to power, there was a period of relative liberalization. At the Seventh Convention of the Union of Polish Writers, in December 1956, Jastrun agitated for freedom of speech, for social and political justice, and for the purification of the Polish language. This speech was later published in the periodical of the young intelligentsia, Po Prostu (Straightforward), No. 50, December 9, 1956.

ON FREEDOM OF SPEECH

(1956)

I would like to speak about what is crucial for all of us as writers, namely, the issue of free speech. Freedom of speech is also freedom of conscience; freedom of speech is the fundamental prerequisite of literary creation. Words must resume their original, their true meaning.

As we know, the life of a nation gives words their meaning. Falsification of that life eviscerates the meaning of words. Not long ago [before the "thaw"] freedom meant bondage, and independence meant dependence. Totalitarianism, in whatever guise it assumes, empties words of their meaning. The Nazis called the heroes of the Polish Underground bandits, just as the tsars had termed the revolutionaries of 1848 and 1905. That Hungarian freedom fighters today are called bandits is a bitter irony of history.

Never before has public awareness been so deceived by words twisted out of their true meaning. . . .

We writers must cleanse this dangerous ambiguity from our language. It endangers not only our moral concepts but also the various nuances of our spiritual life. I doubt that we are sufficiently aware of the growing indistinctness of terms such as "violence" and "force," "weakness" and "decadence." So long as the words used to describe ethical concepts lack definite meaning there can be no serious writing. I am dealing here not only with the problem of free speech; the issue here is how to restore dignity to the writer's craft. The best evidence of the collapse of humanistic values in our time is that the intelligentsia have, as in other totalitarian countries, resigned themselves to virtual complicity with the regime, siding with the strong rather than with the weak and subjugated.

The pervasive and persistent totalitarian way of thinking makes it difficult to liberate speech from government control and distortion. . . . Today a writer's language cannot be distinguished from that of the government. Conformity of this kind leads to strict censorship. Not long ago, censorship confiscated books not only for what was in them, but also for what they failed to include. For us, the control of the unsaid was a completely new kind of coercion. In [the newspaper] *The Tribune of the Peoples* Mickiewicz wrote that after the December Uprising [of 1825], "on the day of the execution of Colonel Pestel [one of the revolutionists], his father, Senator Pestel, not only had to make an appearance at Court but also had to have a cheery countenance and participate in the conversation. Russian law forbade his silence."

Censorship extended its control even into the past. As in Orwell's *1984,* a special Department of Learning undertook to change the past, thus destroying the very grounds of knowledge. Censorship not only appropriated the actual past but also affected our emotional life. Pessimism and sadness were banished as bourgeois and liberal emotions. Even death could be confiscated. The editor of a literary magazine rejected a short story whose protagonist had died. "A positive hero cannot die," he said.

Although a lyric poet might be concerned about the freedom to express various human emotions, I am concerned about something more: the right to judge our age. This right can be realized only by removing the notion of taboos. Avoidance of forbidden themes as if they were plague-infested areas leads through fear to hypocrisy, to demoralization, and ultimately, to disbelief in truth. Because of such prohibitions, twentieth-century dictators have been able to reinstate medieval methods of torture.

Even among writers there are those who do not believe in the need to fight for truth. Frightened by the conflict between the great powers, by the possibility of nuclear war, they say: "It is not worth it." I, however, must contradict this assertion. It *is* worth it; history is more than the arena for slaughter and madness. And even if the triumph of justice is brief, as brief as a human life, nevertheless such a life in justice is worthwhile.

The Polish nation that manifested vitality and wisdom during the days of the "Polish October" has no reason to fear free speech or its writers.

STANISŁAW BARAŃCZAK

(Born 1946)

Poet, essayist, and translator, Stanisław Barańczak is a promi-
nent member of the Polish opposition movement. For years his
books have been banned, but he has published them in the
Polish samizdats and émigré presses. In April 1981 he was al-
lowed to leave Poland, and he has assumed a professorship in
Polish literature at Harvard University.

Barańczak wrote the following article (here abridged) for the
Biennale 1977 in Venice, where unofficial Polish publications
were exhibited.

BEHIND THE FACADE

In 1787 the Tsarina Catherine II took a journey through
the southern territories of her domain. She wanted to see the
country close at hand, to see for herself how simple Russian
people lived. Since they lived in conditions far worse than the
Tsarina was led to believe, Prince Potemkin, her favorite,
had an ingenious idea that would spare his ruler disappoint-
ment. Mock-ups of villages and hamlets were quickly built
along the journey's route: fake facades of peasant cottages
that, seen from afar, looked neat, new, and pretty, though
they concealed the view of the wild steppe behind them, or, at
best, that of a wretched, ordinary farmstead. But since the
Tsarina looked at this strange decor from afar and, moreover,
through the windows of a carriage traveling at great speed,
the illusion was complete. The ruler returned satisfied from
her tour and bestowed new favors on her favorite.

This is how the famous "Potemkin villages" were born.
The term denotes the peculiarity of a political system that
erects contraptions of illusion and mock-ups for the benefit
of the distant observer. They are to give the impression that
all is well, that the country is flourishing and its citizens are
contented. "Potemkin villages" is a key term applied meta-
phorically to anything that presents an impressive facade to

conceal a not very impressive reality behind it. We, inhabitants of Eastern Europe, encounter such phenomena every day. We work on State farms where well-fed cattle, borrowed from independent local farmers, are brought in for the day of a State dignitary's visit. We live in towns and cities where hovels intended for demolition are rendered new for the leader's motorcade. We see gigantic neon advertisements over empty shops. We read newspapers that bring daily reports of universal enthusiasm that we neither feel ourselves nor notice anywhere around. Countless "Potemkin villages" make up our daily experience.

We do not always realize, however, that our culture, too, is one big "Potemkin village." Yet, this very culture, in its schizophrenic dichotomy, erects a system of mock-ups to conceal the reality. One of our writers recently noted that the essence of the system prevailing here is a lie. This mendacity, this Orwellian double-talk, permeates every sphere of our life. The enormous chain of the various authorities who supervise, censor, and agitate produces a minimum of authentic values. Such values appear dangerous to those who govern. In their view a country should present itself as a huge, monolithic facade adorned by all kinds of embellishments that give the overwhelming impression of prosperity and health, while behind its facade there is simply nothing.

The metaphor "Potemkin village" is not entirely apt, in that the facade conceals neither emptiness nor crushing poverty. Instead, it hides less ostentatious but quite adequate conditions. . . . In today's Poland general conditions are neither pluralistic nor monolithic. They are official, artificially constructed, and uniform on the one hand, and unofficial, authentic, and multiform on the other. It is, in fact, the contrast of bondage and freedom. And this antagonism is quite fundamental, since freedom, fighting for its right to speak the truth, is also fighting for its own social role, and in this way, for its very life. Giving up these values, it would condemn itself to its own destruction.

This two-facedness of thinking and speaking, this inner rift, is also evident in our everyday language. The news report uses the fake language of appearances. The citizen hears, for example, that "crews manning the urban bakeries continue their fight to bring provisions to the people." When he then goes to a bakery he sees that the supply situation is hopeless. We are, then, used to two languages: the language of platitudes used with superiors in official circumstances, and the other, more genuine and colorful, everyday language, which often parodies the official double-talk.

A similar split characterizes what we might call the "folklore" of our culture. Unofficial folklore manifests itself in harsh political jokes, songs, and uncensored verse, and through the furtive distribution of foreign books and samizdat publications. . . . To publish a book in Poland inevitably condemns its author to one form or another of dependence on the official managers of cultural policy. What, then, of a painting that "lives" only if shown at an exhibition, or of a play that cannot be performed without a theater? For each of these the system of centralized administration of cultural activities enforces the dramatic choice: either—at the price of various concessions—to knuckle under and compromise, or to condemn oneself to silence, solitude, nonexistence. . . . Censorship pushes all that is authentic into the sphere of the unofficial. But at the same time everything that is unofficial openly strives to make itself publicly known. In the past, if the authorities forbade the printing of a book, the writer put his manuscript in the drawer and suffered in silence, or, what was worse, made the decision to cut and change it by way of compromise. Nowadays, he takes his manuscript to some young friends, who enthusiastically turn the handle of a duplicating machine made out of a do-it-yourself wringer. The book will find considerable underground circulation. It will be read with all the greater voracity, since truth and authenticity are automatically expected from an unofficial publication.

. . . The Poland of 1977 is a truly strange country. There is feverish activity beyond the dead mass of the outward facade, away from all the exasperating cultural activities of the zealous journalists, the obedient scribblers, the sculptors erecting statues and monuments in honor of the all-powerful state, and those who produce "socially committed" songs. There are literary meetings in private homes. Satirical songs and poems are born. Discussions, exhibitions, and theatrical performances are organized. And all this is done without the approval—and even without the knowledge—of the authorities. We have long ago abandoned the hope of taming the Leviathan. Rather it is the State, terrified by the political situation, that tries in vain to tame unofficial cultural activities. But it is too late. A new alternative is now open. Instead of "compromise or silence" we are saying "compromise or independent action, "compromise or authenticity," "compromise or freedom."

THE CHURCH IN DEFENSE
OF HUMAN RIGHTS

Throughout the Communist domination of Poland the Church has consistently opposed the ruling ideology. Even during the most repressive Stalinist period, the Church, carrying on its religious mission, survived persecution and demanded constitutional rights for the oppressed people of Poland. For years the only legal opposition in the country, the Church proved to be an influential moral and political force. During the persecution of students in 1968, the Polish Episcopate addressed the following letter to Prime Minister Cyrankiewicz.

A LETTER OF THE
POLISH EPISCOPATE

(1968)

. . . The most recent student demonstrations have a social and cultural, not a political character. The students' appeal to the academic authorities expresses their confidence in the government rather than revolt against its authority. In fact, young people see in the constitution a guarantee of those very rights they claim.

. . . Both academic and government authorities could, in a fatherly manner, have easily reached an understanding with the students without the intervention of the police. It is thus unfortunate that these agencies intervened in the student demonstrations on the grounds of the university.

. . . For a long time now, people have been seriously troubled by the methods the Public Security Services adopted during the student demonstrations and the Millennium celebrations of the Church. In a free society, a truncheon must not replace common sense and justice. . . .

The student demonstrations further inflamed demands for freedom of opinion asserted by the general public, writers, and the Episcopate. The citizens' right to accurate information, guaranteed by the Constitution of the Polish People's Republic and the United Nations Charter, requires freedom of the press and restriction of censorship. The Episcopate understands the indignation of the young at the dishonesty of the press; the Church itself has experienced the corrosive effects of an unscrupulous press.

Anxious for peace and hoping to avoid deepening the split between the people and the government, we propose the following:

1. freedom for the imprisoned students;

333

2. an end to harsh methods of investigation and punishment;

3. truthful rather than tendentious reporting by the press;

4. termination of the repressive measures of the Public Security Services, which awaken disgraceful memories of the past.

We submit these views to the Prime Minister on the basis of Article 5, Section 2, and Article 73 of the Constitution of the Polish People's Republic, and as citizens of that nation concerned with peace in society and with guarding Poland's good name in the world.

STEFAN CARDINAL WYSZYŃSKI
KAROL CARDINAL WOJTYŁA
Archbishops and Bishops of Poland

LESZEK KOŁAKOWSKI

(Born 1927)

*One of the foremost philosophers of our time, Leszek Kołakow-
ski began his career as a Marxist critic of Catholic philosophy.
In the mid-1950s his social philosophy radically changed. He rejected Communist dogma and was consequently expelled from
the Party. Deprived of his professorship at Warsaw University,
he left Poland during the "cultural pogrom" of 1968.*

*Kołakowski taught and lectured at major universities in Can-
ada and the United States, and at present teaches in England at
All Souls College, Oxford. He has maintained close contacts with
the human rights movement in Poland and in other countries.*

*The following excerpts are from his article "Christian Poland
and Human Rights," published in* Index on Censorship *(Vol. 8,
No. 6, 1979), a London-based journal devoted to the works of
writers banned in their own countries.*

CHRISTIAN POLAND AND HUMAN RIGHTS

Despite all the losses it suffered, along with the entire population, in the persecution and massacres of the occupation, the
Church emerged as spiritually influental as it had been
before the war. It was the confrontation with the Communist
power that brought about formidable changes in all aspects
of Catholic life. If the Polish process of totalitarianism on
the Soviet model never reached the level of other socialist
countries, this is largely due to the popular resistance which
the Church itself symbolised. The extent to which it was
subject to harassment and repression varied, depending on
many internal and external political factors; yet all attempts
to split the Church from within failed. The ruling party
supported and organised—often using police methods—various pseudo-Catholic "progressive" groups intended to break
down the unity of the Church, but despite the enormous
effort invested by the state, the outcome was meagre indeed.
Throughout the post-war years the Church has been subjected to various forms of pressure, but it has remained the

only powerful form of organised cultural activity that has escaped nationalisation, and has managed to preserve its independence from the state. Not surprisingly, it provided an outlet for all sorts of social and political discontent, and though it never encouraged any violent expression of opposition, it naturally absorbed—by the sheer fact of not being state-owned—both the feelings of national humiliation that resulted from the forcible incorporation of Poland into the Soviet empire, and the people's passive resistance towards such oppressive and mendacious a power system.

It cannot be denied that neither in the Stalinist period nor later, when a shaky *modus vivendi* between the Church and state had been reached (systematically infringed by the state though it was), the repressive measures intended to disable religion and the Church in Poland never reached the degree of brutality characteristic of the Soviet state. The forms they took were of a different order: chicaneries to prevent children from receiving religious instruction in proper centres outside the schools (religion is forbidden in the state education, of course); restrictions imposed on the Catholic press, including a particularly devastating and vicious censorship; numerous interdictions and limitations on the building of places of worship; persistent violation of the Church's autonomy to appoint bishops; systematic discrimination against avowed Catholics in all areas of social life.

The point is that no Communist nor, for that matter, any ideological state can afford the separation of Church from state because separation implies that the state is indifferent to citizens' religious views and that their social positions and careers are unaffected by allegiances to a particular denomination. A state that is ruled by a single party professing a particular *Weltanschauung* with all-embracing pretensions—even if no one takes its doctrine seriously any more—is unable, in principle, to treat its citizens as equals, irrespective of their faith. It cannot be a lay state in the true sense, nor can it give up the goal, hopeless as it may be, of converting its citizens to its creed. Those who openly profess a different belief are bound to remain second-class subjects even if they are not directly punished by law. Thus, Poland's citizens are

the fight well beyond its own particular cause. . . .

Once Communism had been reduced to a matter of sheer power, and its doctrinal aspirations were no longer being taken seriously even by its own ruling parvenu class, attempts to wear it out from within became pointless.

This process reached its culmination in 1968, the year of a major cultural pogrom in Poland. After a period of inevitable disruption, the altered situation released new forms of democratic opposition, and the secular/Christian distinction finally, and deservedly, lost its meaning. The current antitotalitarian movement does not operate in perfect unison, and the various groups tend to stress different aspects of their struggle against the dictatorial order. At times, they feud among themselves. But the division into Catholics and non-Catholics, believers and sceptics, is non-existent in political terms. Both in the legal Catholic press and in the numerous illegal (albeit not clandestine) journals, priests and former party members appear side by side. Many ex-Marxists, who are only rarely allowed to appear in print, find refuge there.

Thus in Poland Christianity has become the most unyielding repository of traditional libertarian values. If the authorities view the Church as a kind of rival party that they failed to destroy, this is because they are unable to imagine human actions other than those motivated by greed for power and privilege. Although the Church, due to its independent position, acts as an outlet for a variety of feelings and needs within the opposition, it only does so because the source of its strength lies ultimately in its faith and not in any political doctrine. It must be stressed that many of the young and old who are attracted to the Christian tradition were brought up in an intellectual milieu that was either irreligious or indifferent to the Church. Some find in it an irreplaceable vehicle of cultural continuity, the expression *par excellence,* of historical national identity, and the only reliable source of moral guidance. Others return to Christianity in full response to its religious message.

By a cruel irony of destiny—or of Providence—the official, ruling ideology, once rooted in the ideas of the Enlightenment, has become host to all the vices formerly attributed to the Roman Church. It was the Church which used to be reproached with hampering independent thought, of stifling learning, of upholding indefensible social privilege, of employing massive untruths in order to promote its worldly interests, of persecuting heretics and Jews, of combating democracy. At various periods in history some of these charges were well-founded; some might have been exaggerated, but still they contained a sufficient basis of truth. None of them can justifiably be raised against the contemporary Church in Poland today; all of them are true when applied to the ruling party. It is Communism that has become the incarnation of obscurantism, fear of enlightenment and truth, the persecutor of free cultural expression, the seedbed of falsehood and anti-Semitism. Furthermore, even when the Church was rightly blamed for its intolerance and backwardness, it never had guns at its disposal (as Stalin aptly observed).

The Church in Poland has strenuously maintained its right to perform its evangelical mission, and has asserted man's universal right to spiritual liberty, but has been equally emphatic in its insistence that it does not issue prescriptions on political matters. No doubt it is difficult to clearly divorce the cause of human rights from constitutional questions. In fact, the latter is not in issue in Poland where the Declaration and Covenants of Human Rights are in principle legally binding (much as they may be made void by a number of specific laws or by the deliberate vagueness of other legislation). The concept of human rights suffices both for the democratic opposition to phrase all its claims, and for the Church to struggle for its place in public life and for freedom of expression. Thus the moral foundation of both is essentially the same. Having taken up the cause of human rights as its own, and having given it universal meaning—by no means confining it to Communist countries—the Church does not need to desist from its condemnation of violence even for just ends.

In Poland, both as a matter of principle and for obvious circumstantial reasons, the Church has never endorsed, let alone incited, violent opposition to the regime. In critical moments, when violence was likely or indeed had erupted, the Church used its influence to promote calm. Neither the democratic opposition nor the Church are interested in violent clashes which could have disastrous consequences, including a Soviet invasion; and this is an interest they share with the ruling party. This common interest is strong enough to allow room for a limited agreement between Church and state, although it is insufficient to bring about the removal of various restrictions imposed on religious life, let alone to loosen the intolerable fetters of censorship. But the government, having lost all credibility among the population (even the qualified and shaky legitimacy it achieved by the economic improvements of the early seventies), is compelled to canvass for the support of the Church to avoid an uncontrollable explosion of popular wrath that could bring Soviet tanks on to the streets of Warsaw.

It is common knowledge that the government has lost the battle for what the Poles refer to as "the government of the souls," and that the Church has remained the greatest, unquestioned authority in the country. . . .

Cardinal Wojtyła's election to the Holy See and his recent trip to his native land enormously fortified both the Church's moral authority and the steadfastness of Polish Catholicism. By thus increasing the chances of anti-totalitarian resistance, dangers as well as hopes may breed, especially when the economic failures of the government provoke more and more fury. May we hope that the ruling party, under its self-imposed duress and just to avoid the worst, will seek a minimal consensus by letting the population voice its grievances and by enlarging, even slightly, the extent to which people can influence the way they are ruled? Thus far, experience has not been encouraging, but nothing is absolutely precluded.

Whatever happens, it is clear that the vicissitudes of Christian life in Poland have led to a situation the significance of which goes far beyond the confines of its own borders. This kind of coalescence of Christianity, in its worldly aspects, with the human rights movement and democratic values, has never before been achieved. It might herald dramatic changes throughout the entire Christian world.

THE EMERGENCE OF
OPPOSITION ORGANIZATIONS

THE LETTER OF THE
34 INTELLECTUALS

After a few years of relative liberalization, following the so-called "Polish October" (1956), the Communist regime renewed its suppression of free thought. Władysław Gomułka, the Party leader, began his attacks on liberal intellectuals. The progressive journal Po Prostu (Straightforward) was discontinued, the circulation of other liberal journals limited. Censorship was tightened, many books were banned, and the Crooked Circle, a political discussion club, was closed by the police.

The growing dissatisfaction in Warsaw's cultural circles resulted in the "Letter of the 34," addressed to Prime Minister Józef Cyrankiewicz. It was delivered by Antoni Słonimski, the celebrated poet and former chairman of the Union of Polish Writers, on March 14, 1964:

The limiting of the paper allotment for printing books and journals as well as the tightening of the censorship of the press have created a situation that threatens the development of our national culture. The undersigned, claiming the right to criticism and free discussion as a basic element of progress, and further motivated by patriotic concern, demand a change in Poland's cultural policy in conformity with the rights guaranteed by the Polish Constitution, in the interest of the welfare of the nation.

LEOPOLD INFELD, MARIA DABROWSKA, ANTONI SŁONIMSKI, PAWEŁ JASIENICA, KONRAD GÓRSKI, MARIA OSSOWSKA, KAZIMIERZ WYKA, TADEUSZ KOTARBIŃSKI, KAROL ESTREICHER, STANISŁAW PIGOŃ, JERZY TUROWICZ, ANNA KOWALSKA, MIECZYSŁAW JASTRUN, JERZY ANDRZEJEWSKI, ADOLF RUDNICKI, PAWEŁ HERTZ, STANISŁAW MACKIEWICZ, STEFAN KISIELEWSKI, JAN PARANDOWSKI, ZOFIA KOSSAK, JERZY ZAGÓRSKI, JAN KOTT, WACŁAW SIERPIŃSKI, KAZIMIERZ KUMANIECKI, ARTUR SANDAUER, WŁADYSŁAW TATARKIEWICZ, EDWARD LIPIŃSKI, STANISŁAW DYGAT, ADAM WAŻYK, MARIAN FALSKI, MELCHIOR WAŃKOWICZ, JAN SZCZEPAŃSKI, ALEKSANDER GIEYSZTOR, JULIAN KRZYŻANOWSKI

STUDENTS IN DEFENSE OF DEMOCRATIC FREEDOM

The year of 1968 left a shameful memory of the so-called "cultural pogrom." The entire apparatus of repression was activated to annihilate all traces of independent thought in Poland's social and cultural life. With the closing of Adam Mickiewicz's patriotic drama, Forefathers' Eve, *on charges of being anti-Russian, the repressive forces grew to absurd proportions. Intellectuals, students, and Jews were the first victims of the ruthless brutality that answered protests. Eventually, the majority of Jews were forced to leave Poland.*

The following Resolution of the Warsaw University students was read at the protest rally on March 8, 1968.

RESOLUTION

We, the students of Warsaw's institutions of higher learning, having met on March 8, 1968, declare:

We protest the violations of the Constitution of the Polish People's Republic. The repression of the student protests against the prohibition of staging *Forefathers' Eve* at the National Theater openly violates Article 71 of the Constitution.

We will not be deprived of our rights to defend the democratic and independent traditions of the Polish nation.

We will not remain silent before repression. We demand the annulment of the decision to expel our colleagues Adam Michnik and Henryk Szlajfer.

We demand the annulment of disciplinary proceedings against Ewa Morawska, Marta Petruszewicz, Józef Dajczgewand, Maria Dąbrowska, Sławomir Kretkowski, Jan Lityński, Wiktor Nagórski, and Andrzej Połowczyk, accused of having participated in the student demonstration following the last performance of *Forefathers' Eve.* We demand that Józef Dajczgewand's stipend be restored to him.

We demand that, within two weeks from today, the Minister of General and Higher Learning, Henryk Jabłoński, and the Rector of Warsaw University respond to the above requests.

We, the students of Warsaw . . . express our full support of the resolution of the Plenary Meeting of the Warsaw section of the Union of Polish Writers. They denounced the increase of censorship and the banning of Adam Mickiewicz's *Forefathers' Eve*. We declare our solidarity with these writers in defense of our cultural aspirations and our national freedom.

THE LETTER OF
59 INTELLECTUALS TO THE
SPEAKER OF THE DIET OF THE
POLISH PEOPLE'S REPUBLIC

Warsaw, December 5, 1975
To the Speaker of the Diet,

Herewith, I transmit to you a copy of the letter with reference to the proposed changes in the Constitution of the Polish People's Republic The letter has been signed by 59 persons. I hereby attest to the authenticity of these signatures.

I have been authorized to inform you, Mr. Speaker, that a separate letter concerning the same problem will be sent to you, signed by about 300 research workers, students, and graduates of institutions of higher learning.

With expressions of the highest regard and respect,

PROF. DR. EDWARD LIPIŃSKI

P.S. Copies of this letter are being sent to the Council of State of the Polish People's Republic, the Parliamentary clubs, and to the secretariat of the Primate of Poland.

The "Directives for the VII Congress of the Polish United Workers Party" contained an announcement of changes in the Constitution. After the conference at Helsinki at which the Polish government together with 34 governments of other states solemnly confirmed the Universal Declaration of Human Rights, we consider that the implementation of these basic freedoms should become a new stage in the history of the nation and in the lives of individuals. Motivated by civic concern, we consider that the Constitution and the legislation based on it should, above all else, guarantee the following civil liberties:

—Freedom of conscience and religious practice. These freedoms do not exist when people adhering to religious beliefs or manifesting a conception of life differing from the one officially prevailing are not admitted to a considerable part of the executive posts in public offices and institutions, social organizations and the national economy. Therefore all citizens, without reference to religion, conception of life, or party political affiliation, should be assured equal rights to assume public office. The only determining factors should be individual qualifications and personal integrity. Also, all religious groups should be permitted free exercise of their religious practices as well as erection of places of worship.

—Freedom of work. This freedom does not exist when the State is the sole employer and the trade unions are subordinate to Party agencies which, de facto, exercise state authority. Under these conditions—as the experiences of 1956 and 1970 indicate—attempts to defend the interests of labor threaten bloodshed and can lead to serious disturbances. For this reason, workers should be assured the possibility of a free choice of their own occupational representation, independent of State or Party organs. The right to strike should also be guaranteed.

—Freedom of speech and information. If there is no freedom of speech, there is no free development of the national culture. When all publications are subject to State censorship before they appear, and publications and the mass media are controlled by the State—citizens are unable to take an informed stand on decisions of the State authority, while the authority does not know what is society's attitude toward its policies. The particularly dangerous consequences of the State monopoly on publications as well as the impact of preventive censorship appear in literature and art which are not fulfilling their socially important functions. Therefore, trade unions, creative, religious, and other associations should be enabled to establish publications and periodicals independent of the State. For this reason, preventive censorship should be abolished, and in the event of violations of press regulations action is to be taken only by judicial process.

—Freedom of learning. There is no freedom of learning

349

when the criteria for selection of the academic cadre and the subjects of research are determined by the State authorities and have a political character. Consequently, the autonomy of the institutions of higher learning should be restored and the independence of the academic milieu should be assured.

The guarantee of these basic freedoms cannot be reconciled with the presently prepared official acknowledgment of the leading role of only one of the parties in the system of State authority. Such a Constitutional confirmation would give the political Party the role of a State organ, not responsible to the people, not controlled by the people. Under such conditions the Diet cannot be considered the supreme organ of authority, the government is not the supreme executive organ, and the courts are not independent.

Implementation must be assured of the rights of all citizens to propose and elect their own representatives. The independence of courts from executive authority needs to be assured, and the Diet must in fact be made the supreme legislative power. We consider that the nonobservance of civil liberties can lead to the destruction of our collective effectiveness, to the disintegration of social bonds, to the gradual deprivation of society's national consciousness, and to the breaking of the continuity of the national tradition. It is a threat to the nation's existence.

The statements and postulates which we submit represent our conviction that responsibility for the fate of our society is collective. The recognition of these freedoms, which were reaffirmed by the Helsinki Conference, has at present acquired international importance since there is neither peace nor security where there is no freedom.

STEFAN AMSTERDAMSKI, STANISŁAW BARAŃCZAK, EWA BIEŃ-KOWSKA, JACEK BIEREZIN, IRENA BYRSKA, TADEUSZ BYRSKI, BOHDAN CHWEDEŃCZUK, LUDWIK COHN, ANDRZEJ DRAWICZ, JERZY FICOWSKI, KORNEL FILIPOWICZ, ZBIGNIEW HERBERT, RYSZARD HERCZYŃSKI, MARYLA HOPFINGER, ZDZISŁAW JARO-SZEWSKI, ANNA KAMIEŃSKA, JAKUB KARPIŃSKI, WOJCIECH KARPIŃSKI, JAN KIELANOWSKI, STEFAN KISIELEWSKI, JACEK KLEYFF, LESZEK KOŁAKOWSKI, JULIAN KORNHAUSER, MARIA

KORNIŁOWICZ, MARCIN KRÓL, RYSZARD KRYNICKI, JACEK KU-
ROŃ, STANISŁAW LEŚNIEWSKI, EDWARD LIPIŃSKI, JAN JÓZEF
LIPSKI, ZDZISŁAW ŁAPIŃSKI, REV. STANISŁAW MAŁKOWSKI,
JERZY MARKUSZEWSKI, ADAM MAUERSBERGER, ADAM MICHNIK,
HALINA MIKOŁAJSKA, JAN NIEPOMUCEN MILLER, LUDWIK
MUZYCZKA, ZYGMUNT MYCIELSKI, JERZY NARBUTT, JAN OL-
SZEWSKI, ANTONI PAJDAK, KRZYSZTOF POMIAN, JÓZEF RYBICKI,
REV. JACEK SALIJ, WŁADYSŁAW SIŁA-NOWICKI, STANISŁAW
SKALSKI, ANTONI SŁONIMSKI, ANIELA STEINSBERGOWA, JULIAN
STRYJKOWSKI, JAN JÓZEF SZCZEPAŃSKI, ADAM SZCZYPIORSKI,
KAZIMIERZ SZELAGOWSKI, WISŁAWA SZYMBORSKA, JACEK TRZ-
NADEL, MARIA WOSIEK, ADAM ZAGAJEWSKI, WACŁAW ZAWAD-
ZKI, REV. JAN ZIEJA

THE WORKERS' DEFENSE
COMMITTEE STATEMENT
(1977)

The Workers' Defense Committee was created in 1976 in order to bring legal, financial, and medical aid to victims of the repressions that followed the June strikes and demonstrations. The Workers' Defense Committee demanded that those charged for their part in the demonstrations be granted full amnesty; that those fired be reappointed to their jobs and that their permanency be made secure, that the full extent of the repressions as well as all the other circumstances surrounding the workers' protest of 25 June 1976 be revealed; that all those guilty of violations of law, such as using torture, be exposed and punished; that a Special Parliamentary Committee be called to make an impartial investigation into all the problems that create social unrest. Once all these demands are met, the Workers' Defense Committee will lose its justification for existence.

All the participants in the events of 25 June 1976 who were arrested have been released. The majority of those who had been fired have, with few exceptions, been rehired, but the conditions of their appointment are considerably worse and tenure has not been retained. The demand for official disclosure of the extent of the repressions has not been met, and the government has turned a deaf ear to public demands for a Special Parliamentary Committee to investigate the circumstances surrounding the events of June. The main aim of the Workers' Defense Committee was to provide aid for the victims of the post-June repressions. This campaign has, for the most part, been completed. But the Committee has received appeals from many people who, though unconnected with the June events, have also suffered repressions for political reasons and seek aid in the fight for their rights. All sorts of problems have resulted from the unlawful activities of the secret police, from the questionable dispensation of justice. The Workers' Defense Committee could not refuse to respond to these important social problems; it found various means of doing so, for example, the formation of a Bureau of Intervention and the establishing of a fund for Social Self-Defense.

In this situation we, the undersigned, consider it necessary to expand the committee's range of activities. We have decided to reshape the Workers' Defense Committee into the Social Self-Defense Committee. This Committee will insist on the fulfillment of the Workers' Defense Committee's hitherto unmet demands and will give the necessary aid to victims of the post-June repressions.

The Social Self-Defense Committee, "KOR," has the following aims:

1. To prevent persecution for political, ideological, religious, or racial reasons and to help those who are persecuted for such reasons;

2. to oppose law violations and to help victims of injustice;

3. to fight for guarantees of civil rights and freedom;

4. to support all initiatives made in the cause of human and civil rights.

The year's activities of the Workers' Defense Committee have documented the sorry state of law and order in Poland. This relates, above all, to the abuse of power by the instruments of prosecution, by prison functionaries as well as by law councils and courts. Certain that the most effective weapon against authoritarian constraint is the active solidarity of all citizens, we will continue our activities. The main reason for violations of law practiced by the government is the defenselessness of a society deprived of institutions that, independent of the government, can protect individuals against infringements on their rights.

JERZY ANDRZEJEWSKI, STANISŁAW BARAŃCZAK, KONRAD BIELIŃSKI, SEWERYN BLUMSZTAJN, BOGDAN BORUSEWICZ, ANDRZEJ CELIŃSKI, MIROSŁAW CHOJECKI, LUDWIK COHN, JERZY

353

FICOWSKI, REV. ZBIGNIEW KAMIŃSKI, WIESŁAW KECIK, JAN KIELANOWSKI, LESZEK KOŁAKOWSKI, ANKA KOWALSKA, JACEK KUROŃ, EDWARD LIPIŃSKI, JAN JÓZEF LIPSKI, JAN LITYŃSKI, ANTONI MACIEREWICZ, ADAM MICHNIK, HALINA MIKOŁAJSKA, PIOTR NAIMSKI, JERZY NOWACKI, WOJCIECH ONYSZKIEWICZ, ANTONI PAJDAK, ZBIGNIEW ROMASZEWSKI, JÓZEF RYBICKI, JÓZEF ŚRENIOWSKI, ANIELA STEINSBERGOWA, ADAM SZCZYPIORSKI, MARIA WOSIEK, HENRYK WUJEC, WACŁAW ZAWADZKI, REV. JAN ZIEJA

THE POLISH LEAGUE FOR INDEPENDENCE

The Polish League for Independence (Polskie Porozumienie Niepodległościowe—PPN) is a coalition of people from various backgrounds. Their differing political views coalesce to form a common platform for all those who share the desire for an independent and just Poland. The League's program represents a complete reconstruction of Poland's economic and political system. Its twenty-six points present an analysis of the present situation and a proposal for change. The program is built on the following assumptions:

PROGRAM

(1976)

. . .

1. The nation, in the sense of a group of people conscious of national identity, is sovereign and has an inalienable right to decide its own destiny.

2. All citizens are absolutely equal before the law and should have equal opportunity to organize their own lives.

3. The enormous majority of Poles are people of religious beliefs; the majority of those are Catholics. The political system in Poland cannot be based on discrimination against the majority.

4. The Polish national tradition was based on the progressive expansion of civil rights and the participation of an increasing number of people in government. Polish political thinking has been foremost in the development of democratic ideas since the sixteenth century. The autocratic, anachronistic, totalitarian system imposed on us is humiliating and alien to our tradition.

5. Poland belongs historically to the great family of nations of Western and Central Europe, the inheritors of the Greco-

355

Roman and Christian civilization. We wish to continue within that tradition, strengthening our ties with nations close to us spiritually. . . .

The following are points 13, 14, and 15 of the Polish League for Independence Program:

13. Our relationship with Russia is the most important problem for Polish foreign policy. Officially the relations are based on friendship, mutual help, and our gratitude. The fact that we have suffered innumerable wrongs from Russia during the last two centuries is passed over in silence. Silence covers the unprovoked attack in 1939 in collusion with fascist Germany, the transportation of millions to Siberia, their suffering and often death, the mass extermination of educated Poles in territories annexed by Russia, and the Katyń massacre. We are told to be grateful, but before we can think of gratitude we have to forgive. This is made difficult by the guilty party (whom we have neither attacked nor provoked), carefully covering up its own crimes while continuing a policy of ruthless domination.

Only if Russia sincerely admits the past wrongs and agrees to place Polish-Russian relations on a footing of equality would there be hope for future friendship and the healing of old wounds.

The Russian government must realize that the present situation tends only to increase the dislike, even hatred, felt by the Poles toward Russia and that present tensions may easily lead to tragedy. The interests of the two countries are not necessarily at variance; only greed and stupidity of the governments makes them so.

14. We are not Russia's neighbors. Our eastern neighbors are the Ukraine, Byelorussia, and Lithuania. For centuries we lived together as one state—not always in harmony, occasionally disturbed by our own expansionism—but at least voluntarily. Ukrainians, Byelorussians, Lithuanians, and Latvians are not independent today. Their countries have been forcibly annexed by the U.S.S.R. and they are subjected to much stricter political, ideological, and religious pressures than ourselves. They are exposed to intensive Russification.

It is impossible to remain indifferent or sympathize only silently. We wish to express warm solidarity and support for their attempts to regain independence. Whenever possible, we should aid and assist them.

We make no territorial demands on our neighbors, although the loss of Vilno and Lvov, the two cities linked for centuries with Polish culture, is a great sorrow. We demand, however, from all governments likely to exercise authority over ex-Polish territories that they guarantee to Poles living there equal rights and give them opportunities to preserve their language and national culture. We also demand that Polish citizens should enjoy unrestricted right of access to regions historically close to us.

15. German-Polish relations, still suffering from the horrors of the last war, are aggravated by another factor. The Moscow-directed Party propaganda exaggerates the danger of German revisionism. It conceals from the public that a far-reaching change is occurring in political thinking in West Germany and that an understanding between us is indeed possible. This fact has to be suppressed, because the Polish people have to be convinced of the need for constant military readiness. This involves the costly alliance with the U.S.S.R. and the maintenance in Poland of a large contingent of the Red Army said to be necessary for our own safety.

German acts of expiation are concealed from the Polish public. This discourages the Germans from making further friendly moves and the hope of a lasting genuine improvement in our relations is lost.

Better information and free movement of people and ideas are necessary if old enmities are to be buried. . . .

The Program of the Polish League for Independence ends with the following appeal:

The Party does not even try to satisfy the people. The only thing it wants from them is inactivity, indifference to what is being done to the country. It is supremely important that those who disagree with what the Party stands for should adopt an active role. To start with, let it be at least an intellectual exercise: constant attention to the possibility of different courses of action, better decisions, and more sensible personal conduct. To oppose is not the same as to complain or to grumble. Our aim is to provide alternative solutions.

The task has to be undertaken by the whole of the intelligentsia, historically responsible for the spiritual life of the nation. The most powerful section of society, the industrial workers, must share in the responsibility. The events of the last thirty years have amply demonstrated that they represent an invincible force.

POLISH LEAGUE FOR INDEPENDENCE
(WARSAW)

INTERNATIONAL SOLIDARITY OF THE OPPOSITION MOVEMENT

Polish revolutionaries have always maintained close ties with dissidents in other countries that endure Russian repression.

The following documents demonstrate the solidarity among kindred nations.

JOINT STATEMENT BY CHARTER 77 * AND KOR
(1978)

Ten years have passed since the troops of five Warsaw Pact countries occupied Czechoslovakia to suppress the aspirations of its people to freedom. A brake was put on the democratization process and on the hopes of all democratic Europe. In the name of humanistic values, the people of Czechoslovakia had developed an alternative to the totalitarian system. In the same year, the aspirations for freedom of the Polish intelligentsia were suppressed by force.

The ten years that have passed have clearly proved the viability of the ideas of the Prague Spring and the democratic movement in Polish society—despite all that the spokespersons for the antidemocratic order and lack of national sovereignty can say. Many people from both countries have, because of their support for these ideas, paid and still pay a very high price. They have been removed from public life, deprived of work and freedom and some even of life. Continuing repression is part and parcel of the life of our friends in the U.S.S.R. and other countries who fight and suffer for the same aims.

In the days around this tenth anniversary we are standing together in defending truth and freedom, in defending true human rights, democracy, social justice, and national independence. We declare our common intention to maintain

* Charter 77 is a Czechoslovakian dissident group.

faith in these ideals and to act in the same spirit. Human dignity as an inviolate value which gives meaning to the lives of individuals and nations is the source of all our aspirations and actions. And it is from this source that our profound feelings of solidarity with our many friends in the world who cherish the same ideas spring.

AN APPEAL BY RUSSIANS AND POLES TO FREE THE SIGNATORIES OF CHARTER 77
(Moscow-Warsaw, July 1979)

We, Russians and Poles, united in our common struggle for human rights, address ourselves to our Czech and Slovak friends, Charter 77 signatories, illegally imprisoned by the authorities of the Czechoslovak Socialist Republic. We appeal to all people of good will in Poland and throughout the world. We appeal to the governments and the people of all countries.

We believe that every person imprisoned and persecuted for defending justice is morally victorious by virtue of his sacrifice. We believe that the ideas, for which Jarmila Belikova, Václav Benda, Otka Bednařova, Jiři Dientsbier, Václav Havel, Ladislav Lis, Jiři and Dana Němec, Petr Uhl, Jaroslav Sabata, and other defenders of human rights in Czechoslovakia, Russia and Poland are persecuted, will be considered victorious in the hearts and minds of Czechs and Slovaks, Poles and Russians; that those ideas will serve to bring our peoples closer—in spite of our governments' policies. We believe that through our work, our testimony, and our sacrifice we will achieve—all of us together—the victory of truth and justice in the life of our countries.

We know that our friends, detained in Czechoslovakia at the end of May, will regain their freedom only through pressure from the public. We shall do our utmost to reduce the length of their stay in prison. We hope that all people of good will throughout the world will help us in this task.

Members of Social Self-Defense Committee (KOR): JERZY ANDRZEJEWSKI, STANISŁAW BARAŃCZAK, KONRAD BIELIŃSKI, SEWERYN BLUMSZTAJN, BOGDAN BORUSEWICZ, ANDRZEJ CELIŃ-

SKI, MIROSŁAW CHOJECKI, LUDWIK COHN, JERZY FICOWSKI, REV. ZBIGNIEW KAMIŃSKI, WIESŁAW KECIK, JAN KIELANOWSKI, LESZEK KOŁAKOWSKI, ANKA KOWALSKA, JACEK KUROŃ, ED-WARD LIPIŃSKI, JAN JÓZEF LIPSKI, JAN LITYŃSKI, ANTONI MACIEREWICZ, ADAM MICHNIK, HALINA MIKOŁAJSKA, PIOTR NAIMSKI, JERZY NOWACKI, WOJCIECH ONYSZKIEWICZ, ANTONI PAJDAK, ZBIGNIEW ROMASZEWSKI, JÓZEF RYBICKI, JÓZEF ŚRENIOWSKI, ANIELA STEINSBERGOWA, ADAM SZCZYPIORSKI, MARIA WOSIEK, HENRYK WUJEC, REV. JAN ZIEJA

Members of the Moscow group for the monitoring of the Helsinki Agreements: VICTOR NEKIPIELOV, TATIANA OS-SIPOVA, MALVA LANDA, HELENA BONNER, JURI JARY AGEJEV, NAUM MEIMAN, SOFIA KALISTRATOVA

Representative of the Assistance Fund for Political Pris-oners: IRINA VOLKOVSKAYA-GINZBURG

Member of the Group for the Defense of the Rights of the Handicapped: JURI KISIELOW

Members of the Working Committee for the Study of the Abuse of Psychiatry: LEONARD TERNOVSKY, VIACHESLAV BAKH-MIN, ANDREI SAKHAROV, TATIANA VIELIKANOVA, GRIGORI VLADIMOV, ALEXANDER LAVIET, IVAN KOVALOV, NINA KOMA-ROVA, VLADIMIR MALINKOVITCH, MARIA PIETRIENKO, IRINA GRIVNINA, IGOR KHOKHLUVKIN

HUNGER STRIKE IN SOLIDARITY WITH IMPRISONED
(1979)

We, the undersigned, in order to bear witness to our sol-idarity with our imprisoned Czech and Slovak brothers as well as with our friends in Polish jails, have begun today, 3 October 1979, a hunger strike in the Church of the Holy Cross in Warsaw.

We earnestly appeal to all people of good will in Poland and the rest of the world, to join us in defending the arrested members of the Czechoslovak Committee for the Defense of the Unjustly Persecuted: Rudolf Battek, Otka Bednařova, Jarmila Belikova, Václav Benda, Albert Černy, Jiři Dienst-bier, Václav Havel, Dana Němcova, Jiři Němec, Ladislav Lis, Václav Maly and Peter Uhl;

—in defending priests arrested in Slovakia and the Czech lands for performing their pastoral duties: Aleš Březina, Josef Mrovcak, Josef Zverina and many others;

—in defending the Czechs and Slovaks arrested for participating in Pope John Paul II's pilgrimage to Poland;

—in defending all political prisoners in Czechoslovakia, among them: František Hrabal, Jiří Lederer, Jaroslav Sabata, Jaromir Havrda, Jiří Wolf, Jan Zmatlik, Aleš Machaček and Tomáš Petrivy, who is being held in a psychiatric hospital.

We ask you also to take a stand in defense of Adam Wojciechowski and Edmund Zadrożyński, who are under arrest in Poland. We believe that human solidarity is capable of effectively defending the rights and dignity of man.

We have chosen to carry out our hunger strike in a Catholic church since in the Polish People's Republic only the Church can give sanctuary to people of various persuasions, to people who act in defense of the inalienable rights of the human person.

We have asked Professor Jan Kielanowski and Dr. Jan Józef Lipski to act as our representatives.

JACEK BIEREZIN, ANDRZEJ CZUMA, KAZIMIERZ JANUSZ, ANKA KOWALSKA, JACEK KUROŃ, JAN LITYŃSKI, FATHER STANISŁAW MAŁKOWSKI, JERZY MARKUSZEWSKI, ADAM MICHNIK, HALINA MIKOŁAJSKA, MARIUSZ WILK

WORKERS' DEMANDS

In a Communist totalitarian country a one-party system always subordinates organizations of any kind to the dictates of the Party. Therefore, the independent trade unions that became a reality in Poland in August 1980 were without precedent in the Soviet bloc.

The workers' revolt of 1980 resulted from economic crisis. The Gdańsk shipyard workers formulated their demands first on economic and then on political issues. During the strikes, the workers were a cohesive, well-organized force led by men mindful of their responsibilities, and supported by workers from other industries and by society as a whole.

Under these circumstances the Party was compelled to sign the Gdańsk Agreement, which acknowledged the formation of an independent workers' union—Solidarity. There has been an ongoing struggle to put into effect the terms of the Gdańsk Agreement. The workers, misled by the Party so many times, demanded the immediate implementation of the agreement. Strikes, some of which were authorized by Solidarity, were widespread. The workers' determination to achieve their goals by defying the government was tempered, however, by the fear of a Soviet invasion and by further deterioration of the country's economy.

The following are the key points of the Gdańsk Agreement.

THE GDAŃSK AGREEMENT
(August 31, 1980)

The Government Committee and the Inter-factory Strike Committee, after considering the twenty-one demands of the striking crews of the coastland, have arrived at the following agreement:

Regarding point one, "Acceptance of free trade unions independent of the Party and employers in accordance with convention no. 87 of the ILO [International Labor Organization] concerning trade-union freedoms, which has been ratified by the Polish People's Republic," it has been agreed:

1. Since the trade unions of the Polish People's Republic have failed to satisfy the hopes and expectations of the workers, the creation of self-governing trade unions as authentic

representatives of the working class is therefore justified. No one is to be denied the right to remain a member of the existing unions; future cooperation between unions is envisaged.

2. The ISC [Inter-factory Strike Committee] declares that in the formation of new, independent and self-governing unions it will abide by the principles stated in the Constitution of the Polish People's Republic. The new unions will defend the material interest of the workers. They do not intend to act as a political party. They accept the principle of social ownership of the means of production, the foundation of the socialist order in Poland. Recognizing that the PUWP [Polish United Workers' Party] plays a leading role in the state and without undermining the existing system of international alliances, the unions will strive to secure for the workers the free expressions of views and the defense of their rights.

The Government Committee declares that the Government will respect the independence and self-government of the new trade unions, both in their organizational structure and their functioning at all levels. The Government will provide the new unions with adequate means for fulfilling their basic functions in the defense of workers' interests, as well as in the realization of their material, social, and cultural aspirations. It also declares that the new unions will not be subject to any discrimination. . . .

5. The new union should be kept informed about such important decisions that might affect the living conditions of people, that is: about apportionment of the national product and the proportion of production to consumption; about how health, education, and cultural activities are funded by the latter; also about basic principles of wage and salary policy, as well as about investment plans and price changes. The Government will create conditions under which this agreement will be implemented.

6. The Inter-factory Strike Committee will call into being a center for social-vocational affairs that will provide objective analyses of the employment situation, living conditions, and means for protecting workers' interests. The center will also provide expertise concerning the wage and price index

and suggest forms of compensation. The results of the center's research will be publicized, and the new unions will issue their own publications.

Regarding point two, "To ensure the right to strike and for the security of strikers and persons helping them," it has been agreed:
The right to strike will be spelled out in the new trade-union law now in preparation. This law should specify the conditions for calling a strike and for methods of resolving controversial issues.

Regarding point three, "To respect the freedom of speech and the issuance of publications guaranteed in the Constitution of the Polish People's Republic, and therefore not to suppress independent publications but to provide access to the mass media to representatives of all denominations," it has been agreed:
1. Within three months the Government will present in the Seym a bill dealing with newspapers and all publications and artistic performances. It will be based on the following principles: Censorship should protect the interests of the state and the country's security, the range of which will be specified; it should protect the religious feelings of both believers and nonbelievers; and it should prevent the disseminating of morally offensive material. The bill will secure the right to contest censorship decisions in the Supreme Administrative Court. This right will also be embodied in a revision of the Code of Administrative Procedure.
2. The Government will ensure the Church's access to the mass media, in particular the transmission of the Sunday Mass on the basis of a detailed agreement with the Episcopate.
3. Both radio and television, as well as the press and other publications, should express a variety of opinions.
4. The press, as well as individual citizens and their organizations, should have access to governmental documents such as economic plans or administrative bills.

Regarding other demands, it has been agreed:

365

—to investigate the lawfulness of dismissals from work after the strikes of 1970 and 1976; if in such investigations irregularities are found, the persons concerned will be reinstated;

—to investigate the lawfulness of any arrest and to free those persons listed in the supplement [of this document];

—to ensure gradual pay increases for all groups of employees, especially for those earning the least;

—to improve the meat supply by increased agricultural production, by limiting meat exports to the indispensable minimum, and also by meat imports;

—to discontinue the sale in hard-currency shops of such home products in common use that are in short supply;

—to select the executive cadres from among both Party members and non-Party candidates only on the basis of their qualifications;

—to increase investments in health services, augment the availability of medical supplies through increased imports of required raw materials, and to develop without delay a government program for the general raising of health standards;

—to introduce work-free but paid Saturdays.

With the above settlements, the following points have been agreed upon:

The Government also undertakes

—to guarantee the personal safety of all persons involved in the present strike, as well as the safety of those who supported the strike. It also guarantees to maintain the prevailing conditions of employment;

—to publish in the national mass media (press, radio, and television) the full text of the present agreement.

The Inter-factory Strike Committee will terminate the strike on August 31, 1980 at 1700 hours.

Praesidium of the ISC: Chairman–Lech Wałesa, *Vice-Chairman*–Bogdan Lis, *Vice-Chairman*–Andrzej Kołodziej.

Members: Lech Badkowski, Wojciech Gruszewski, Andrzej Gwiazda, Stefan Izdebski, Jerzy Kwiecik, Zdzisław Kobyliński, Henryk Krzywonos, Stefan Lewandowski,

ANNA PIEŃKOWSKA, JÓZEF PRZYBYLSKI, JERZY SIKORSKI.

The Government Commission: *Chairman*–MIECZYSŁAW JAGIELSKI, Vice-President of the Council of Ministers of the Polish People's Republic.

Members: ZBIGNIEW ZIELIŃSKI–*Member of the Secretariat of the CC of PUWP,* TADEUSZ FISZBACH–*Chairman, National Council of Gdańsk Voivodship,* JERZY KOŁODZIEJSKI–*Voivod of Gdańsk.*